I/S 7/14

Newcastle College Library

02797046

KU-284-851

Newcastle College
Library Services

to get
castle
y app

be returned by the date stamped below
If you wish to renew your books
call 0191 200 4020   email – libraries@ncl-coll.ac.uk
Online - http://library.ncl-coll.ac.uk

– 8 FEB 2017

academia

An AVA Book

Published by AVA Publishing SA
Rue des Fontenailles 16
Case Postale
1000 Lausanne 6
Switzerland
Tel: +41 786 005 109
Email: enquiries@avabooks.com

Distributed by Thames & Hudson (ex-North America)
181a High Holborn
London WC1V 7QX
United Kingdom
Tel: +44 20 7845 5000
Fax: +44 20 7845 5055
Email: sales@thameshudson.co.uk
www.thamesandhudson.com

Distributed in the USA & Canada by:
Ingram Publisher Services Inc.
1 Ingram Blvd.
La Vergne TN 37086
USA
Tel: +1 866 400 5351
Fax: +1 800 838 1149
Email: customer.service@ingrampublisherservices.com

English Language Support Office
AVA Publishing (UK) Ltd.
Tel: +44 1903 204 455
Email: enquiries@avabooks.com

© AVA Publishing SA 2010
The author asserts his moral rights to the work.
www.branddriveninnovation.com

All rights reserved. No part of this publication may be reproduced,
stored in a retrieval system or transmitted in any form or by any means,
electronic, mechanical, photocopying, recording or otherwise, without
permission of the copyright holder.

ISBN 978-2-940411-28-3

10 9 8 7 6 5 4 3 2 1

Design by Borries and Leo H. Schwesinger
Original title concept devised by Kathryn Best

Production by AVA Book Production Pte. Ltd., Singapore
Tel: +65 6334 8173
Fax: +65 6259 9830
Email: production@avabooks.com.sg

All reasonable attempts have been made to trace, clear and credit the
copyright holders of the images reproduced in this book. However, if any
credits have been inadvertently omitted, the publisher will endeavour to
incorporate amendments in future editions.

LIBRARY
NEWCASTLE COLLEGE
NEWCASTLE UPON TYNE

Class 658.827

BARCODE 02797046

BRAND–DRIVEN INNOVATION

Required Reading Range
Module Reader

strategies
for development
and design

Erik Roscam Abbing

Ethical: aware-
ness/
reflect-
ion/
debate

academia

4

Contents

PART I

**The merging worlds
of branding,
innovation and design**   10

CHAPTER 1

**How branding
and innovation
are connected**   16

CHAPTER 2

**How branding
and innovation are
connected to design**   40

PART II

**Brand-driven innovation
in practice**   68

Foreword

When exploring the topics of branding and innovation, there are a wealth of different possible definitions and approaches that can be taken – reflecting the diverse nature of the business of creativity (such as design, branding, marketing, research and development, for example), the disciplines involved in the creative industries (design, arts and crafts, advertising, architecture, fashion, film, music, TV, radio, performing arts, publishing and interactive software), and the academic contexts in which these subjects are studied (art schools, business schools and universities). The result is that there are variations in the emphasis and approach taken to how students are taught to link theory with practice, and how they view and engage with the concepts of branding and innovation. The need for understanding and awareness of a range of approaches is critical for anyone learning about and working within the creative industries today.

Because of the particular challenges faced by organisations in light of changing global economic and political conditions and their local impact, and the increased sense of responsibility towards the environment and society, companies are looking for new ideas and new ways to do more with fewer resources. Identifying these opportunities to do 'more with less', will be what drives future strategies for development – in companies and countries all over the world. In the context of design management, there are tremendous opportunities for demonstrating how design can help to link creativity, innovation and branding, in a way that can both add value and *create* value. If we think of creativity as developing new ideas, innovation as exploiting these new ideas, and branding as a tool for differentiation and communication, then design becomes the way in which companies can make tangible customer propositions that can be experienced and touched – that is to say, in forms that can be taken to market.

This book addresses the need for understanding how branding, innovation and design are connected, in theory and in practice, inside and outside companies and enterprises, in a way that connects with the real needs of people. Taking a visual approach to the subject of brand-driven innovation is particularly suited to students from a range of creative disciplines, where a practice-led approach to academic learning forms the main component of the search for knowledge and meaning. Helping students to understand the underlying framework of brand-driven innovation also enables students to act as 'agents of change', initiating and facilitating a wealth of new cross-disciplinary projects, processes and conversations about innovation.

Kathryn Best

Introduction

In literature, conferences, online debate and in practice, design is often discussed in the context of branding. Design, in all its varieties, has the potential to bring brands to life in a way that can be tangibly experienced. In a comparable manner, design also plays a leading role in innovation. It helps to infuse innovations with meaning, usability, sustainability and emotion. Design, in fact, appears to bridge the gap between branding and marketing on the one hand, and innovation, product and service development and research and development (R&D) on the other.

However, in existing literature on the fields of branding and innovation, this connection is hardly mentioned: literature on branding makes little mention of the role of innovation, and literature on innovation mentions branding only as an aside.

This book fundamentally sets out to fill this conceptual gap. Brand-driven innovation demonstrates how branding and innovation are necessarily connected, and introduces a method to forge a strong synergy between the two, using design management and design thinking.

Organisations need to constantly develop new products and services to keep up with changing markets and user needs. In order to do this, they must have a keen understanding of what it is they're especially good at, and how that brings value to users and customers. They need to find the sweet spot where their vision and capabilities meet user needs and desires. In brand-driven innovation, that sweet spot is their brand. So rather than using branding to add emotion and recognition to an otherwise undifferentiated product or service, in this book it is used to represent the vision that drives sustainable and meaningful growth.

While a deeply ingrained vision is required in order to innovate in a meaningful way, that same innovation is required to bring that vision to life and fulfil the promise it sets forth. Innovation in this context is not necessarily about high-tech, high-risk endeavours. It can be any new product or service that adds value or meaning to users' or customers' lives.

In the first part of this book, this intricate relationship between innovation, branding and design is explained by looking at how their meanings have changed over the years. It first explores existing literature in the fields of branding and innovation to establish connections between them and to find a foothold for the new, synergistic relationship that is proposed in *Brand-driven Innovation*. It then goes on to explore that synergy: how can branding and innovation learn from each other, and what benefits might be gained from them working in unison?

Next, the role of design management in establishing this collaborative process is explored. It looks at existing frameworks for design management and establishes a plausible connection to current branding and innovation discourse. *Brand-driven Innovation* aims to demonstrate how designers already possess the competencies and character traits required to add value to the domains of branding and innovation and connect them meaningfully.

The second part of this book proposes a process for brand-driven innovation that was developed through intensive research by the author and tested in the field through numerous projects. The four stage process demonstrates how the relationship between branding and innovation might be brought to bear in practice, and explores the practical tools and methods that might enable this new approach to flourish.

This book is enriched with many case studies and interviews with expert practitioners in the fields of design management, branding and innovation that will enable you to gain a valuable and useful insight into how each field operates and how they might fruitfully interconnect.

Brand-driven Innovation was written with an academic audience in mind; as such, it will be useful for those studying design, design management, marketing and business. But it will certainly also be of great benefit to a practising reader currently working or consulting in design management, branding or innovation strategy.

Erik Roscam Abbing

How to get the most out of this book

About the use of certain terms

The user

A person or an entity using a product or service is referred to in this book as 'the user'. This is to avoid the words 'consumer' or 'customer', and to prevent us from looking at the user solely from a business transaction point of view.

Brand

With the term 'brand', we mean a vision that is shared amongst people and that defines the relationship an organisation aspires to have with its stakeholders.

The offering

A lot of the thoughts and frameworks in this book apply both to products and services. Sometimes the term 'the offering' is used, meaning that which the company offers to the user, in terms of both product, service and all the interactions around it, to the extent that they are staged by the company.

Innovation

Innovation in this book refers directly to the creation of new offerings that are valuable, original and meaningful. Innovation can concern products, services, markets, processes and business models, and does not necessarily include new technology.

Organisations

These can be commercial or non-commercial companies or institutions, in business-to-business markets or consumer markets, large or small, delivering products, services or both.

Design

Design is the process of creating meaningful interactions between people and products, communications, environments, interfaces and services.

Using this book

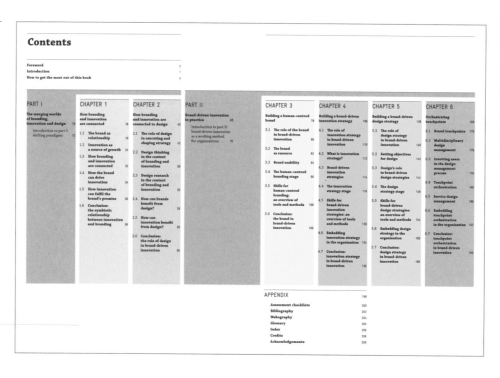

Contents

TABLE OF CONTENTS
The book has two parts: Part I dives deep into the theory behind brand-driven innovation, while Part II builds up a practical approach to applying brand-driven innovation in organisations. The chapters are colour-coded to aid navigation.

In addition to the explanatory text, special features within the book include:

INTRODUCTORY ESSAYS
These introduce the two parts of the book by discussing the context and premises on which the subject matter is based.

IN PRACTICE
These sections represent structured assignments and exercises with a clear, set purpose and deliverables, to be used as input for workshops or group discussions among students or colleagues.

CASE STUDIES
These give practical examples of the theory or methodology that is discussed. There are 12 case studies in this book (two within each chapter).

SUMMARY INSIGHTS
Each chapter ends with a set of key insights from the preceding chapter. They function as both a summary and conclusion of each chapter's main content, as well as providing a solid, at-a-glance overview of the main structure of the book.

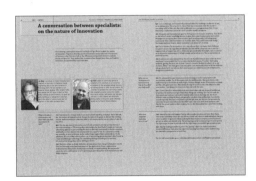

CONVERSATIONS BETWEEN SPECIALISTS
Two specialists practising in a certain area engage in conversation to explore a specialised topic that supports the theory in the book, in order to find out how their views overlap or contrast.

DISPLAY QUOTES
Provide additional insights into the book's main content and themes.

PAUSE FOR THOUGHT
These sections represent structured assignments and exercises with a clear, set purpose and deliverables, to be used as input for workshops or group discussions among students or colleagues. Upload your work and compare it to that of others on ‹www.branddriveninnovation.com/book›.

GLOSSARY
Explains the meaning of key terms introduced in and employed throughout this book.

PART I

The merging worlds of branding, innovation and design

What the terms branding, innovation and design mean depends largely on the context in which the words are used. In this introductory essay, we will explore these different contexts and meanings in order to come to an agreement about what the terms mean for us in the context of brand-driven innovation.

This book explores the premise that branding, innovation and design are merging disciplines; that they benefit from each other and in many cases even need each other. In order to explore this premise in a sensible and critical way, we first have to explore what 'branding', 'innovation' and 'design' actually mean. The three terms are used liberally in modern-day business lingo, often with a broad spectrum of potential meanings and avoiding too precise definitions. It's a common handicap of buzzwords: they lose their 'buzz' when confined to a precisely defined meaning. In addition, what the three terms mean is defined by the context in which they are used.

Introduction to part I: shifting paradigms

Branding

There are as many meanings of the word 'brand' as there are books on the subject (a good list of must-read branding books and articles can be found in the Bibliography on pages 202–203). The meaning of the word 'brand' essentially depends on the context in which it is used. Is it used by a professional or a consumer? Is it used in a strategic sense or on a more operational level? Is it used by someone in marketing, sales, research and development (R&D) or design? Is it used in the context of fast-moving consumer goods (FMCG), durable goods or services? Is it used in a business-to-consumer context or in a business-to-business context?

Depending on these different contexts and their unique environments, the brand may operate as the logo of the company. Or it may be seen as the corporate identity of which that logo is a part. To some, the brand is a collection of perceptions in the mind of the consumer (<www.buildingbrands.com>) to be influenced by shrewd advertising. To others, the brand may be seen as belonging exclusively to the domain of marketing. Its function may be considered to add intangible benefits to the core offering of the company. Or the brand's expression may be considered to be limited to the fields of graphic design, advertising and packaging design. Although for many people such views on how a brand may function may be perfectly acceptable, from a brand-driven innovation perspective they are not. A different understanding of the term is required if we want the brand to drive innovation.

First, the brand in our context is not the logo itself, but what that logo symbolises. Often, this is a set of values or insights, or it might even be a vision. These values may be embodied in a corporate identity, but hopefully they will also find their way into a lot of other things that the company does, too: the way it does business, the way it hires and treats its employees, the way it deals with the environment and social issues, and yes, the way it develops new products and services (Ind, 2002; Roscam Abbing, 2005). This also implies that the brand is not something that lives entirely in the mind of the user. The user will have an image of the organisation in his or her mind, based on the organisation's behaviour. But this is not the brand; it is the brand's image. The brand itself may be focused on the user, but it is a part of the organisation. For a brand to drive innovation, it should also not be solely confined to the marketing department: it has to be understood and used by everyone who is involved in the innovation process. And it should not only be concerned with adding 'intangible benefits' to the company's products or services, it should also add tangible benefits, and drive what these products and services are in the first place. This means that the brand is expressed in many ways, through service, product, retail, interaction and experience design, for example.

For brand-driven innovation to make sense, we have to look at the brand in a certain way, as outlined above. This view responds to the shifting paradigms of brand creation and brand management that are apparent in contemporary design management discourse. This might be best expressed through a consideration of how thoughts about branding are changing (see figure 1, below).

1 BRANDING PAST AND PRESENT
The way brands are discussed both in theory and practice has changed over time, as shown here.

Brands were previously often referred to as being	Brands in current thinking are considered to be
A sign of ownership	A representation of a vision
Connected to their owner	Connected to their owner and their user
Facades behind which the company could hide	Lenses through which a company is seen more clearly
Created by their owner	Co-created by their owner and their user
Managed and controlled	Coached
An addition to the product or service	A core asset, with huge balance sheet value
Constructed to influence the user	Grown from within the company

Innovation

A comparable analysis to that we have just made of branding discourse can also be made for the subject of innovation. This term is similarly used in many different ways, with many diverse meanings associated with it, depending very much on the context in which the word is used. A list of books to consult on the topic of innovation can be found in the Bibliography on pages 202–203.

Depending on the context, innovation is often seen as something that involves highly complex technology. Some consider it to be the exclusive domain of research and development. The result of innovation is often seen to be a new product or a new technology. Regarding the issue of why organisations innovate, many see innovation as inevitable: to keep up with competition, or to meet changing users' needs. What is more, innovation is often considered as a process that starts with an idea and moves on from there to bring that idea to market.

Although these ways of looking at innovation are common, for brand-driven innovation we need to understand the concept in a slightly different manner. Innovation can be involved with new and complex technology, but more often than not, it isn't. Innovation is about creating sustainable value, and sometimes a new way of using *existing* technology creates more value than the invention of *new* technology (Apple, famous for its innovations, is very clever at applying existing technology, for instance). Innovation is not limited to the labs of R&D. Anyone can innovate, no matter whether you're in human resources, accounting, sales or marketing. And the result of innovation can be a product or a new technology, but very often it's a process (a new way of doing things), a service or a business model. Some of these results are never seen by the user: they are internal innovations.

Lastly, innovation in the context of brand-driven innovation doesn't start with an idea, it starts a long time before the first idea has even been formed: the processes and insights leading to the idea (exploration) are as much a part of innovation as the processes aimed at developing that idea (exploitation). This way of looking at innovation directly corresponds to how its meaning has shifted in the post-industrial western world (see figure 2, below).

Innovation was previously often referred to as being	Innovation in current thinking is considered to be
About technology	About value
About products	About anything that can carry value
About management and calculating risks	About creativity, entrepreneurship and vision
Owned by R&D	A part of the organisation's culture
Something taking place inside the company boundaries	Taking place both inside and outside the company
Hard, risky and a nuisance	Hard, risky and fun

2 INNOVATION PAST AND PRESENT
The way innovation is discussed both in theory and practice has changed, as highlighted here.

Design

The third concept to be explored in this book is design. If ever there was a word with different meanings attached to it, it surely must be the word 'design'! Designers often have to explain what they do because of this: design can be a verb ('to design something') or a noun ('the design looks good') and a designer can be an engineer, an artist, a philosopher and anything in between. Let's explore some common understandings about design and see how the term is seen from a brand-driven innovation perspective.

Design is frequently seen as the look of something. Design, in these cases, is about aesthetics. It is worthwhile to note here that this view is not a layman's view: many designers think of their own profession as dealing with the look of products, environments and identities. Some also see design as an addition to something that already exists. This view leads to design being seen as a luxury addition to a 'normal' product: a 'designer' corkscrew, a 'designer' garden chair. Some, upon hearing the word 'design', will think of product design, while many others will tend to think of interior design or graphic design. Most people, however, will probably see design as an expression of an individual's taste or opinion.

Again, many of these views are common and sensible. However, in the context of brand-driven innovation, we have to redefine what we mean by design to understand it fully. First of all, in the context we are referring to here, design operates much more as a verb than as a noun: when we say 'design', we usually mean designing as a practical activity or conceptual process. This process in turn involves much more than aesthetics: it is also concerned with functionality, interaction, usability, the use of materials and construction. Design in this sense is not an addition to something already existing; it is a creative process that defines the essence of objects, expressions, services and environments. Design, seen from this perspective, serves not to express an individual's view on the world, but rather to solve problems, create meaningful interactions and to generate value for users and organisations.

This way of looking at design matches the current discourse on design among scholars and many practitioners, although there is still a fair amount of disagreement on what design actually is. Figure 3 (below) summarises the main shifts that have taken place in thinking about design.

3 DESIGN PAST AND PRESENT
The way that design is discussed both in theory and practice has changed in recent years, as evident here.

Design was previously often referred to as being	Design in current thinking is considered to be
A noun	A verb
A result	A process
About aesthetics	About aesthetics, interaction, functionality, usability, construction and meaning
A luxury addition to things	Essential to the value of things
About products	About processes, products, services and experiences
An individual's expression	A collective effort to solve problems

Conclusion

In this introduction, the broader meaning of branding, innovation and design in the context of brand-driven innovation has been explored. This meaning might be different from some common understandings about the terms, but it certainly reflects the shifting paradigms in the fields of branding, innovation and design, and responds to current discourse on these topics. The purpose of this discussion has been to help you understand how branding, innovation and design mean different things in different contexts, as well as to gain a sense of how their meaning has changed over the years, to arrive at their commonly held meanings today.

Pause for thought: reflections on paradigm shifts

Purpose

This exercise will enable you to critically reflect on what you've read so far and also to embed it within your own experience and knowledge. Working through this exercise will enable you to consolidate your understanding of branding, innovation and design and their interrelationship, before moving on to chapter 1.

1

Do you agree with how branding, innovation and design have been explained in the previous pages? And if you disagree, can you make it clear why you see things differently? Can you give examples that oppose the reasoning in this introduction?

2

Do you recognise the various opposing views people have when describing the three terms? Do you see how context defines the way that someone understands the concepts of branding, innovation and design? Can you give examples of these different contexts?

3

Do you recognise the way that the meaning of the terms has shifted over time? How have these shifts affected your perception on branding, innovation and design as a student or practitioner? Can you give examples of these shifts from practice by looking at brands, innovations or manifestations of design around you?

CHAPTER 1

How branding and innovation are connected

In this chapter we will delve into the connection between branding and innovation. Brands need innovation to fulfil the promise they implicitly make to users. Innovation needs branding to give guidance and meaning.

Having explored how branding, innovation and design can be understood in the context of brand-driven innovation, it's time to learn how the three are connected to each other. How do they need each other and in which ways can synergies be forged? In this chapter, we will delve into this connection between branding and innovation. You will learn why this mutual dependence exists, how brands can drive innovation and how innovation can fulfil the brand's promise.

1.1 **The brand as relationship**

Brand process and brand content

As we have so far discussed, the brand has some very special qualities in brand-driven innovation. Let's take a closer look at these qualities, by looking at what function the brand performs in brand-driven innovation, and what that teaches us about the qualities it should have.

If a brand drives innovation, it means that the brand sets in motion a process of change, with the intention of improving a situation and/or creating value. This implies two things:

1 | the brand inspires and sets in motion that process of change

2 | the brand challenges the people involved in the innovation process to improve something or create some kind of value.

In other words, the brand has a dual role to fulfil; firstly, it plays a process role and secondly, it performs a content role. The process role is designed to trigger and inspire a climate of change; while the objective of the content role is to give direction to the changes that may need to be made. Take a look at the innocent smoothies case study (on pages 20–23) for an example of how these two roles may come to be played out in practice: the brand inspires the constant devotion to the development of new drinks (process), but it also gives direction to what kind of drinks these should be (content); they should be healthy, as well as environmentally friendly, and ultimately, they should also have an element of fun in them.

1   THE BRAND
     AS RELATIONSHIP
     The brand forms
     the relationship
     between the internal
     organisation and the
     external world. It also
     forms the relationship
     between the
     marketing function
     and the innovation
     function within an
     organisation.

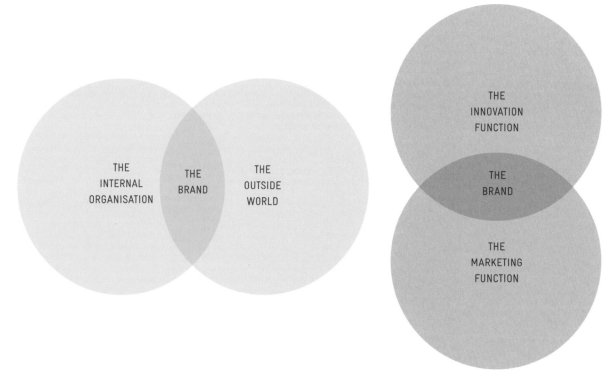

The brand can best be defined as the relationship an organisation has with the outside world. It is the platform for the shared understanding between marketing and innovation, and between organisation and user.

The brand has a bridging function

If we look at these two roles of the brand more closely, an interesting pattern emerges. From the process point of view (where the brand sets processes in motion and inspires people to innovate), the brand must bridge the gap between the marketing department (where the responsibility for the brand lies in most organisations) and the departments where innovation takes place (maybe R&D, or the design department, or maybe even manufacturing). The brand must function as a bridge between marketing on the one hand and the departments where innovation takes place on the other. It is not implied that no innovation ever takes place within marketing, but for a brand to inspire innovation, it is inevitable that departments outside marketing will have to be able to work with it and be inspired by it. In a sense, the brand establishes the relationship between marketing and the rest of the organisation. It creates the shared understanding that connects one to the other (see figure 1, below).

Looking more closely at the content role of the brand, a similar pattern can be discerned: to drive innovation, the brand must challenge those people who are involved in innovation, to improve an existing situation, to solve an issue or to create a product or service that has value to someone. This implies that the brand has to mobilise those qualities and skills in the organisation that enable these improvements. It must bring out the best in the organisation. But it has to mobilise these qualities in such a way that they generate value for the user of the product or service. In other words, the brand has to encompass a deep understanding of the organisation's user group. Again, the brand has a bridging function, this time between the organisation's inner strengths and qualities on the one hand, and the organisation's current or future users' values and preferences on the other. Once again, the brand establishes a relationship, this time between the organisation and the outside world. And again, the brand should be based on a shared understanding between these two poles, this time focusing on the organisation's qualities and how these can be of value to the user (see figure 2, below).

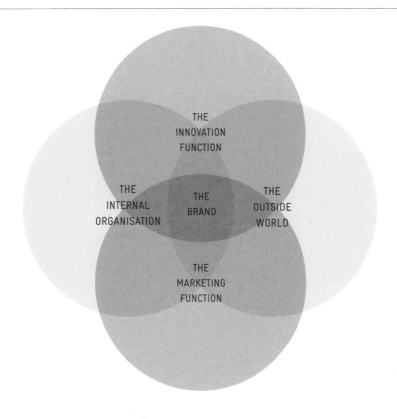

2   THE BRAND
    CONNECTS
    Brands (as they are
    discussed in this
    book) connect the
    organisation to the
    outside world, and
    connect its marketing
    function to its
    innovation function.

Case study:
innocent smoothies

The purpose of this case study

In this case study, you will have the opportunity to meet a modern brand, to experience how the relationships described in section 1.1 (pages 18–19) come to life in practice, and to see how the brand drives the way that an organisation behaves.

About innocent

innocent drinks is a UK company that produces and markets smoothies and other healthy food and drink. innocent was founded in 1998 by Jon Wright, Adam Balon and Richard Reed and now employs 275 people, sells two million smoothies a week and has a yearly turnover of £ 100 million (US $ 144.5 million). In 2009, Coca-Cola made a minority investment in innocent drinks. Take a look at <www.innocentdrinks.co.uk> for more information.

The innocent brand

The innocent brand is a rich cocktail of health, ethics and humour. The first two ingredients are taken very seriously. The last one, obviously, isn't.

Health

The company's founders came to the realisation that it was very hard for them to lead a healthy lifestyle as busy working men. This realisation impacted upon their approach to the products that they create. Innocent aims to make healthy food accessible and pleasant to consume, with an emphasis on using healthy and 100 % natural ingredients.

INNOCENT FOUNDERS AND TOUCHPOINTS
innocent founders Jon Wright, Adam Balon and Richard Reed (far left) have built a brand that is a rich cocktail of health, ethics and humour. The brand forms the foundation for everything the company does.

Richard Reed,
innocent

The idea was to make it easy for people to do themselves some good. We wanted people to think of innocent drinks as their one healthy habit; like going to the gym, but without the communal shower afterwards.

Ethics

innocent's ethics policy runs deep within the company and literally touches upon everything that they do, from producing the drinks, distributing them, hiring people and heating their offices, to dealing with investor relations. It's built on working with five essential tenets: natural ingredients, responsible ingredients, sustainable packaging, resource efficiency and sharing profit.

Humour

The innocent brand is light-hearted and personal, and has a very British tongue-in-cheek sense of humour about it; not only in its communications but also in other expressions of the brand, such as the company offices, packaging, events – and innocent vans designed to look like cows and fields of grass.

The brand as relationship at innocent drinks

It's hard to look at innocent as a company and say: 'this particular thing forms the essence of the innocent brand'. The company, in its entirety, appears to be the brand. The brand's vision on health, ethics and humour is so completely ingrained in everything that innocent does, that there is no clear distinction between the brand vision on the one hand and its manifestations on the other. Marketing at innocent is very much about doing rather than talking: the innovation function and marketing function circles in figure 3 (below) have a huge overlap.

Innocent also naturally combines insights about what users value (authenticity and accessible health) with a very strong sense of how they want to do business. In other words, the innocent brand is able to trigger the values and beliefs of the organisation internally, as well as user needs externally. The brand connects what the company believes in with what the user values, and offers a shared vision of what's meaningful and worthwhile pursuing. This shared vision is both broad and inspiring for the organisation and its users alike.

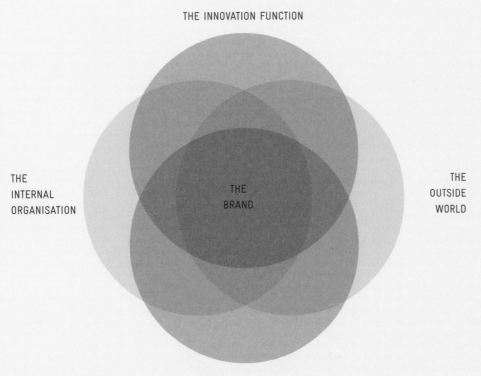

THE INNOVATION FUNCTION

THE INTERNAL ORGANISATION

THE BRAND

THE OUTSIDE WORLD

THE MARKETING FUNCTION

3 THE BRAND AS RELATIONSHIP AT INNOCENT DRINKS At innocent, both the relationships between the company and its users, and between the marketing and innovation functions, are very close.

Richard Reed, innocent

We sure aren't perfect, but we're trying to do the right thing. It might make us sound a bit like a Miss World contestant, but we want to leave things a little bit better than we find them.

Fruit Towers, the headquarters of innocent drinks in Shepherd's Bush, reflects the company's DNA in many ways. The use of brands to harness the energy of employees and to inspire them into doing things that fit the company is called 'internal branding'. Modern companies like innocent seem to be extremely aware that the power of a shared brand vision is not only directed outward, for use in brand communications, but is also directed inward, for use in teamwork and new product development, as well as for designing new business strategies and exploring possible futures.

Brands are not only about product marketing and communication. They can also define the way that an organisation does business. In 2009, innocent chose the giant multinational company, Coca-Cola, as an investor. Coca-Cola paid £30 million (US $45.9 million) for a stake of 10–20 per cent of the company. This is an interesting business and branding case, because at first sight this business partnership would appear to go against everything that innocent believes in. However, innocent believe that in order to put your beliefs into practice, you have to be willing to 'play with the big guys'. The founders of innocent are on a mission, and the money that Coca-Cola brings in and the (lack of) conditions that they set, will ultimately enable innocent to fulfil that mission. Of course, sticking to your original values while growing bigger as a company is a fundamentally difficult challenge that every growing brand has to deal with.

Pressed on why innocent chose Coca-Cola, one of innocent's managing directors, Richard Reed, responded thus: 'For several reasons. One is we liked the people we met from Coke – they were smart and honest. Secondly, Coke were prepared to invest the money with no unpleasant conditions attached (we spoke to lots of other possible investors and it was amazing how many wanted to put conditions on their investment – one said they would invest the money, but we would have to stop our donations to charity. Another said we would have to let them have control of the business.) Thirdly, Coke can help us with our mission to get our healthy drinks out to as many people as possible, by introducing us to customers in Europe and maybe helping us with distribution. And with the deal we remain a stand-alone business with Adam, Jon and I continuing to lead it in the same way as before. Overall, the deal brings security and opportunity to the business, and allows us to step up our mission of getting more healthy drinks out to more people.'

We strive to do business in a more enlightened way, where we take responsibility for the impact of our business on society and the environment, and move these impacts from negative to neutral, or better still, positive.

Conclusions to be gained from the innocent case

1 | innocent's brand vision is so completely ingrained in everything the company does, that there is no clear distinction between the brand on the one hand and its manifestations on the other.

2 | The innocent brand connects what the company believes in with what the user values, and offers a shared vision of both what's meaningful and worthwhile to pursue, for all parties involved.

3 | The innocent brand drives marketing communication and new product development, as well as more internal strategic decisions, such as partnering with Coca-Cola.

FRUIT TOWERS, INNOCENT'S HEAD OFFICE innocent's head office reflects the company's vision, and is an example of how the brand can guide the way that an organisation does business, which is with an emphasis on fun and an integrity to their core brand values. Pictured are innocent employees happily enjoying innocent products at a staff party; and rebranded innocent products at Christmas, with knitted 'hats' supplied by innocent-loving consumers.

1.2 **Innovation as a source of growth**

The purpose of innovation

Innovation, just like branding, has a specific meaning in brand-driven innovation. Having laid the groundwork for this on pages 12–15, we will now look at innovation up close, by analysing its role in brand-driven innovation. Innovation, just like branding, is never a goal in itself. Innovation has a role to play in the organisation: 'Innovation has become perhaps the most important source of competitive advantage in advanced economies,' as Michael Porter (2002) has put it. In the end, the purpose of innovation is to enhance the continuity of organisations, by increasing long-term turnover and profit. It does this by creating value. Value, in organisations, can be created by exploiting a new technology, fulfilling new or previously unmet user needs, differentiating from competition, or improving internal processes. Innovation starts with looking for opportunities to create value.

Innovation drivers

These opportunities for creating value are often referred to as innovation drivers. They are the factors that set the process of innovation in motion. There are internal innovation drivers and external innovation drivers. Internal drivers are changes within the organisation, such as the invention of a new technology, the appointment of a new manager, or a merger. External innovation drivers are changes outside of the organisation, like demographic developments, competitive behaviour, or changing user needs.

It is interesting to make this distinction because an organisation can often be defined by the sort of drivers that set its process of innovation in motion. Technology-focused companies will be urged to innovate on the basis of new inventions, materials or technological possibilities. Marketing-oriented companies will use market research as a source for opportunities to innovate. A company that wants to be the best in its class will keep a close eye on what the competition is doing, and will innovate to outperform them.

In the context of brand-driven innovation, an organisation should try to internalise external drivers and externalise internal drivers. This means looking at internal drivers for innovation from an external point of view (what value would this new technology generate for our users?) and looking at external drivers for innovation from an internal point of view (what would this competitor's new move mean if we were to look at it from our point of view, with our values and beliefs?). This way, both internal and external drivers for innovation create opportunities to generate value that match the qualities of the organisation as well as the desires of the users.

Proactive and reactive innovation

There are many innovation drivers that initiate the process of generating new value. The trick is to stay on top of the game: often, the search for opportunities to create value is not the proactive process it would appear to be. Organisations are busy; competition doesn't stand still, markets change at high speeds, consumer preferences fluctuate, and technology keeps developing. As a consequence, the process of looking for opportunities to create value sometimes conversely operates with a false logic, whereby companies attempt to *avoid* situations where value may potentially be lost. Innovation then turns into the unpleasant business of reacting to an ever-changing commercial environment, hastily copying every competitor or seizing every opportunity that presents itself, in a frantic attempt to regain control. Innovation in these cases becomes merely an inevitable reaction to change instead of the proactive search for opportunities to create value that it could more usefully be.

In the context of brand-driven innovation, we try to see innovation not as something that's inevitable and has to be dealt with, but as something that's part of an organisation's natural and healthy ambition for sustainable growth.

	Products	Service	Process	Business model	
Transformation	cars instead of horses	internet banking	Pilkington's floating glass	<www.amazon.com>	4 DIFFERENT TYPES AND LEVELS OF INNOVATION Bettina von Stamm distinguishes between different types and levels of innovation (2003, based on Tidd et al.), as shown in the table here.
Radical	hydrogen-powered cars	a new kind of mortgage	gas-filled, thermo-glass panes	online sales and distribution of computers	
Incremental	new car model	different mortgage feature	differently coloured glass	selling in business parks vs. town centres	

In practice: distinguishing between types of innovation

Purpose

The purpose of this exercise is to learn to distinguish between different types of innovation, and to learn to see innovation as the search for new opportunities to create value.

Required

A group of six–eight people, 30 images of innovative products and services printed on large cards and a flip-chart with figure 4 (above) drawn on it.

1

Take turns in drawing a card from the stack. Put the card in the right place on the chart and explain why you believe that it should go there. Discuss this position in the group.

2

Discuss what you think were the drivers behind the innovation. Were they internal drivers such as a new technology, or were they external, such as competition or a market development? Was the innovation proactive or reactive?

3

Then discuss in the group how the position in the chart could be changed. For example, what would be needed to move the innovation a 'new car model' to the service column? (The Saturn car brand, for example, combined their product offer with an extensive service portfolio <www.saturn.com>) Or what would be needed to make the innovation more radical? (You could, for instance, introduce a new concept such as Toyota's hybrid car engine.)

4

Move innovations to the upper right corner of the chart, but also move them to the lower left corner: sometimes innovations are too radical and it would help them to make them more incremental (at the beginning of the 20th century, the Zeppelin was perhaps too radical an innovation in the world of transport. How could you make it a less radical innovation today? What kind of products could Amazon potentially make?)

Case study: Icebreaker

The purpose of this case study

In this case study, you will have the opportunity to understand the brand as a relationship, and innovation as a source of growth, and to recognise how they manifest themselves in practice.

About Icebreaker

Icebreaker is an active clothing brand from New Zealand that manufacturers and markets clothes made from New Zealand merino wool. The Icebreaker website details the company's origins and development: 'Launched in 1994 by Jeremy Moon, Icebreaker was the first company in the world to develop a merino wool layering system for the outdoors. It was also the first outdoor apparel company in the world to source merino direct from growers, a system it began in 1997. Icebreaker is sold in more than 2000 stores in 24 countries throughout Europe, Asia, Australasia and North America. Based in Wellington, New Zealand, Icebreaker uses only pure merino hand-picked from 120 high country stations in the country's Southern Alps to create outdoor clothing that combines nature's work with human technology and design' (<www.icebreaker.com>).

A DIFFERENT APPROACH TO OUTDOOR CLOTHING Icebreaker designs, manufactures and markets technical high-performance outdoor apparel such as that pictured here, without the use of any fossil-fuel-based material such as nylons or polyesters: every garment is made entirely from natural materials.

Jeremy Moon, founder and CEO of Icebreaker, puts it this way: 'The plan was simple: let's be what the others weren't. They were synthetic; we were natural. They were about sweaty men; we were gender neutral. They were about hard adventure; we were about kinship with nature. They were about function only; we were about design and creativity.'

The Icebreaker brand

Icebreaker is a brand-driven company in the sense that its actions essentially stem from a clear vision. In fact, the brand was created before the product portfolio actually existed. 'Investing most of our seed capital, over $100,000, to define and express our brand identity was beginning to pay off. People were connecting with our identity – we were different from the others, and this was meaningful to customers.' Moon started the company by assembling a clear and integrating, long-term vision through a 'brand blueprint.' Moon, with brand consultant Brian Richards, created an overall, multi-year architecture for his brand and then 'reverse engineered' the year-by-year details that he could actually implement on an operational level (Lassiter, 2006).

The Icebreaker brand is captured and communicated in the company's philosophy. It is a narrative combining internal values and vision (why Icebreaker does what it does), an understanding of what outdoor enthusiasts value (for whom they do it), insights into the company's supply chain (how they do it), and the rationale behind the products and their design (what they do). As Jeremy Moon says: 'Our brand is about creating new relationships between people, people and nature, and between merino wool and the human body. From this thought sparked our ethos: "It's about our relationship to nature and to each other."'

The plan was simple: let's be what the others weren't. They were synthetic; we were natural. They were about hard adventure; we were about kinship with nature. They were about function only; we were about design and creativity.

Jeremy Moon,
founder, CEO.

Icebreaker's brand philosophy has five pillars (they can all be found online at <www.icebreaker.com/site/philosophy>).

1. Discovery

Tells us about the history of Icebreaker. When you want to build a durable relationship with someone, you share your background, and discuss what made you into what you are today. This pillar also has an internal function, to enable new employees to become part of the brand's heritage and narrative.

2. Nature as inspiration

Tells the story of how natural resources (the typical New Zealand merino wool, and the natural setting in which the merino sheep live) are Icebreaker's main source of inspiration. Jeremy Moon asks: 'If nature is a system and we as people are part of nature, and a business is a collection of people, then can business be a nature-centred system? We believe the answer is yes.'

3. Design ethos

Rob Achten, creative director, discusses the brand vision in prosaic terms: 'Nature is the best designer in the world. Have you ever seen anything in nature that isn't elegant, beautiful, balanced and perfect? If it isn't all these things, it won't last long – it dies and is redesigned. Nature is a restless system of change. But so is being human. So we put design at the centre of the company, and we go from there.'

4. Sustainability

This is a very important brand pillar for Icebreaker, and they take it to a high level, involving raw material, sourcing, supply chain management, manufacturing techniques and taking it all the way to animal welfare, ethical manufacturing and corporate social responsibility. Viv Feldbrugge, sourcing manager for Icebreaker, says: 'We take responsibility for the whole process because most of the environmental damage caused by the apparel industry is in the creation of fabrics, and most apparel companies are manufacturers who start with fabric. Starting with the raw fibre isn't just a luxury; to us, it's a necessity.'

5. Culture

The fifth Icebreaker brand pillar, interestingly, is culture. Kimberley Gilmour, HR manager, asserts that: 'Icebreaker is about innovation, inspiration and opportunity. We work here because we love it, because it has meaning, because we feel challenged and inspired, because we have a strong compelling vision, and because we all matter, every one of us. And because it's fun!'

THE SOURCE AND
THE PRODUCT
Icebreaker garments are made from 100 per cent pure New Zealand merino wool. Merino sheep, as pictured above, have evolved to withstand severe mountain conditions, giving them very fine quality wool.

Nature is the best designer in the world. Have you ever seen anything in nature that isn't elegant, beautiful, balanced and perfect? If it isn't all these things, it won't last long – it dies and is redesigned.

STRESSING
THE DIFFERENCE
Icebreaker is proud
of its use of 100 per
cent merino wool and
likes to emphasise the
difference between their
raw material and that
of other outdoor apparel
brands, as shown in this
campaign image which
seeks to highlight the
natural base of their
working materials.

PEOPLE AT ICEBREAKER
Icebreaker staff live and
breathe the brand: they
are outdoor enthusiasts
themselves, enabling
them to test their own
products first hand.

Innovation at Icebreaker

Icebreaker looks at its brand not as a carrier for a marketing message, but as a guideline for how to innovate and operate a business. Jeremy Moon claims that: 'Innovation is about how a company is designed, and how the parts within a company interact to create new and meaningful change. Ideas can come from anywhere, and relate to anything – innovation isn't just about products.'

Icebreaker's commitment to be inspired by and learn from nature is taken very seriously. Moon continues: 'The way each species arranges itself in nature tends to follow three distinct rules. At Icebreaker, we call these principles of nature 'ASS' – Adaption, Symbiosis and Sustainability. We constantly refer to them within the business to teach us the next steps. These principles that guide us aren't from a textbook. They come from thinking and talking about this stuff over a glass of wine, or while we're mountain biking, or in our sleep. They have real meaning to us. But also to our users. That's why they purchase their first Icebreaker.' Rob Achten, creative director and vice president of global product, explains: 'Our products reflect our values. We design for a purpose. Sometimes, the purpose is purely functional and sometimes it's aesthetic. Mostly it's both, but it's always directed by an idea. The product you wear is a physical expression of your beliefs.'

Icebreaker's main differentiator compared to other outdoor clothing manufacturers is the use of a natural renewable resource (merino wool) versus a chemical non-renewable resource (polyesters and nylons). Therefore, they invest in getting the most out of the merino wool fibre, and to ensure its constant quality. 'Our system was based on the knowledge that the merino wool we were sourcing was created by nature to keep an animal alive in the mountains. If it didn't work, the animal would die. Ever since then, we've seen our role as turning this fibre into a clothing system that enables people to return to the mountains. We can't design a better fibre – in fact, we don't want to. Our challenge is to make merino relevant for another species – us.'

*Nature is a restless system of change.
But so is being human. So we put design at the centre
of the company, and we go from there.*

Rob Achten,
creative director

This means that Icebreaker invest in the processes of harvesting, cleaning, combing, dying, spinning, knitting and sewing. But Icebreaker also innovates in other areas. For example in the way it lets users trace the origin of their garment back to the sheep farm where the wool was originally harvested. Icebreaker garments are tagged with a unique 'Baacode' that will match each Icebreaker garment to the batch of merino fibre from which it was produced (the name 'Baacode' comes from the 'baa' bleating sound made by sheep). A tag on the garment invites customers to enter their Baacode on <www.icebreaker.com/baacode>, where they can trace the fibre back to the New Zealand sheep stations that produced the fibre. Customers can meet the farmers and learn about the living conditions of the sheep, then follow the fibre to the factories that knit, dye, finish, cut, manufacture and ship the garments. This innovation may sound like a gadget, but it is in fact yet another opportunity for Icebreaker to manifest its commitment to transparency with regard to the entire supply chain. 'Icebreaker is proud of its supply chain. We believe that introducing transparency and traceability into the production of our garments will give consumers further assurance that their Icebreaker was made with deep integrity,' declares Moon.

Conclusions to be gained from the Icebreaker case

1 | The brand has a multi-layered, multi-faceted architecture, containing elements of vision, values, ambition, technology, product, user insights, code of conduct, design and innovation.

2 | The brand is very active: it's constantly connected to practice and to making its vision tangible.

3 | The brand makes no distinction between what the organisation values and what its users value. They are treated equally, and the brand seems to connect the two seamlessly.

4 | Icebreaker is a brand-driven company. Everything it does stems from the brand vision. The product's role is to bring the brand vision to life.

5 | Design is central in Icebreaker's branding and innovation processes. Design for Icebreaker is not about just adding an aesthetic layer to its products. Rather, design is seen as a way of thinking about creativity and innovation, and draws upon nature for inspiration.

6 | Icebreaker consciously builds a culture around its brand philosophy, realising that it's the people within the organisation whose job it is to translate the company's vision into value for its users.

'BAACODE'
TRACING SYSTEM
Icebreaker puts codes in all their garments, such as those pictured above. If you type in this unique code online, you will get to see the sheep farm that provided the wool for your garment. Clicking further will give you the background stories of the farm and its operators.

A conversation between specialists: on the nature of innovation

The following conversation between Jan Buijs and Igor Kluin is about the nature of innovation. Together, they discuss what innovation means and how it forms part of business today. They also look at the differences and parallels between academic theory and practice. They explore how innovation has changed over time, and explore innovative entrepreneurship and leadership.

Jan Buijs is professor in Product Innovation and Creativity at the School of Industrial Design Engineering (IDE) of the Delft University of Technology (DUT). He was educated as an industrial design engineer (MSc in Delft 1976), and received his PhD (also in Delft) in 1984. Before working at Delft University, he spent ten years working as a management consultant. Jan is the author of several books and the originator of the Delft Innovation Model.

Igor Kluin worked in advertising before he embarked on his adventure as an innovative entrepreneur in the renewable energy business, by founding Qurrent in 2006. Qurrent enables its customers to generate their own energy locally from renewable sources, using solar panels, micro-wind turbines, heat pumps and hydrogen fuel cells. In 2007, Qurrent won € 500,000 starting capital in the picnic green challenge, handed out by Virgin's Richard Branson.

What is the nature of innovation, and what makes you both successful in the field?

Jan: Innovation is a strange word. It can mean almost anything nowadays. But if you ask me, the essence of innovation is to change the rules of the game, to disrupt the existing system. And innovation is subjective: what is very innovative for one is a piece of cake for the other.

Igor: For me, my career in innovation started with personal curiosity and fascination. I saw a documentary on TV in 2005 about alternatives for fossil fuels. It made me leave my advertising agency, to start tracking the sources that were mentioned in the documentary, and finally, to start Qurrent. So innovation is not a goal for me. It's a means to satisfy my curiosity, to solve problems, and to make things happen that I personally feel to be necessary. It's not rocket science either; one of my starting points was that I didn't want to create breakthrough technology. I'm combining existing technology in a new way. It's really about being smart about solving problems.

Jan: That's the oldest academic definition of innovation, from Joseph Schumpeter (1908): 'Die durchsetzung neuer kombinationen' or 'the application of new combinations'. Innovation has always been closely associated with entrepreneurship: this purposeful search for new combinations to solve problems is something that most entrepreneurs will likely recognise.

Igor: I see a challenge, and I intuitively assess whether that challenge can be met by me, as an entrepreneur. Then I go for it. I hear from my environment that the course I am taking is full of risk, and that that would make me a courageous man. But it's not something I really worry about so I don't consider myself courageous.

Jan: Designers and innovators are good at feeling secure in insecure situations. They thrive on the lack of certain knowledge because it gives them opportunity to play and explore. Managers are occupying their time too much with securing profits and taking away uncertainty. That's why innovation is so hard for them. They could learn from things like improvisational theatre, where insecurity is the source of creativity.

Igor: As to whether I'm successful or not I can only say that I am happy that I followed the path I am on now, regardless of whether Qurrent will be a huge success or not. So I suppose that as long as I am able to follow my gut and do what feels right, I am successful as an innovative entrepreneur. I've had a vision and acted upon it. That is my version of personal success.

Jan: Academic success is measured by the amount of publications in your name. By those standards I'm successful. But I'm not after that kind of success. I'm after challenging students, getting the most out of them. I want to transfer the love for what I do to my students. When I see them grow, I am successful. I am immensely proud of all the students who graduated with me and who have now become successful innovative entrepreneurs, designers or consultants.

What are new developments in innovation and how do they affect your daily work?

Jan: I'm interested in open innovation in relationship to intellectual property (IP) and business models. The IP discussion, and the confidentiality that goes with it, kills explorative open innovation in early stages. Partners change, ratios of investments change, and the costs grow over time. This means the way IP is used needs to be adapted to this new context. I am doing a lot of projects that deal with this issue.

Igor: I have a love-hate relationship with open innovation and new forms of intellectual property: it is necessary and good that these things are evolving, but I'm not ready for them yet in my business. I do look for outside influences to challenge me, but that's different from opening the doors and going for complete cross-pollination. I work with outside expertise because I need them to get the job done, not because I'm intrinsically interested in open innovation. On the other hand, I do try to work with students a lot. Not for the actual results of their projects, but for the discussions that come from working with them.

What does innovative leadership mean to you?

Jan: Innovation can only happen if you're able to make mistakes and learn from them. Innovative leadership means that you allow yourself and others to make mistakes; that you create a culture of openness where pushing the boundaries is accepted, even if it doesn't get you to where you wanted to be. The wrong steps are as necessary to get to your goal as the right steps, because if you only took the right steps, you wouldn't get anywhere new.

Igor: Exactly: making mistakes is part of the journey. I don't see them as mistakes, more as differences from what was expected. Learning from them is what makes being an innovative entrepreneur so much fun.

For the full conversation, go to ‹www.branddriveninnovation.com/book/conversations›.

1.3 How branding and innovation are connected

Having established what branding and innovation mean in the context of brand-driven innovation, we can move on to an understanding of how they are connected and how they in turn influence each other. Let's start by looking a bit closer at what it means to see the brand as a relationship. Relationships are based on a shared understanding of value, and a shared vision of how that value can be enjoyed or benefited from. Relationships thrive if the shared understanding grows, and if the opportunities to benefit from that value develop over time. Relationships in which shared understanding diminishes, or where the opportunities to benefit from this value decrease, grow stale over time. Two rules can be derived from this understanding:

1 | Organisations have to demonstrate a clear understanding of the people they aspire to do business with and what these people essentially find of value. They also have to possess a vision of what role their organisation can play in delivering that value to their intended users.

2 | Organisations have to capture this value and turn it into actual propositions (products, services or experiences).

Rule 1 implies a pledge of the organisation to its user group, which might be expressed in the following way: 'I understand what you find valuable, I understand my role in delivering that value to you, and I will do my best to perform that role.' In brand language, this is called 'the brand promise'. Rule 2 implies that the organisation can put this pledge into action. That it can create products, services and experiences of which the user says: 'You have succeeded in delivering what I find valuable.' In brand language, this is called 'the fulfilment of the brand promise'.

In branding, the concept of brand promise is essential. Walter Landor, of international strategic branding consultancy Landor, phrases it like this: 'Simply put, a brand is a promise. By identifying and authenticating a product or service, it delivers a pledge of satisfaction and quality.' It's the promise that makes a brand meaningful to the user and connects it to their values. And, as we have seen, fulfilling the brand promise through the delivery of new products, services and experiences (through innovation) is essential in keeping the brand-as-relationship alive. The brand needs innovation to be meaningful.

Now, let's look at what it implies to see innovation as the proactive scouting for opportunities for creating value. In practice, this means that 'willingness to change' must be part of an organisation's culture. This requires a very solid and shared foundation of norms, values, beliefs and vision. You can only jump high if you stand on firm ground. This in turn implies that at the core of what drives an organisation's innovation are its beliefs and values, and its vision of the role it can play in creating value for its stakeholders.

In innovation, the concept of proactively seizing opportunities that match an organisation's qualities and the desires of users is crucial. We have seen that in order to do this, an organisation needs to have a strongly ingrained set of values and beliefs. It needs to have a unique vision of where it stands in the world and what it can mean to others. Innovation needs the brand to be meaningful.

Willingness to change must be part of an organisation's culture. This requires a solid and shared foundation of norms, values, beliefs and vision. So at the core of what drives an organisation's innovation are its beliefs, vision and values.

In practice: brand promises and how they are fulfilled

Purpose

The purpose of this exercise is to learn to recognise the kinds of things that brands promise the user through their various communication channels, and to understand how they fulfil this promise.

Required

A group of four–six people, a notebook and pen, and some time.

For three days in a row, keep track of the brands you encounter in your daily life. For each brand write down the following:

1

What does the brand promise me? (For example, Volvo promises 'for life'.)

2

What does this promise intend to communicate to me? (Volvo wants me to be a lifelong customer but also claims that their cars save lives. And their cars are made to be a part of the way I live my life.)

3

On what internal qualities is this promise based? (Volvo is an expert in safety, and a company that have changed their portfolio from manufacturing family cars to the creation of a wide range of models designed for personal use over a whole lifetime.)

4

How is the promise relevant to me? (I like to feel safe in a car but I don't want it to be boxy and boring, I want my car to show I care about my life without compromising on dynamics or design.)

5

On what vision is the promise based? (Volvo moved away from safety as an issue having to do with accidents towards an attitude of facilitating and safeguarding life on the road.)

6

How is the promise fulfilled through product innovations? (Side Impact Protection System, a model for each life stage, the YCC, a concept car designed for and by women.)

After three days, get together in a group and discuss your findings. Be critical and constructive, as if you are acting as a creative consultant helping each brand to improve its promise and fulfilment. Try to come up with new ways of phrasing the promise, or with new innovations fulfilling it (such as Volvo child seats, or the possibility to expand the compact C30 model to a larger version when the time's ripe, for example).

1.4 **How the brand can drive innovation**

Branding and innovation are closely connected and need each other to have meaning inside and outside the organisation. But how does this work? How can the brand drive innovation? In chapter 3 (pages 78–107), we will look at the issue of building brands that drive innovation from a more practical point of view. Firstly, we will turn to explore what it takes to enable a brand to drive innovation.

In order for the brand to drive innovation it has to have certain characteristics. Very little solid research has been done on these characteristics, so we have to instead rely on empirical data. Case studies, interviews and student work over the past five years have led to the following insights into what characteristics a brand needs to have in order to drive innovation. The list is split up into characteristics, in terms of content, form, and the process through which the brand was built.

Brand content

Brand content is about the story the brand tells, its 'brand narrative'. It is what the brand is about. (BMW's brand content, for example, is about driving pleasure; Levi's brand content is about American ruggedness). In order to drive innovation, in terms of content:

1 | The brand has to be authentic. It has to be original and close to the real 'DNA' of the organisation.

2 | The brand has to be meaningful. It has to connect to what users really want or need.

3 | The brand has to be understandable. It has to be accessible and simple; it shouldn't require too much effort to understand the brand's story.

4 | The brand has to be inspiring. It has to be exciting; it has to trigger and challenge.

For brand-driven innovation, the stakeholders of the brand are not only the users of the organisation's products and services. The other very important stakeholders of the brand are those people who have to work with it every day, to create compelling new offerings that fulfil the brand's promise: the people within the organisation who are involved in innovation. For them, too, the brand has to be authentic, meaningful, understandable and inspiring. In chapter 3 (pages 78–107), we will look more closely at what these brand characteristics mean for the various brand stakeholders, as well as at how to build brands that have these characteristics.

Brand form

Brand form refers to the way that the brand is captured and shared within an organisation. A brand can be captured in a set of words, a story, a movie, a set of visuals or even in the form of a person (think, for example, of Bibendum, the Michelin tyre-man, or of Jamie Oliver, the man behind the lifestyle cooking brand in the UK). In order to drive innovation, in terms of form:

1 | The brand has to be layered. Both snappy and easy to remember one-liners, as well as deeper and richer insights have to be present.

2 | The brand has to be visual. Experience shows that a brand captured in images is more inspiring and easier to work with than a brand captured solely in words.

3 | The brand has to be connected to real data. Brands that are captured in a way that shows real people interacting with the brand, or real research data (images and quotes) trigger creativity and the urge to innovate more than brands that are abstract and detached from reality.

4 | The brand has to be dynamic. If the brand form is adapted over time (to new insights, new markets, new target groups, new product concepts) it is easier to apply in everyday work than when it's static and untouchable.

Brand process

Brand process is the way in which and by whom a brand is built, communicated and maintained, especially within the organisation. (Unilever, for example, includes deep-dives in their brand building process: marketers stay with households for a weekend to refresh the brand and connect it to the real world.) In order to drive innovation, in terms of process:

1 | The brand has to be co-created by those who work with it. The building of a brand should be a shared process where everyone involved can contribute their own insights and requirements.

2 | The brand has to be shared by those who work with it. It should not be owned by a single entity in the organisation, although it might be wise to install a brand steward who safeguards its quality.

3 | The brand has to be based on experiences both inside and outside of the organisation. If the process of brand building is connected to real-life people and experiences, the brand will gain stature among those involved in innovation.

4 | The brand has to be lived by management (Ind, 2002). If leaders in the organisation demonstrate that they take the brand seriously and put it into practice, it is much more likely that others will follow.

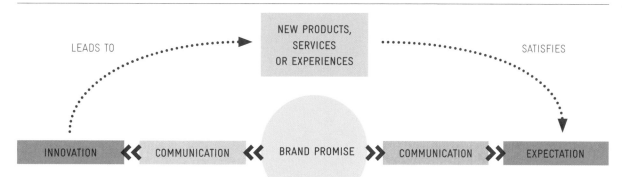

5 EXPECTATION AND INNOVATION Communicating the brand triggers user expectations about that brand, and requires a creative team to satisfy these expectations through the creation of new products and services.

1.5 How innovation can fulfil the brand's promise

In section 1.4, we observed how the brand can drive innovation given that it fulfils certain characteristics regarding content, form and process. But what does it take for innovation to fulfil the brand's promise? This question is answered from a practical point of view and in greater detail in chapter 4 (pages 109–137), but we will use this section to begin to formulate an answer to it.

In order for innovation to fulfil the brand's promise, it has to be part of a sequence of events: first, the brand promise has to satisfy the characteristics mentioned in section 1.4. Then the brand promise has to be communicated both internally and externally. Internally, this should set in motion a process of innovation; while externally this should trigger a set of expectations. Internally, the innovation process then leads to innovations that are brought to market, while externally, if all is well, these innovations satisfy the expectations (see figure 5, page 35).

This implies that the kind of innovation we're talking about here is challenged from two sides: it has to be able to respond to the triggers of the brand promise, and it has to meet – and preferably exceed – the expectations in the user's mind, that are set by that promise. In order for innovation to respond to the brand, it has to be clear within the organisation that branding is not exclusively a marketing-communication activity. Marcom, as it's called in organisations, is concerned with communicating the brand promise to the target audience through various media. But that, as we have learned, is only one side of the coin. The other side of it, to fulfil the brand promise, is innovation's responsibility. This is something that the innovation capacity within the organisation has to be aware of. Its task is not to scout randomly for opportunities for growth but is rather to create these opportunities, with the brand's vision as a guide and the expectations of the user as the goal. This requires a more visionary and aspirational mindset on the part of the innovators. In fact, it may require innovation staff that are less left-brain oriented, technology-driven and opportunistic, and more right-brain oriented, people-driven and creative. As Roger Martin so aptly points out in *The Opposable Mind* (2007), this is a new, but upcoming and essential set of qualities in innovation leaders.

In order for innovation to meet the expectations of users that were set by the brand promise, it has to break free from the notion that innovation is limited to the domain of products. As Pine and Gilmour point out in *The Experience Economy* (1999), we live in an age where much economic value is created by services and experiences (see figure 6, page 37). And even where products still form the core business of an organisation (as with BMW, for example) these products can't be seen independently from the services and experiences that surround them. (In the case of BMW, think of dealerships; leasing, maintenance and insurance services, and the BMW museum in München.)

This implies that innovation, if it wants to fulfil the brand's promise, must be a very integrative discipline. It must be able to combine the development of break-through technological solutions with human-centred services and embed them in meaningful experiences. This kind of innovation has been referred to as 'value-innovation' (Kim and Mauborgne, 1997). This, in itself, puts a huge challenge on innovation and marketing teams within organisations and requires them to work in unison like never before. But the biggest challenge of all is that products, services and experiences must tell the same story, each fulfilling the brand promise in their own special way, but together forming an orchestrated whole that is authentic to the organisation, makes sense to the user and adds value to his or her life.

This implies that innovation, if it wants to fulfil the brand's promise, must be a very integrative discipline. It must develop technological solutions, combine them with human-centred services and embed them in meaningful experiences.

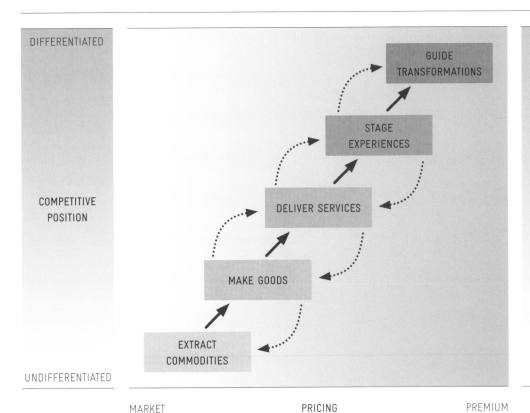

6 THE PROGRESSION
   OF ECONOMIC VALUE
   When using
   innovation to fulfil
   a brand's promise,
   it's not enough to
   think about product
   innovation alone.
   Pine and Gilmour,
   in The Experience
   Economy (1999)
   distinguish several
   stages of value
   creation, ranging
   from extracting
   commodities,
   making goods,
   delivering services,
   staging experiences
   to guiding
   transformations.
   All these stages
   play a role in meeting
   what users expect
   of a brand.

Pause for thought: reflections on how innovation fulfils the brand promise

Purpose

To critically reflect on what you've learned so far about how innovation can fulfil the brand promise through exploring products and services in your everyday life.

1

A good way of reflecting on how innovation fulfils the brand promise is to think about this as you go about your everyday life. Choose a day when you're travelling, visiting a city or doing a lot of shopping. Take a notebook with you and keep track of the innovative products and services you encounter. Think of public transportation, the goods in shops and so on.

2

It may help you to write down how these products and services are connected to the brands they belong to. Is there a connection? Do they fulfil the brand's promise? What do you think that you would you have done differently?

1.6 Conclusion: the symbiotic relationship between innovation and branding

In this chapter, we have explored the meaning of branding and innovation in the context of brand-driven innovation, and we have looked at how they affect and need each other. Both case studies and a discussion between experts have shown us in more detail how branding and innovation work together to create meaning and value.

Branding is not limited to marketing communication: it's about developing a guiding vision of the relationship an organisation aspires to have with its stakeholders. Branding is about creating a compelling brand promise that combines insight into what users aspire to, with insights into the role that the organisation can play in meeting these aspirations. We have learned that this bridging function of the brand requires it to have certain characteristics; in content, form and in process.

Innovation can be driven by many factors, some internal and some external. We've learned that for innovation to fulfil the brand's promise, it has to internalise external innovation drivers, and externalise internal innovation drivers. And rather than innovation occurring as a reaction to changes, organisations should proactively look for opportunities to create value. Furthermore, we have seen that innovation is not limited to technological innovations: it's also fundamentally about delivering value through new products, services and experiences. This puts high demands on the innovation function within organisations, requiring innovation leadership to be creative, holistic and human-centred.

But the key discovery that we have made in this chapter is a better understanding of the symbiosis between branding and innovation. Branding and innovation need each other and are mutually dependent on each other (von Stamm, 2003). Brand communication only promises value, it doesn't deliver it. A brand needs innovation to fulfil its promise and to deliver value. On the other hand, innovation without vision is innovation for innovation's sake. It needs the brand as a guide, in order to connect what the organisation is good at and what it believes in, to what the user desires or needs.

7   THE INNOVATION-
    BRANDING LOOP
    Innovation and
    branding need each
    other, derive value
    from each other, and
    strengthen each other
    in an ongoing synergy.
    They are caught in
    an eternal loop of
    mutual symbiosis.

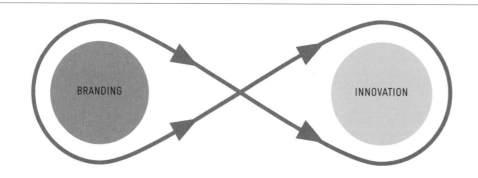

Summary insights
from chapter 1

1   Branding and innovation are closely connected concepts.

2   The brand forms the relationship between the organisation and the user, and between marketing and innovation.

3   A key concept in branding is the brand promise. It is based on insights into what the organisation values and is capable of on the one hand, and what the user values and aspires to on the other.

4   In branding, marketing communication creates the brand promise, but innovation fulfils the brand promise.

5   Brands that are suitable as drivers for innovation satisfy certain characteristics regarding their content, form and process.

6   The purpose of innovation is to find opportunities to create value.

7   Innovation should make use of an organisation's qualities, and translate them into value for the user.

8   Innovation can be triggered by external and internal drivers.

9   External drivers have to be internalised, while internal drivers have to be assessed from an external point of view.

10   Innovation must be proactive if it wants to fulfil the brand's promise.

11   Innovation can be focused on processes, products, services or experiences. Sometimes a combination of these is best.

12   Innovation that fulfils the brand promise requires special organisational and human conditions.

13   Branding and innovation need each other to generate value for the organisation and the user.

CHAPTER 2

How branding and innovation are connected to design

Design plays a vital role in bringing strategy to life, through inspiring brands and meaningful innovation. In this chapter, we will discover why innovation and branding need design – making the triangle on which this book is based complete.

In chapter 1 (pages 16–39), we established that branding and innovation need each other. In this chapter, we will explore the role of design and design management in the context of branding and innovation. We will also explore the role of design in corporate strategy, and we will look into building and executing the concepts of design strategy, design thinking and design research by meeting some of the leading specialists operating in the field of design.

2.1 The role of design in executing and shaping strategy

Aligning vision with execution

Brand-driven innovation stipulates that it is vital to have a strong vision in modern business ventures. Having a strong vision will set you apart from the pack, and it will give meaning to your offerings in an already over-crowded market. It is imperative to then translate that vision into a well-defined strategy. This strategy will help you to turn your dreams and ambitions into concrete plans by providing you with a clear focus, and will enable you to skilfully direct resources. But without execution, both vision and strategy are worthless. Making strategy work is more difficult than the task of strategy making, however (Hrebiniak, 2005).

Execution – acting upon a plan, getting things done, making dreams come true – is the main challenge facing businesses in the 21st century. There are many factors that play a role in successful execution. Between a good business strategy and a happy user lies a world of insecurity. Does the product work as it's supposed to? Can it be serviced? Are our sales personnel able to clarify the benefits of the product? Do users understand it? Can our manufacturing facilities cope with demand? Can we ensure that quality remains stable? Can we make it to the market in time? These are only a few of the questions that you are likely to hear when a strategy needs to be acted upon.

In executing strategy, the contribution of design is often overlooked. This is frequently because of the amalgam of meanings attached to the word 'design'. Making things a bit 'prettier' does not seem crucial in making a plan come together. Yet, as we discovered from our discussion about design on page 14, making things a bit prettier is not design's only role. On the contrary, design can also offer a very important contribution to execution. Let's take a look at some reasons why.

1 | Design enables things to get done in an integrated manner. Design, by its very nature, connects disciplines that might be separated organisationally, but that are required to work together to reach their goal. The word silos is used in a design management context to describe any management system that is incapable of reciprocating with other, related management systems. When developing a new product, for example, designers often have to work together with R&D, marketing, manufacturing and sales to collectively bring their efforts to a good end. Designers are experts at integrating the often diverse interests of these different stakeholders. The key to their skill lies in synthesising these differences into an integrated solution: the product works well, it can be easily manufactured, it looks great, is easy to use, it occupies a clear and open space in the market and it generates a decent margin. Design, in short, connects silos (see figure 1, page 43).

2 | Design can turn abstract ideas into concrete solutions. Design, by its nature, translates the abstract into the concrete. It turns ideas into realities and visions into facts. Design always starts with a problem, a vision, an idea or a hunch. It then goes through an iterative process of creation, resulting in a concrete solution of some form. This process may not be unique to design (a carpenter or an artist or an entrepreneur may similarly claim to work in this way); but the extent to which design applies it in both a structured and reliable way is in fact quite unique in a business context.

Hence, design plays a very significant part in turning the initial vision into reality and making plans come true. Occupying this crucial role, design is thus indispensable to brand-driven innovation. 'Design as process' hereby becomes a strategic activity: to design something is to essentially execute strategy. This understanding of the design process also establishes 'design as skill' as a strategic resource: design competency within a company is a valuable asset. So it makes good sense to treat design strategically. Despite this, it's hard to grasp what people mean when they talk about a 'design strategy'. In chapter 5 (pages 138–167), we will explore this issue at greater length.

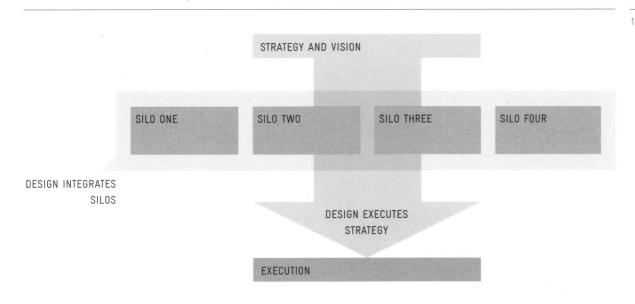

DESIGN INTEGRATES SILOS

STRATEGY AND VISION

SILO ONE SILO TWO SILO THREE SILO FOUR

DESIGN EXECUTES STRATEGY

EXECUTION

1 TWO DESIGN FUNCTIONS
This diagram demonstrates how design executes strategy and design integrates silos.

Case study: Fatboy

fatboy ® the original

The purpose of this case study

In this case study, you will have the opportunity to learn how design and strategy are inter-related. Through reading this case study, you will come to understand how design helps to explore and shape strategy as much as strategy helps to guide design.

About Fatboy

Fatboy is a Dutch lifestyle company that has become a well-known brand based on its flagship product, 'the original'. 'The original' is a redesigned beanbag in bright colours, tactile fabrics and bold Marimekko prints, which has sold 700,000 items worldwide. Fatboy was founded in 2003 by Dutchman Alex Bergman and is located in Den Bosch, the Netherlands, in a brand new factory and studio that houses 60 employees.

The challenge

It is dangerous for a company to base its entire success on one product alone. Slowly but steadily, Fatboy has explored new territories: garden products, bags and products for pets have been added to the collection. Grown into a well-known brand with a worldwide distribution network, it was time for Fatboy to get a strategic grip on the future without them giving up on the brand's spontaneity and intuition. The central question to their defined project was: 'Where will we be five years from now, given that we are a lifestyle brand that is not attached to a specific product category, market, technology or manufacturing technique? Where will our brand take us?'

DESIGNING A STRATEGY FOR FATBOY
The process of designing a strategy for Fatboy consisted of internal design research sessions with the company's creative team, external contextual inquiry sessions featuring <www.7daysinmylife.com>, house visits (page 101) with users, and deep-dive sessions with the creative team.

explorative creative sessions
soaking up the company's past, culture, ambitions and vision

house visits
get a deeper understanding of how the participants lived and used their Fatboy products

Grown into a well-known brand with a worldwide distribution network, it was time for Fatboy to get a strategic grip on the future without them giving up on the brand's spontaneity and intuition.

The process

Fatboy hired Dutch creative consultancy, Zilver, to help them to explore their future. The consultancy set out to develop a research and strategy development process for Fatboy that would fit with their existing beliefs and values, and that would also do honour to Fatboy's intuitive and creative approach to doing business. In the early meetings between client and consultancy, it was decided that a strategy for Fatboy could not be born out of rigorous left-brain analysis. The strategy needed to emerge from a more intuitive, design-led exploration of brand ingredients and user insights.

The process of developing a strategy happened like this:

1 | Soaking up the company's past, culture, ambitions and vision took place over several explorative creative sessions. Zilver's sessions with the Fatboy team never consisted solely of plain interviews, but always included visuals and the making of collages.

2 | Based on these sessions, a user-insight research project was started on ‹www.7daysinmylife.com›, an online environment where users keep and maintain a visual diary of their week in images and text (see also page 101).

3 | Results from the diaries were used to prepare house visits, to gain a deeper understanding of how participants lived and how they used their Fatboy products. The house visits generated a significant amount of data in the form of videos, photos, quotes and recorded conversations.

4 | These results were shared by Zilver with the Fatboy team in several data-immersion sessions, leading to clusters of insights about different Fatboy user contexts, the meaning of Fatboy products in users' lives, and users' aspirations and dreams.

5 | Zilver combined these findings with the internal insights gathered to develop a brand vision and to present a number of possible strategic directions to the company. The final insights were shared with the international Fatboy team in a creative session comprising 40 people, all of whom were focused on building the ultimate Fatboy experience.

FATBOY FUTURE CONCEPTS
Based on the insights that followed from the research into the brand and its users, a designer made concept sketches of possible future product directions. These sketches, pictured left, formed the basis for further discussion and design exploration. Sketches by Roy Gilsing.

The results of the project were so richly diverse and meaningful that they couldn't be squeezed into a report: a more tangible and inspiring approach of capturing them had to be chosen.

The result

The project resulted in a box that was filled with all of the insights, directions, ideas and thoughts that were uncovered during the course of the project. The consultants deliberately chose not to attempt to squeeze this wealth of information into a report. They felt that the results were so richly diverse and meaningful that a more tangible and inspiring approach to capturing them ought to be chosen.

The box contained the following items:

– A photo book that captured the process covered during the six-month project. The photo book explained the different steps of the process and illustrated each of them with photos taken during the various meetings.

– A booklet containing the results of the <www.7daysinmylife.com> user-insight online research, as well as photos and quotes obtained during the house visits.

– Delft Blue tiles illustrated with aphorisms representing the various resolutions that were shared during sessions and that made participants laugh, sigh, or jot a quick note down.

– An 'insight fan': a set of triangular cards depicting all of the insights regarding Fatboy's users, Fatboy's entrepreneurial vision and possible markets for the company to operate in that were uncovered during the process.

– A game board for playing the Future Brand Interaction (FBI) game. This game board depicts two concentric circles in three zones. First, the insight fan cards are laid out in their respective zone in the outer circle. The inner circle is then filled by brainstorming about possible combinations of two insight cards. Final ideas are then brainstormed again by integrating these combinations. The game provides support to the process of working out how to assess ideas based upon a number of brand, user and business criteria. It also helps players to map ideas out and develop them into strategic directions, product ideas, service ideas and marketing ideas.

– A sketchbook containing concept sketches that were made on the FBI game, by designer Roy Gilsing. Gilsing was briefed about the strategic directions that were discovered while playing the game, and worked from there. These sketches demonstrated how combining insights from the fan produced concrete new directions for growth.

THE FUTURE BRAND
INTERACTION GAME
As a result of the design
research project, the
consultants delivered
a game (pictured, right)
that could be played
and used by Fatboy's
creative team. It was
designed to help usefully
combine various research
insights concerning users,
markets and brand vision
into successful future
interaction concepts.

Alex Bergman explains: 'What we learned from this project is a sense of how tremendous the scope of our brand is. We have re-discovered the potential of our brand, by creatively exploring its implications in the future. This has given us the freedom and confidence to trust our intuition and to design those products that we think fit the brand.'

Conclusions to be gained from the Fatboy case

1 | Design thinking, design research and design tools can help to define strategy, by:

- Gathering user insights that are inspiring and usable

- Providing clarity in complex situations

- Combining internal resources and vision with user insights and market trends

- Prototyping and visualising possible futures

- Designing processes and tools for strategy exploration

2 | A company like Fatboy is truly brand-driven: their future will be defined by how they interpret and gain leverage for their brand, not by the market that they operate in nor by what manufacturing resources or technologies they own.

3 | The Fatboy brand consists of a mixture of entrepreneurial vision and deep user insights. This brand is brought to life through the use of design.

PLAYING THE FUTURE BRAND INTERACTION GAME
The Fatboy creative team playing the Future Brand Interaction Game in order to explore new strategic design and innovation opportunities for the Fatboy brand.

A conversation between specialists: designing strategies and strategic design

Design is great at executing strategy: design's 'downstream territory'. But design can also help to shape strategy and the management of organisations. This is design's 'upstream territory'. This conversation between Ralf Beuker and Fred Collopy focuses on the role of designers in the process of creating strategy.

Ralf Beuker holds a diploma in Business Administration from the University of Paderborn, Germany; Ralf is a Professor for Design Management and Dean at the University of Applied Sciences School of Design in Münster, Germany. Ralf also consults in the areas of strategy consultancy, design management and technological innovation. Ralf teaches at many leading design management programmes in Europe, and since 1998 runs <www.designmanagement.de>, the first blog worldwide dedicated to design management.

Fred Collopy is Professor and Chair of Information Systems and Professor of Cognitive Science at Case Western Reserve University in Ohio, US. He received his PhD from the Wharton School of the University of Pennsylvania. He does research on business forecasting, visualisation, and the application of design ideas to management. Fred co-edited the book Managing as Designing. He is a contributor to the Business Week and Fast Company blogs dealing with innovation, design and management.

Fred, you're at the forefront of the discourse on managing as designing. Can you briefly explain what this means?

Fred: Everything about organisations is designed: personnel policies, marketing plans, financial instruments, presentations, supply chains, organisational structures, strategies and so forth. We speak about 'managing by designing' to draw attention to the designed character of these things, many of which are typically seen as outside the standard province of design. If these things are designed, we ought to get good at designing them. We need to learn to understand where decision makers find the options they select from, and how new options can be designed.

Ralf, in your practice as a design management consultant, you distinguish between managing design and designing management. Can you explain what you mean by this?

Ralf: Historically the notion of 'managing design' stems from the 70s of the last century and aims at making sure that design, as a critical discipline to a company, is managed to produce optimum results. Accordingly, for quite a while managing design focused around contributing to operational excellence and effectiveness in organisations. However, limiting management only to effective decision-making means that you are neglecting the strategic responsibility management has. 'Strategic' means that management needs to develop a sense for looking into the future and preparing the organisation accordingly. This is where 'designing management' comes into play. It means that managers do not only rely on traditional MBA decision-making frameworks (mostly looking at data from the past) any more, but instead recognise that 'design thinking' helps them to address their very often paradoxical challenges far better. Instead of finding 'the right solution' designing management means to find 'a right solution in time'.

*What does it take
for designers to play
this upstream role
in organisations?
And what sort of
managers does it
take to allow design
to play this role?*

Fred: Design is always contextual. So, just as someone designing a new physical product needs to understand the context in which the product will be used, so too does someone designing a corporation's strategy need to understand how companies function, what employees are like, and how particular industries shape their participants. Not all designers will be interested in these things. They must follow their interests if they are to be personally satisfied and successful at their work. As for managers, at this point those most likely to take an interest in design are those who recognise the limits of analytic models in dealing with the complex and dynamic problems that we face. As these managers become more familiar with what design actually is, they become more open to design and to designers.

Ralf: In order to make a case for the value that design is adding to business, designers need to be able to show management the nodes within the structures and systems of the organisation within which design can play a role. I quote my former colleague from Westminster University's Design Management MBA Peter Gorb: 'What designers need to learn, is the language of the business world. Only by learning that language can you effectively voice the arguments for design.' From the management side, I don't think that we should expect managers to attend any specific classes in design thinking. I'm completely in line with Fred here: let the complex problems be the reason for management to feel the need for a change in thinking. Smart design thinkers will do the rest.

*What is the role
of design and
management
education in making
this shift happen?*

Fred: Our goal in bringing design into our programmes is to produce graduates who use more of themselves in managing. Humans are not merely information gatherers and decision-making machines. We are drawn to take actions that make the world better. We have interests in stories, in that which is beautiful and elegant, and in making the future better. It is important to be great analysts. But it is also important to be able to create something new, to understand when we should trust our intuition, and to recognise when new ways of viewing old problems are likely to be more productive.

Ralf: Sara Beckman and Michael Barry (from Stanford University Product Design Program and Berkeley Institute of Design at the University of California, respectively) state that design thinkers should be able to think on two continua: the continuum between 'abstract and concrete' and the continuum between 'analysis and synthesis'. This results in four quadrants or areas that design management education should invest in:

– understanding contexts: combining the analytical with the concrete

– generating insights: combining the abstract with the analytical

– crafting ideas: combining the abstract with synthesis

– creating artefacts: combining synthesis with the concrete

I think that this framework offers nice options for both design and management education, preferably in an integrated form: good design has always demonstrated a comprehensive integration of the four quadrants.

For the full conversation, go to <www.branddriveninnovation.com/book/conversations>.

2.2 Design thinking in the context of branding and innovation

Design is an essential part of brand-driven innovation because it resolves one crucial dilemma: how do you create a brand that is visionary and inspiring, and then bring it back to earth with real, tangible products? So far, we've learned that design can resolve this dilemma by connecting silos (design's bridging function), by turning abstract ideas into concrete solutions (design's downstream territory), and by playing a role in shaping strategy and management (design's upstream territory) (see figure 2, below).

In this light, it is worthwhile distinguishing between design results (the products, services, logos and environments that are designed) and design processes. Both contribute to resolving the dilemma mentioned above, but it's design processes that play the more durable role; because what designers ultimately contribute to a company's culture and assets is their way of thinking. Let's explore this concept of design thinking a little bit further.

The power of design thinking

Design thinking is widely discussed by both academics and practitioners alike: the question of what goes on in a designer's head apparently stirs up debate, not least among designers themselves! Designers feel the urge to better explain the value of the process and thinking behind their work, and rightly so: it's hard to be part of the economic system if your value depends on more or less random bouts of genius. But a more interesting discourse is taking place throughout the management world, with managers slowly discovering that designers are capable of dealing with reality and facing problems in ways that people with MBAs do not always master. In management schools such as Case Western Reserve's Weatherhead School of Management (US), the Rotman School of Management (Canada) and Stanford University's Hasso Plattner Institute of Design (US), design – and more explicitly design thinking – is centrally embedded in course programmes. Slowly but surely, business schools are really starting to recognise the power and importance of design in tackling contemporary business issues.

2   DESIGN'S UPSTREAM AND DOWNSTREAM TERRITORY
Design is good at executing strategy, but also at shaping it. Executing strategy takes place in design's downstream territory, through managing design. Shaping strategy takes place in design's upstream territory, through designing management.

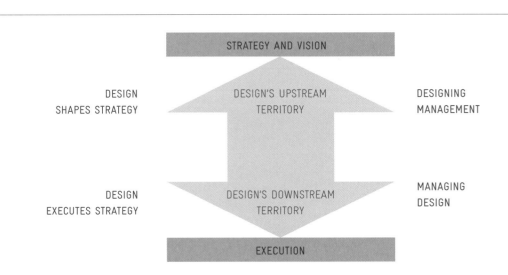

Design thinking helps you to be creative while facing constraints, by encouraging paradoxes to be used as inspiration – rather than being seen as an intrinsic limitation.

Wicked problems and how to solve them

In his book, *The Designful Company: How to build a culture of nonstop innovation* (2009), Marty Neumeier talks about today's problems as 'wicked problems'. Neumeier lists ten of these problems as a result of a 2008 Neutron/Stanford survey amongst 1500 top executives. The executives were asked to identify those problems they found the hardest to deal with, as well as the most persistent and complex to solve. Neumeier concluded that the top ten such problems are necessarily ill defined, because they inevitably change while you're working on them. In essence, they amount to problems that can't be solved in a traditional, rational or binary way, such as: 'How do I combine long-term vision with short-term success? How do I predict the returns on innovative concepts? How do I combine profitability with social responsibility?'

Such problems can be compared to design problems, which are also ill defined and need creative, lateral thinking to be used in order for them to be solved. Neumeier goes on to demonstrate that dealing with 'wicked problems' in a design-led manner will yield much better results than dealing with them purely in a 'business school manner'. Roger L. Martin arrives at a similar conclusion (albeit less explicitly so) in his book *The Opposable Mind: How successful leaders win through integrative thinking* (2007), by demonstrating that successful entrepreneurs tend not to treat problems as dilemmas. Martin asserts that successful leaders don't look for 'either-or' solutions, but rather for 'and-and' solutions; he then describes a process that can be used to arrive at insights useful for resolving dilemmas, a third option that closely resembles the way in which designers think. Design is the process of resolving paradoxes by finding new approaches, and in *Managing as Designing* (2004), Richard Boland Jr and Fred Collopy go as far as to suggest that managers should learn to behave more like designers. By observing the way in which the world-renowned architect, Frank Gehry works, thinks, solves problems and works in teams, Boland and Collopy go on to distil thinking patterns and processes that are applied intuitively by designers but that can, in turn, be learned by managers.

A consensus has emerged that design thinking can resolve those 'wicked problems' that Neumeier claims managers face nowadays. But how exactly? What do designers do that is so relevant? What is 'design thinking'? Ultimately, design thinking is an umbrella term for a way of thinking that is 'structurally creative' and can be said to combine both business thinking and creative thinking. Design thinkers have the ability to switch at will between left-brain, structured, rational, analytical thinking and right-brain, creative, emotional, holistic thinking. They are not limited to one mode of thought, but can instead choose their mode of thinking to match the situation at hand. They will, for example, analyse a given problem in a very structured way, then generate many out-of-the-box ideas in a very intuitive and creative mode, before then judging and selecting ideas with a rational and structured approach once again.

Design thinkers also deal with problems in a special way: they know that to learn to understand and redefine a problem is part of the process of solving it. They will play around with the problem and look at it from different sides, without jumping to conclusions or trying to 'decide' their way out of the problem. They know that in order to solve the problem they need to really understand the essence of the problem. They also have the tendency to see possible solutions as prototypes. They will visualise a solution, quickly test it in their head, and either discard it or use it as input for a new iteration of ideation. But they also use these cycles of ideation, prototyping and testing to redefine the problem at hand. In other words, they don't think of a problem as something static and well defined. For design thinkers, a problem is seen rather as something that grows and becomes more defined with each iterative cycle of analysis, ideation, prototyping, testing and evaluation. Often this leads to a new understanding of the problem, which in turn leads to very creative solutions. Or it leads to new opportunities by identifying inspiring 'problems' that no one saw before. This is why design thinkers are so well equipped to deal with Marty Neumeiers' 'wicked problems' and turn Roger L. Martin's 'either-or' dilemmas into 'and-and' solutions.

The overview of contemporary design thinking that we have just explored (on pages 50–51) is, of course, somewhat simplified: many businessmen are certainly very creative and many creative people are undoubtedly very structured in their approach. Maybe design thinking can best be defined as the ability to switch at will between the business and design modes of thinking. Figure 3 (below) clarifies these differences between business, design and creative thinking.

Having explored what design thinking is, let's now look at what it means for brand-driven innovation. Design thinking is the oil in the brand-innovation symbiosis we discussed in section 1.6 (pages 38–39). It works both ways: it helps brands to generate meaningful innovations, and it helps innovations to become more infused with the brand. It also helps to create a solid basis for brand-driven innovation by creating brands that form a fertile soil for innovation. The three key benefits of design thinking for brand-driven innovation are explained in greater detail in the following paragraphs.

Design thinking helps brands to generate meaningful innovations

It helps to turn vision into value and it facilitates the transition between the abstract brand and concrete innovations. It does this by combining right-brain, more holistic and visionary thinking with left-brain, more structured and concrete thinking. Design thinking can analyse and structure an abstract vision in such a way that it provides a handle on it that can later be rationally acted upon. This step-by-step journey from the abstract to the concrete is something which design thinkers feel very comfortable with. For each step, they will prototype and test many possible alternatives in their mind in order to find the one which best reflects their original vision. They don't make a giant leap from the abstract into the concrete but slowly iterate and prototype their way forward. In chapter 3 (pages 78–107), we will look more closely at how this process works.

	Business thinking	Design thinking	Creative thinking
3 DESIGN THINKING This table explores the essential components or characteristics of design thinking as compared to business thinking and creative thinking.	Left brain	Using both sides of the brain to solve problems	Right brain
	Rational and structured	The ability to switch at will between a rational and structured approach to a more emotional, intuitive approach	Emotional and intuitive
	Focused on analysis	Iterating between analysis and synthesis	Focused on synthesis
	Dealing with well-defined problems	Dealing with ill-defined problems	Dealing with undefined problems
	A problem is something to get out of the way	A problem is the start of the process	There is no problem
	Analyse › decide	Analyse › ideate › prototype › evaluate › decide	Perceive › ideate › decide
	Focused on parts of the problem	Zooming in and out, taking the problem apart to reassemble it in a different way	Holistic focus

Design thinking helps innovations to become more infused with the brand

It helps to embed vision in innovation and provide it with a sense of direction. Innovation is often a concrete and rational business. The dreamy, visionary part of ideation usually doesn't last too long; soon enough there are problems to be solved, deadlines to be met and operational issues to be dealt with. In short, innovation often doesn't leave much room for a brand vision. But design thinking can help to connect innovation back to the initial design vision. It does this by understanding the constraints in technology, time, budget and other resources, while at the same time understanding what the brand vision can actually add to enrich the status of the innovation at hand in a productive manner. Design thinking helps you to be creative in the face of constraints, by encouraging paradoxes to be used as inspiration – rather than being seen as an intrinsic limitation.

Design thinking helps to create a solid basis for brand-driven innovation by creating brands that form a fertile soil for innovation.

It helps to create brands that are a source of inspiration for people involved in innovation and new product development. This is not a small feat, as we shall see in chapter 3 (pages 78–107): very often, brands don't connect to those involved in the innovation process because they are too abstract, generic and language-based. Design thinking helps to create brands that are genuine, inspiring, visual, authentic, concrete and inviting. It does this by continuously reality-checking the abstract brand values with the concrete real world. What does it imply if we say we value authenticity, or entrepreneurship, or performance or social responsibility? What would that brand value look like in practice? How could we implement it in reality? By continuously asking such questions and prototyping possible answers, design thinking helps to filter out those values that don't really mean anything in practice.

Pause for thought: reflections on design thinking

Purpose

This section will enable you to recognise design thinking and its value, as well as to critically reflect on what design thinking means and on the results that it generates.

1

One way of reflecting on what design thinking means and how it can be of value, is by gathering together examples of it to look at and consider. Think about the objects, media, environments, services and experiences you've encountered or read about in design journals and magazines, in school or at your business, or simply in your vicinity.

2

Then consider how you might answer the following questions:

– Why is it an example of design thinking?

– Is the design thinking in the process or in the result? (If all of your findings are results-based, look a bit closer for design thinking in processes.)

– Was there a paradox resolved?

– Could you have thought of it? What processes, skills, resources and specialists do you maybe lack?

3

Go to <www.branddriveninnovation.com/book/examples-of-design-thinking> to follow the discussion, or maybe add some of your own findings.

A conversation between specialists: Oliver King and Arne van Oosterom on design thinking in practice

Design is no longer a process that only leads to physical artefacts like products or visual expressions such as logos. Design, and more specifically design thinking, is now put to use to create services and experiences. Service design, an upcoming discipline, has been at the forefront of the design thinking debate. In this conversation, Arne van Oosterom and Oliver King talk about what design thinking means to them in their daily practice.

Arne van Oosterom is owner and strategic design director at DesignThinkers, a strategic design agency based in Amsterdam, the Netherlands, that specialises in social innovations, service innovations, customer-centred design, marketing 2.0 and branding. Arne is also lecturer and chairman of the Service Design Network Netherlands, founder of Wenovski, the design thinkers network and guest lecturer at various European institutions. Arne has a background in communications design.

Oliver King is co-founder and director of Engine, the London based service design consultancy. Engine helps organisations to identify where, when and how they can provide better, more meaningful and valuable services. He works with organisations to formulate strategy and deliver service innovation by improving or interconnecting the things that their customers experience – from products to processes and people. With over 18 years' experience, Oliver is a pioneer in his field. He speaks internationally and writes about service design and innovation.

What does design thinking mean to you personally and what value do you attach to it?

Oliver: I think it is a fantastic term and I wish I had thought of it myself. I don't think it is a new concept for the design community, but it certainly does open doors in the business community. I think we have the good and the great to thank for that because design is now seen as a process, as a way of tackling problems, rather than design being only about artefacts. Arne, what do you think?

Arne: Personally, I find it liberating. As a designer and strategist coming from a creative background, I always found it very frustrating that I was doing something in a grey area. It never had a name. When I first heard of the term 'design thinking', I said 'Wow, this is what I do.' Design thinking has now been a part of my work for many years. But it's like a new notebook you've just bought: it's still a blank, white piece of paper that needs to be filled. It gives me a feeling of endless opportunities and unlimited possibilities.

Why is design thinking especially relevant for service design?

Oliver: The relationship between design thinking and service design is interesting. Service design, by its nature, goes beyond the artefacts I mentioned before. It is much more strategic, much more holistic. You are designing processes and behaviour. You are tackling corporate and social challenges. Service design is about solving very complex issues. Design thinking is a very good way to describe how we think, and the principles we apply, in order to solve these issues.

Arne: For me, design thinking acts like a sort of glue between different disciplines. Especially during the last few years, activities like design, R&D, marketing, communication, branding and product development, have all become connected to each other. So much so that you cannot tell them apart. But within companies and corporations they are sometimes completely different islands.

When you design services you design processes from the customer's point of view. And from this point of view the islands aren't relevant. Design thinking has the ability to build bridges between the islands in organisations. These bridges enable our clients to develop the emphatic abilities that are required to design meaningful services. It helps them to start with a blank sheet and to really focus on the customer and the service.

The business world is slowly becoming interested in design thinking and applying it to management problems (see the conversation between Fred Collopy and Ralf Beuker on pages 48–49). Do you think you need to be a trained designer to apply design thinking?

Oliver: No, I don't think you have to have studied design to apply design thinking. We are very happy to recognise and support other people becoming design thinkers, because we realise that we're experts at it and the more people that experience it and get results from it, the greater the demand for design thinking will be.

I compare our situation to the rise of TV chefs. Most people enjoy cooking and so want to learn more about it. The fact that TV chefs share their expertise increases our appreciation of them. But if you put me in their kitchen, give me their recipe books, pans and ingredients, I still could not cook a meal like the chef could... They create demand by sharing their 'secrets'.

We need to build demand for design thinking in the same way. We should encourage people out there to become design thinkers so they understand what we do and will therefore appreciate it more. That's also why the design community needs to make more connections with non-designers. We need to engage more with the academic community, for example, so that we can begin to understand the science behind what we do.

Arne: I am relieved to hear you talk about it in this way, Oliver. My work is also very much about making connections and building new collaborations. We don't want service design to become an isolated discipline. We don't want to claim to have all the expertise. In order to make the cultural and organisational shifts that service design sometimes requires, it must reach out and connect to other disciplines and schools of thought. Maybe sometimes these connections are unorthodox. But then, isn't design thinking all about building unorthodox connections?

For the full conversation, go to <www.branddriveninnovation.com/book/conversations>.

2.3 Design research in the context of branding and innovation

We have thus far discussed design strategy and design thinking. Both are expansions of the traditional demarcation of the design domain and both, as we have seen, are important to brand-driven innovation. A third expansion that merits discussion here is the concept of 'design research'. In order to create a brand that is relevant to the user and to develop innovations that the user will want to buy and use, organisations have to do quite a substantial amount of research. They need to develop an understanding of who their users are and what their lives look like; and they have to develop an understanding of how they can be of value for those users. This information is often not readily available, which means that research necessarily has to take place.

Criteria for design research

There are many types and forms of research. In the context of brand-driven innovation, the research has to fulfil a number of requirements:

1 | Research content
The research has to lead to insights into the identity of the organisation and their users that are sufficiently deep and true to build a brand and innovation strategy upon. Insights that are too generic, shallow or insufficiently underpinned will not be able to support this demand.

2 | Research form
The research results have to be accessible, understandable and inspiring to those involved in building brands and generating new products and services. Research results that are hard to understand, difficult to access or uninspiring will not be used. As a consequence, brand development and innovation may not be connected to what the organisation and the end user are all about.

3 | Research process
The research process itself has to be open and inviting to those who have to work with the results. Experience shows that research that is carried out by those who have to work with its results tends to be generally much better understood and used in the long term than research results that are 'thrown over the wall' from the research party to those who will work with it.

In a sense, design research has two faces:
it is both research by design and research for design.

The benefits of design research

The type of research that answers and meets these demands has been called 'design research' by authors such as Brenda Laurel, Sam Ladner, Pieter Jan Stappers and Elisabeth Sanders. Design research is more inspiring, authentic, inclusive and richer in results than most other types of research, it can be argued, because:

1 | It involves close contact between researcher and subject (such as house-visits, going shopping with consumers, or undertaking creative sessions with users).

2 | It uses research techniques that trigger creativity and that are fun to use (for instance, through the use of diaries, games, play-acting or modelling).

3 | It embarks upon the research without any fixed assumptions or the use of narrowly defined hypotheses. It entails the search for embedded needs and values, which only reveal themselves to open minds.

4 | It empowers research subjects to reveal valuable truths by providing them with the means to express themselves. Rather than asking users for their opinions or having them fill in questionnaires, design research gives them the means to express what's really on their minds.

In a sense, design research has two faces: it is both research by design and research for design. Research by design means it uses techniques that are also used in design, such as sketching, making models, storyboarding, creating scenarios and personas, and so on. It uses design techniques not to create new artefacts, but rather to create new insights. Research for design, on the other hand, means that the research results generate great feedback for designing brands and their products and services. (A third face of design research is research into design: that is, researching design processes and methods. This field is less relevant in this context.) Several design research techniques are discussed later in the book, in section 3.5 (pages 100–105).

2.4 How can brands benefit from design?

In this chapter, we have so far established that design, design strategy, design thinking and design research are all important to brand-driven innovation. But how can brands benefit from design? Is it even possible in the 21st century to skip design and just engage in branding? It doesn't appear so. Brands are constructed by organisations, but they do have to reach the hearts and minds of users. They also have to reach the hearts and minds of internal stakeholders, such as personnel. Thus, some kind of transfer of meaning has to take place between the creator of the brand and the user. Traditionally, this transfer of meaning is modelled and understood from a communications point of view, and was originally framed by Claude Shannon in 1948. The transfer of meaning takes place between the sender, the medium and the recipient, in a linear sequence (see figure 4, below). The sender (the creator of the brand in a given case) operates with a certain intention. The recipient, in turn, will generate a particular interpretation of this message.

Shannon's model explains how communication works from the point of view of the sender, who acts with a specific intention and wants their message to be understood by the intended recipient. But in the world of brands there is more at stake than just getting your message across and being understood: you want users to derive value from the message, too. You want to tap into their emotional world. So conveying your message successfully is more than just a question of the functional transfer of information. Additionally, the message is not always communicated directly via the spoken or written word. Branding is often seen as 'just' brand communication, but in reality the written and spoken communication around a brand constitutes a fraction of what that brand ultimately communicates. Products, services, environments and people play a much larger role in getting the brand message across than do the written and spoken word. This is where design comes in: in order to get across messages that are both emotive and embedded, and that can be carried by non-verbal media, design is essential.

Semantic transformation

Toni-Matti Karjalainen modelled this role of design – conveying embedded messages in media such as products and environments – in his work *Semantic Transformation in Design* (2003) (see figure 5, facing page). Karjalainen's model is intended to facilitate bringing a certain set of values (or brand 'character') across. These values have to be embedded in the medium that is used, in the form of design features. The process of translating values into design features is called 'semantic transformation'. This is hardly a scientific process; what is more, there is always a certain amount of distortion involved as the written values turn into designed features (decreasing this distortion is one of the topics discussed in chapter 5, pages 138–167.) The recipient (the user) then experiences these embedded values through perceiving the design features.

4   SHANNON'S
TRANSMISSION
MODEL OF
COMMUNICATION
(1948)

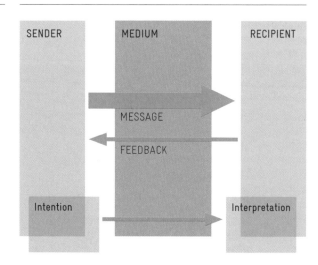

If the purpose of brands is to build a relationship between the organisation and its stakeholders by adding value and meaning to the transaction and interaction between them, brands need design more than anything else.

Semantic attribution

The process of interpreting the design features and assigning value and meaning to them is called 'semantic attribution'. Again, a certain amount of distortion is involved in turning design features into meaning. Decreasing this distortion is virtually impossible because it occurs as a direct result of differences in cultural backgrounds and taste preferences. Educating the user to interpret design features in a particular way is a slow process and has its limits. The next level in modelling the transfer of brand meaning to users results from the fact that users not only perceive the design features and 'read' them, but physically interact with them, too, so becoming part of the system that carries the brand meaning. When certain types of users interact with an object or an environment, that use adds specific meaning to the design of that object or environment. Look at the two images of the BMW (below). In one, we see the clean, intended, design features of the BMW without interaction; in the other, we see how the object is interpreted by its users.

Getting brand values across requires the skill of semantic transformation, and it requires empathy to visualise the use of the object or environment and the meaning it will thereby add to the equation. Both are part of the designer's skill set. Designers know how to turn abstract ideas into concrete forms, as we saw in section 2.1 (pages 42–49). They know how to transform words into shapes in such a way that the shapes embody the words. But what's more, they know how to turn ideas into valuable and meaningful interactions, turning an organisation's values into relationships between the user and his or her environment. If the purpose of brands is to build a relationship between the organisation and its stakeholders by adding value and meaning to the transaction and interaction between them, brands need design more than anything else.

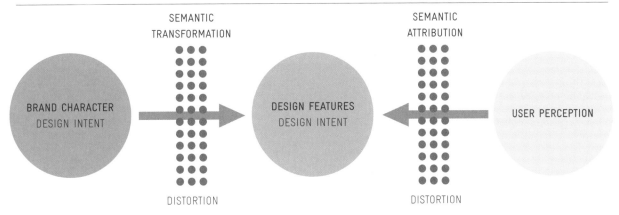

SEMANTIC TRANSFORMATION

SEMANTIC ATTRIBUTION

BRAND CHARACTER DESIGN INTENT

DESIGN FEATURES DESIGN INTENT

USER PERCEPTION

DISTORTION

DISTORTION

5   KARJALAINEN'S SEMANTIC TRANSFORMATION IN DESIGN (2003)

USE AS PART OF DESIGN BMW users (left) add meaning to the brand's design (far left) and the way in which the brand is commonly seen.

2.5 How can innovation benefit from design?

As Marty Neumeier snappily puts it in his book, *The Designful Company* (2009): 'If you wanna innovate, you gotta design'. But why is this so? Why is design so essential to innovation and what does it bring to the table? Innovation is generally considered to be about adding value by implementing products, services or processes that are new to an organisation, or by presenting a significant improvement to an existing situation. According to Peter Drucker (1993): 'Innovation is the specific tool of entrepreneurs, the means by which they exploit change as an opportunity for a different business or a different service... Entrepreneurs need to search purposefully for the sources of innovation, the changes and their symptoms that indicate opportunities for successful innovation.'

All right. So we have to learn to be inspired by change and we have to learn to leverage this change into new value propositions. That sounds easy and even promising. And in very many cases, innovation isn't as hard and groundbreaking as some make it sound. But to really do something new and to really add value with it *is* hard, otherwise everyone would do it all the time. So, to put it a bit less promisingly: innovation is about turning what's uncertain and continuously changing into value that doesn't yet exist for a group of people that don't yet know they need it. This sounds a lot like the 'wicked problems' we talked about in section 2.2 (pages 50–55). But innovation is not only out to solve these wicked problems, it even wants to generate value by solving them. It wants to take a wicked problem, resolve the paradox, and turn it into something that a user will attach meaning and value to.

This is again where design comes into play. As we've discussed, design thinking lends itself well to deal with wicked problems. And designers are good at understanding what users may want or need and are able to capture that in their design. Innovation needs design to solve issues that are inherently hard to solve, and to create solutions in such a way that they will be of value to the user. Or, as John Moravec of the University of Minnesota puts it: 'innovation is the purposive application of creativity' (Moravec, 2009). As previously discussed, this mix of the creative and the purposive is exactly where design feels most at home.

Innovation needs design

The notion of design as essential to innovation is closely connected to the paradigm shifts we discussed in the introduction to this part of the book (see page 14). It was also discussed by Clive Grinyer in his talk 'Lipstick on a pig' (see Webography, page 204) in which he declared that: 'Design is a vital tool for increasing the success of innovation and product development that is often ignored, badly managed or simply applied too late.' Innovation needs design, Grinyer argues, because 'when we develop technical products we have to deal with humans', and because the technologists working on the innovation at hand are not the same people who will use it. Design can make technology usable, provided you start with it early enough in the innovation process.

Marty Neumeier also makes a strong case for why innovation needs design, stating: 'Design contains the skills to identify possible futures, invent exciting products, build bridges to customers, crack wicked problems and more.' Neumeier claims that design has been 'waiting patiently in the wings for nearly a century, relegated to supporting roles and stand-in parts', used as a 'beauty station' for identities and communications, or as a last stop before a product launch – while in fact design's true power lies in generating growth and attracting users to innovations. As Herbert Simon, a leading social scientist and Nobel Laureate, wrote in *The Sciences of the Artificial* (1969): 'Everyone designs who devises courses of action aimed at changing existing situations into preferred ones.' In Simon's definition, design is innovation, and design is change.

Innovation is turning what's uncertain and continuously changing, into value that doesn't yet exist for a group of people that doesn't know they need it.

Design needs innovation

Neumeier and Grinyer are amongst a growing group of consultants who put design centre stage, and consider it to be essential to innovation. These people are doing admirable work for the design community from their business backgrounds. Fortunately, institutions such as the European Community and the UK Design Council are picking up on the trend. As the European Union report, 'Design as a driver for user-led innovation' states (see Webography, page 204):

'...The results are compelling: companies that invest in design tend to be more innovative, more profitable and grow faster than those that do not. At a macro-economic level, there is a strong positive correlation between the use of design and national competitiveness... Although often associated with aesthetics and the "looks" of products only, the application of design is in reality much broader. User needs, aspirations and abilities are the starting point and focus of design activities. With a potential to integrate, for example, environmental, safety and accessibility considerations – in addition to economic considerations – into products, services and systems, design is an area which deserves public attention.'

The UK Design Council supports the role of design in making organisations more innovative and competitive with some compelling statistics: 'Research has shown that design is a significant source of competitive advantage... In the UK, 45 per cent of firms that don't use design compete mainly on price; only 21 per cent of firms where design is significant do so... In UK businesses where design is integral to operations, 84 per cent say they've increased their competitiveness through design; and 79 per cent think that design's importance to competitiveness has risen over the past decade... 55 per cent of manufacturing firms see design and development as one of their most important sources of competitive advantage in five years' time.'

In practice: the role of design in brand-driven innovation

Purpose

This exercise will enable you to think about how innovations are connected to brands and to discover what role design plays in both establishing this connection, and in making the innovation worthwhile or significant.

Required

A camera, an empty wall, 16 blank postcards or large post-its, tape, felt pen, and a group of four people.

Steps

During the next few days keep track of the innovative products and services that you find valuable or meaningful. Take a snapshot of each innovation and print it. Then take four blank postcards or post-its and write or draw on them some answers to the following questions:

1 | Why is the innovation worthwhile for you?

2 | How is the innovation connected to the brand it belongs to?

3 | What is the role of design in establishing this connection?

4 | What is the role of design in making the innovation worthwhile for you?

All participants hang the cards or post-its next to the images, in the same order. Then, in the group, take turns to present your findings, and discuss the differences and similarities between them amongst yourselves. Try to come to a definition by completing the sentence: 'the role of design in brand-driven innovation is...'. Once you've come to a satisfying definition that you reach agreement upon, you're done... for now!

Upload photos of your innovations with your comments to <www.branddriveninnovation.com/book/the-role-of-design-in-bdi>.

Case study: BALTIC
Centre for Contemporary Art, UK

BALTIC

The purpose of this case study

In this case study, you will come to understand more about the role of design in building brands through innovation, and will learn about the various roles that design can play in relation to delivering tangible results: that is, through designing strategies, processes, services and cultural change.

THE BALTIC CENTRE FOR CONTEMPORARY ART
The BALTIC in Gateshead, UK is a contemporary art gallery that is housed in an old industrial flourmill on the south bank of the River Tyne, and it is the biggest gallery of its kind in the world.

About BALTIC

The BALTIC Centre for Contemporary Art in Gateshead, UK is an art gallery housed in an old industrial flourmill on the south bank of the River Tyne, and it is the biggest gallery of its kind in the world. BALTIC has no permanent collection, providing instead a changing programme of exhibitions and activities that provide an insight into contemporary artistic practice from around the world. BALTIC's vision is of a gallery that 'exist[s] to enrich people's lives with a programme that deepens their knowledge, understanding and love of contemporary visual art while increasing and broadening its impact'. This is a good example of a brand vision that invites innovation, and that will only have value if BALTIC actually succeeds in reaching the lives of people through art.

The challenge

This in turn poses the 'wicked problem': how to connect people to art in a meaningful way, despite their full lives and lack of time and despite the fact that art, and more particularly, art galleries, tend not to feature as part of most people's everyday lives. Although BALTIC has welcomed over three million visitors since it opened in 2002, it was soon apparent that it wasn't consistently achieving its ambition to bring contemporary art to the local community – from art lovers to art virgins. BALTIC believed that many visitors were not receiving the welcome, expertise or information that they expected or hoped for and that would be likely to lead them to return regularly, despite the best efforts of staff. Put simply, BALTIC was not fulfilling its brand promise. There was obviously a need for a more enriching and engaging experience among visitors to the gallery. It isn't enough to merely display the very best art if there isn't a means available for personal connection to it. Who better to 'design' that connection than the visitors themselves, in conjunction with the front of house staff that aim to deliver it?

Hiring a service design agency

BALTIC asked London service design agency, live|work, to help them to attract more visitors, particularly from amongst the local community, to improve their visitor experience and to secure a regular, loyal audience. As discussed earlier on pages 54–55, service design is an upcoming discipline that uses the best tools that design has to offer, and applies them to the development of new services and experiences. As live|work say: 'A service is made up of several interactions through a range of touchpoints over time.' These touchpoints need to go beyond people's individual expectations, but they also need to work together to create wonderful common experiences. Ben Reason of live|work explains how this is envisaged: 'Our work is driven by deep insights into people and how they behave with services. Our designers and ethnographers engage with both staff and users to uncover hidden opportunities. We enjoy complex problems and make cross-channel experiences tangible. We use creative methods and design to solve these problems.'

The project

The project aimed to improve the existing customer experience by working closely with a group of 16 members of staff from different levels across the whole organisation. The project began with the staff being given 'camera probes' (instant cameras and a photo book to store the images in), in order to record what they believed to be the good and bad customer experiences both inside and outside BALTIC. The results provided the group with a set of key customer 'needs' and possible 'opportunities' on which to base the new service proposals.

At the next stage, staff were asked to act as customers when they were sent out on 'service safaris' (going out to experience services first hand, as if experiencing wild animals on a safari!). These highly diverse experiences from all sorts of services allowed the participants to understand how services work outside BALTIC and to reflect on how they compared to the services provided by BALTIC.

DESIGN RESEARCH TOOLS AND WORKSHOPS
Live|work used various design research techniques and creative workshops to help BALTIC understand itself and its relationship with its visitors better.

Working with live | work has not only set us on course to define an outstanding visitor experience at BALTIC, but started us on a journey of wholesale cultural change.

The output of these tasks was used as the inspirational material for the next stage of the project. Using the needs and opportunities uncovered from the service safaris, the staff rapidly generated over 140 ideas on how to improve the BALTIC visitor offer. These ideas were then sketched out to make sure that the project didn't merely drown in abstract words.

Having voted on which concepts to take forward, the staff created rough prototypes of their ideas (including the use of cardboard and sticky-backed plastic) to test on the public and other BALTIC staff in real time during gallery opening hours, in order to quickly assess their viability and success. Each group recorded the impact and findings from their prototyping session, which in turn led to the next prototype iteration. In this way, staff successfully prototyped and implemented four service propositions.

In order to sustain the use of service design in improving the customer experience, live | work introduced an ideas wall and an in-house innovation team, who held regular sessions in which to review progress, set targets for getting more ideas implemented and built an ideas blog on their intranet.

Conclusions gained from the BALTIC case

1 | A brand vision is not free of consequence: companies need to deliver their vision, in the public services sector as well as in all other environments.

2 | Delivering a vision almost always requires innovation. If you can fulfil your brand promise by just doing what you've always done, your vision probably isn't very aspirational.

3 | Everything can be designed, not merely artefacts, environments and communications, but also services, too.

4 | Service designers use the same methodologies, processes, thinking modes, skills and tools as other design disciplines. However, one could argue that service designers use them more intensely because of the nature of the services they are providing (see point 5).

5 | Service design requires the understanding of a series of interactions across a range of touchpoints. These interactions have to be orchestrated into a compelling consumer journey. Service design is very much about facilitating human behaviour through design.

6 | Design more and more involves stakeholders – both users and staff – in the process. This creates involvement and participation in the project, and it makes results more immediately relevant to those who will benefit directly from them.

7 | Design research tools are fairly easy to apply in practice because they are fun to use and produce quick results that are simultaneously visual and inspiring to work with. There is, however, a trade-off between the fun and inspirational elements of qualitative research and the precision and reliability of quantitative research. It is often wise to use the two together.

BALTIC REVISITED: live/work encouraged greater audiences to the art gallery, using devices like this enormous poster attached to the exterior of the building, which reads 'You cannot help looking at this'.

Stimulated by the tools they gave us to empower staff, improvement for visitors and staff alike is not just being driven by a few, but [has been] embraced enthusiastically by all.

Clare Byers,
BALTIC's Director
of Communications

BALTIC OFFICES
BALTIC's information desk in the reception foyer reflects the gallery's vision and the way that it wants to treat its visitors and staff. Part of the research that was done to improve BALTIC's services was to directly ask the visitor for their opinions in a clear and frank way, such as this sandwich board poster which asks candidly 'Did you love us?'.

2.6 Conclusion: the role of design in brand-driven innovation

In this chapter, we've discussed the role of design in brand-driven innovation. We've learned that design is important for strategy: first of all, it has an essential role to play in the execution of strategies; it has the capacity to turn the abstract into the concrete, thus turning vision into value; and it has the capacity to connect silos and thus create synergy between the various resources of an organisation. Design thus has an execution function and a bridging function, and both are vital to brand-driven innovation.

We then explored design's third task, which lies in what we called design's 'upstream territory': to help create strategy, and to design management. This is not so much the domain of design as an operational activity, but more the domain of design thinking. We've looked at what design thinking entails and how it helps to crack wicked problems. Design thinkers have the ability to quickly switch between different modes of thinking and they follow an iterative loop of analysis, ideation, prototyping, and testing. This enables them to visualise and try out strategies, a valuable addition to the more traditional business school approach of analysis and choosing a strategy.

We went on to explore the function of design in research, defining design research as research both for and by design. The first aims at feeding designers with the necessary information and inspiration to do their jobs well. The second aims at using the designers' toolbox to undertake research, resulting in data that is accessible and inspiring, generating a process that is at once inviting and fun. We then explored how innovation and branding need design, demonstrating how design makes brand visions real and makes innovations relevant.

In conclusion, then, we have made a case for design being much more than a way to make things look prettier. We've assigned a strategic role to it and we've seen that as well being a process for creating things, it is a way of thinking about and a way of researching the world around us. In its capacity to connect, to make the intangible tangible, to visualise and prototype what might be and to create value out of vision, design provides the magnetism that holds branding and innovation together. It enables brands to innovate and it enables innovation to be infused with vision. Design is the music to which branding and innovation perform their magic dance.

In its capacity to connect, to make the intangible tangible, to visualise and prototype what might be, and to create value out of vision, design is the magnetism that holds branding and innovation together.

6   THE INNOVATION-
    BRANDING
    LOOP REVISITED
    As discussed in
    chapter 1 (pages
    16–39), innovation
    and branding are
    caught in an eternal
    loop of mutual
    symbiosis. Design
    is the magnetism
    that keeps the
    symbiosis going.

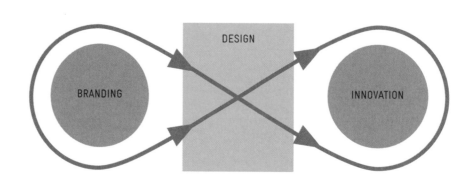

Summary insights
from chapter 2

1   Design is great at executing strategy through its ability to turn the abstract into the concrete and to integrate silos.

2   Design has a downstream territory, a bridging function and an upstream territory. All three are equally important.

3   Design's strategic role is not only to design strategically, but also to design strategy.

4   In addition to design as the creation of artefacts, communications and environments, there's design thinking and design research.

5   Design thinking is defined by the ability to switch between modes of thinking at will and the use of iterative analysis, ideation, prototyping and testing.

6   Design research is defined by doing research for design and research by design, the first leading to inspiring results and the second leading to an inviting process.

7   Brands need design because it helps them turn vision into value, and the abstract into the concrete. It fulfils promises.

8   Innovation needs design because it can connect it to the brand vision and the very real needs and aspirations of the user. It makes innovation meaningful.

9   Design, design strategy, design thinking and design research are all vital to brand-driven innovation.

PART II

Brand-driven innovation in practice

It is useful to establish a formula for brand-driven innovation that streamlines the process and helps to avoid pitfalls and re-inventions of the wheel. On the other hand, one-size-fits-all methods can be very tricky. Real life has a stubborn tendency not to adapt itself well to frameworks, processes and methods. Where pre-set methods may suggest a smooth, linear progression of events, real life is conversely chaotic, iterative and parallel.

The second part of this book builds on the theoretical foundation that we laid down in the first part. After an extensive exploration of the synergy between branding and innovation, and of the vital role that design plays in fostering that synergy, we will now look at brand-driven innovation from a practical perspective. We will look at the concrete steps that need to be taken in order to build that synergy between branding and innovation in practice, and we will establish ways in which design can help this process.

The objective of this part of the book is to help students and practitioners alike to build a concrete, step-by-step working method for brand-driven innovation that you can readily apply in your daily work. The four-step method of brand-driven innovation proposed in this book is preceded by an introductory essay that looks critically at the validity and reliability of such a method.

Introduction to part II: brand-driven innovation as a working method for organisations

A working method for BDI

The second part of this book presents the reader with a practical, step-by-step working method for brand-driven innovation. It will prove very useful to the reader as both a checklist and guideline that provides direction and facilitates processes in building a brand-driven organisation. At the same time, it should be used critically and creatively. In the following section, we'll explore why.

We need methods

Modern life is complex. The sheer number of tasks we have become accustomed to performing in parallel in our everyday lives is enormous. The number of factors we have to take into account with every daily decision is already large, and seems to be increasing over time. The number of stakeholders involved in the issues we are dealing with is also on the rise. We need specialists to deal with the specific pieces of the puzzle, but we need generalists to put them together. But do the generalists still understand the specialists? The problems we are dealing with today are often ill defined and full of paradoxes, and they also change while we work at them (see section 2.2, pages 50–55).

If each new task required us to build up an approach from scratch we would never get anywhere. We would be too busy devising approaches to problems all day, without ever reaching any solutions. The solution to such a creative impasse is to devise methods. Methods generalise, simplify and chop up complex processes. Methods tell us: 'You are not the first person to have to deal with this problem; others before you have dealt with it too. Looking at all those before you from a distance, you'll see that they've performed certain steps in a particular order, advancing to the next step when a certain result has been achieved.' Because that's exactly what methods provide: they are prescriptions to perform tasks with allocated sub-goals in a certain order, to reach a specified end-goal. They provide you with support when performing complex tasks by taking away any incipient insecurity and complexity, and restoring a sense of structure and overview.

What methods don't do

Methods don't solve problems. At most, they help you to solve the problem. Methods are instruments that are useful for meeting certain objectives, and which have been developed from strategies built by, and for, other people. It's important to view methods as such: tools that help perform the task, without replacing common sense, good judgement and genuine expertise. A carpenter doesn't expect his hammer to drive in the nail for him. He needs to operate it. Nor does he expect the hammer to adapt itself to different types of woods or different nails. He needs to apply his expertise to the situation at hand, and adapt how he handles the hammer accordingly. Strangely enough, we do make this mistake with methods sometimes: we expect them to do the work for us, and we expect them to do this regardless of the specific context of the problem at hand. There's a good reason for this: it's called wishful thinking. Methods, like complex problems, abound. If only we could stick an off-the-shelf method onto each complex problem we encountered so that – hey presto! – they simply vanished, well, that would make life a lot easier and more productive, wouldn't it?

Unfortunately, there are also some very good reasons why this doesn't work. These reasons lie in the very nature of what makes methods so useful: that they generalise, simplify and chop up complex processes. Let's look at these qualities in a bit more detail.

1 | Generalising: if methods didn't create generalities, a new method would be required for each new situation. A method presupposes that if problem A resembles problem B, we can use the same method to solve them, even though there are differences between A and B. No one tells us how large the differences between A and B may be, compared to the similarities between them. This is where scrutiny is required: although we use the same method to solve both problems A and B, A might benefit from a slightly different approach, a slight shift in focus, a minute change in the order of tasks, compared to B. We need to generalise to create and apply methods. But we need to adapt them to the situation at hand in order for them to work properly for us.

2 | Simplifying: methods ignore some of the complexity of the problem at hand, in favour of overview and clarity. A problem may be so complex that in reality it needs a sequence of a thousand steps to solve it. If a method were to prescribe these thousand steps it would ultimately be of no help in providing overview and clarity, not to mention that it would be only suited to solving that one specific problem. It's therefore important to understand where a method simplifies, in order to make sure that the real complexity is sufficiently dealt with.

3 | Chopping up: methods chop processes up into smaller chunks. This gives overview, makes it easier to plan, and it allows for sub-goals and sub-deliverables. In truth, the individual chunks of the process can't really be separated: they influence each other, take place at the same time, or depend on each other's result to function. Again, the trick is to use the chopping up to create overview and structure, without losing sight of the interconnectedness of the individual pieces and the way in which they form the whole.

Proposing a method for brand-driven innovation

Brand-driven innovation, as already discussed in chapters 1 and 2, is a complex process. It deals with many levels of abstraction, numerous stakeholders each with diverse interests and playing different roles within the organisation, over a long stretch of time. That's why a method for brand-driven innovation was developed, based on academic research and extensive testing in business practice.

The brand-driven innovation method can be seen as an innovation method (as opposed to a branding method or a design method): in essence, it sets out to provide organisations with a smart way of innovating. It does this by using the brand as a driver of innovation, by using 'design thinking' in the innovation process and by using 'design doing' in the innovation output. It builds on existing innovation methods (see Swamidass, 2000, for examples) by proposing a process that consists of several stages, and by explicitly seeing innovation as the conversion of ideas and vision into realistic and valuable solutions. But, according to Forest (1991; cited in Swamidass, 2000), many innovation models overlook the pre-innovation stage, fail to take into account how the innovation process relates to strategic planning, present innovation as a process that's isolated from internal and external contexts, ignore the human element in innovation and overlook the inherently chaotic nature of innovation. The method proposed in this book tries to avoid these shortcomings by proposing four stages that iterate between an external and an internal view, each stage successively providing input for the next.

1   THE BRAND-DRIVEN
    INNOVATION (BDI)
    MODEL
    This model represents
    the four stages of
    BDI, and iterates
    between looking at
    the organisation (the
    inside of the model)
    and looking at the
    user and its context
    (the outside of the
    model). The four
    stages are cyclical:
    new touchpoints and
    a changing world
    influence the brand
    and require stage 1
    to be revisited
    time and again.

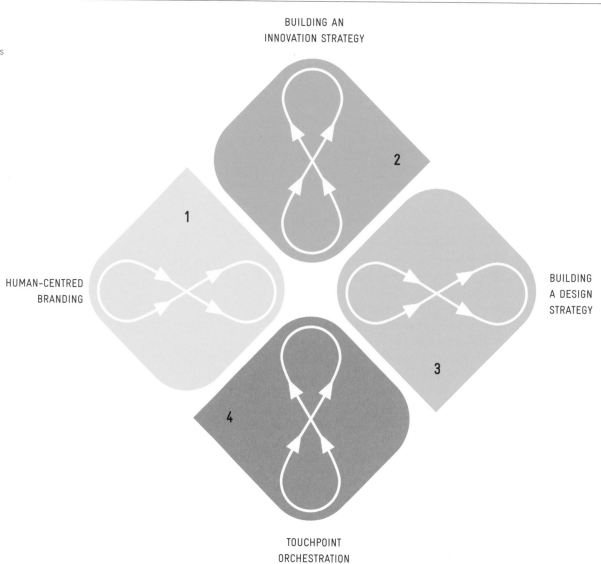

BUILDING AN
INNOVATION STRATEGY

2

HUMAN-CENTRED
BRANDING

1

BUILDING
A DESIGN
STRATEGY

3

4

TOUCHPOINT
ORCHESTRATION

The first stage: building a human-centred brand

The brand-driven innovation method starts with the premise that if the brand is to be used as a driver for innovation, then the brand first needs attention. The existing brand will need to be adapted to its new role as a driver for innovation. Or maybe a new brand will be created to execute this role. Either way, a brand that provides the foundation for innovation is different from a brand typically used in a classical marketing communication role. And it should be built and used in a different way, too. It should be built around the people who will use it as a foundation for their work, as well as around those who will derive value from the products and services that are based on it. The best way to do this will be explained in chapter 3 (pages 90–99).

The second stage: building an innovation strategy

The brand-driven innovation method next builds upon the brand-driven innovation strategy and the foundations for it laid out in the first stage. An innovation strategy maps out what an organisation plans to do in the future and how it plans to do it. What the brand-driven innovation method adds here is the essential question of why it plans to do just that. It asks: 'If this is our brand's promise, how can we fulfil that promise?' It then presents innovation as the action that naturally follows the vision for the brand. It works from the premise that the connection between the innovation strategy and the vision as laid out in the first stage is essential to its success. Thus the second step in the brand-driven innovation method sets out to build an innovation strategy that fulfils the brand's promise, and that takes into account the aspirations of both the organisation and the stakeholders it wants to create value for. It is further characterised by the fact that it uses design techniques to formulate this strategy and to make it understandable, inspirational and usable. The way to build a solid brand-driven innovation strategy is explained in detail in chapter 4 of this book (pages 108–137).

The third stage: building a design strategy

The third stage of the brand-driven innovation method is based on the premise that branding and innovation need design, as laid out in sections 2.4 (pages 58–59) and 2.5 (pages 60–61). In this third stage, design's task is to bring the innovation strategy of stage two to life in a meaningful way. It makes sure that the plans set down in stage two actually do see the light of day. Building a design strategy helps you to decide why and how to use design and what to do with it, in the context of the strategies laid out in stage two. It looks at design as an instrument to help roll out these strategies to reach your given objectives. The way to build a fruitful brand-driven design strategy will be fully explained later in chapter 5 of this book (pages 138–167).

The fourth stage: orchestrating touchpoints

The fourth stage of the brand-driven innovation method is all about execution. It operationalises all that has been decided in the preceding three stages, and provides tools to manage the roll-out of the design strategy in concrete touchpoints. It is about managing design projects and working out ways to connect them in ways that makes sense. This stage is built on the premise that in order to create a meaningful brand experience, one has to bring all the touchpoints around that brand in tune with each other. One has to orchestrate the way these touchpoints work together over time to create a total, compelling experience. This requires an understanding of the entire consumer journey (see section 3.5, pages 100–105), plus a very good understanding between the various design disciplines. The way to orchestrate touchpoints is explained in chapter 6 (pages 168–197) of this book.

Limitations of brand-driven innovation as a method

Brand-driven innovation is not always the best innovation strategy to choose. Even when it is, it's never wise to bet on one strategy alone at the expense of all the other options. And when you've chosen brand-driven innovation as a method to work with, it is wise to be aware that it is only a method, and that just like any other method, it generalises, simplifies and chops up.

First, let's look at those situations in which it makes sense to choose brand-driven innovation as an innovation strategy. The issue depends on two factors in the specific context of the organisation at hand: the extent to which the brand is suitable as a driver for innovation, and the extent to which there is room for innovation to be led by the brand (Roscam Abbing and van Gessel, 2008). The first is what we've come to call 'brand usability': the extent to which the brand is understood by designers, developers, engineers, R&D staff and others involved in the innovation process; as well as the extent to which it has sufficient depth, breadth and authenticity to inspire meaningful innovation. The second factor represents the organisation's innovation potential: the extent to which an organisation has room in its competitive field for the proactive creation of new meaningful value.

If brand usability is low, an organisation should first work on its brand before using it as a driver for innovation. Meanwhile, it should look for opportunities for innovation based on other drivers, such as market potential, technology, leveraging of intellectual property, or user trends. It would be smart for such an organisation to use these innovations to build their brand and to increase brand usability. This process is called 'innovation-driven branding': the innovation is a foundation to build the brand on, instead of the other way round.

If innovation potential is low, an organisation will not have the luxury to use its brand as a driver for innovation. It will need to grasp any opportunity for innovation it gets, regardless of what drives it. Organisations thus compromised must make strategic moves to increase their potential for innovation by diversifying into new product groups or by linking their brand to a different product category.

If brand-driven innovation *is* your innovation strategy of choice, you should still take into account what other innovation strategies have to offer and maybe combine your approach. There is, for example, a lot to learn from the online debate on user-driven innovation (UDI) (see, for instance, Prahalad, 2004, 2008, and Von Hippel, 2005). In UDI, the wishes and needs of the user form the central focus, and the organisation is required to adapt to the user, not the other way around. Where BDI looks at the relationship between the organisation and the user (= the brand) as the driver for innovation, sometimes this unremitting focus on the user is necessary.

Another school of innovation discusses the importance of design-driven innovation (DDI) [see, for example, Roberto Verganti's book by the same title (2009)]. In DDI, innovations aren't reactions to outside changes: rather, they create opportunities and new markets through a combination of design and entrepreneurship. This strategy is very close to BDI, but it depends largely on the presence of a visionary design leadership. In some cases, DDI can be an inspiring strategy to follow. And sometimes there's nothing wrong with good old technology leading the way: if you have a great new invention or technology that no one else has discovered or marketed yet, and that your users will find valuable, by all means use it!

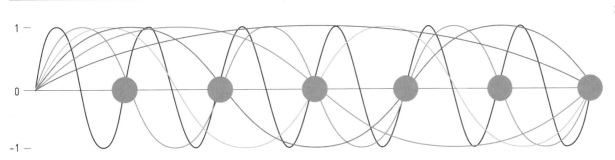

1

0

-1

2 THE FOUR STAGES
   OF BDI ARE
   NOT ALWAYS
   SEQUENTIAL
   They vary in length
   and intensity like
   the waves in this
   diagram. They may
   occur in parallel
   to each other.

BRAND USABILITY HIGH

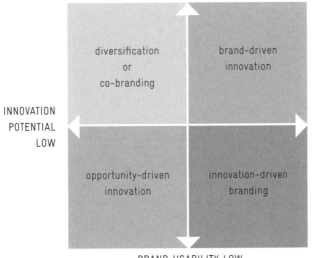

diversification
or
co-branding

brand-driven
innovation

INNOVATION
POTENTIAL
LOW

INNOVATION
POTENTIAL
HIGH

opportunity-driven
innovation

innovation-driven
branding

BRAND USABILITY LOW

3 DETERMINING
   WHETHER BDI IS
   THE RIGHT STRATEGY
   Brand usability and
   innovation potential
   determine whether
   BDI is the right
   strategy to follow.

Lastly, there are the methodological pitfalls to look out for when applying the brand-driven innovation method to your situation:

1 | Generalising: the BDI method, by its nature, does not take into account the specificities of your situation. Maybe you have several brands to work with, maybe a competitor is eating your market share, maybe your designers have no problem at all working with the brand, or maybe you only control a few of the touchpoints of your brand. In those cases, adapt the method to your needs: twist it, squeeze it and stretch it until it does what is good for you.

2 | Simplifying: the BDI method simplifies the process of deriving innovations from brands, which is in fact a very tricky process that requires a healthy dose of human ingenuity and visionary entrepreneurship. It also assigns new and somewhat simplified roles to branding, innovation and design, when in fact these are complex concepts. This is partly so because they still have their 'old' roles to fulfil in organisations.

3 | Chopping up: BDI is chopped up into four stages because in each of these stages a different type of work takes place and a specific kind of outcome is desired. This does not mean, however, that these stages are always sequential in time, or that they necessarily take place in the assigned order. Sometimes, the branding process takes a long time and requires years of building and exploring. In the meantime, innovation strategies deriving from it may be adapted every two years or so, depending on changes in the internal or external environment. Then, several different design strategies may evolve from one innovation strategy, each related to specific product categories or market segments. And they might change yearly. The touchpoints that flow from those design strategies form continuous small projects that have to be managed and orchestrated in time, and then connected back to the changing strategies they stem from. You could see the intensity of each stage fluctuating in time, like a wave (see figure 2, page 75). The first stage has the longest wavelength and the fourth stage the shortest.

Conclusion

The brand-driven innovation method as presented in the following chapters is solidly anchored in the existing discourse on branding, innovation and design. Furthermore, it flows naturally from the theory as laid out in chapters 1 and 2 and was applied and tested both in practice and on an academic basis, in an international context. Still, it is healthy to be critical about methods, and to be very aware of their scope and applicability. This introductory essay has set out to discuss both the method and its scope in a way that will enable you to judge for yourself when, where and how BDI is the strategy that will work best for you.

Pause for thought: reflections on methods

Purpose

In this section, you will have the chance to critically reflect on what you've read so far and embed this within your own experience and knowledge.

1

Looking back at chapters 1 and 2, do you think that the four phases presented here flow naturally from the preceding theory?

2

It may help you to answer this question if you visualise the contents of the four stages. Can you imagine yourself playing a role in them? If not, what would be required for you to be able to or to want to play a role in them?

3

Has the critical reflection on methods presented here been useful to you? Do you agree with the points made? Can you give examples of where methods were taken too literally and didn't work for the situation at hand?

In practice: creating your own brand-driven innovation method

Purpose

Working through this exercise, you will learn to develop methods and tools based on a given challenge in a specific context and to learn to translate what you've learned from chapters 1 and 2 into a practical way of working.

Required

A small group of three – five people, a flip chart or a large sheet of paper, many post-it notes of different colours.

1

Individually, take ten minutes to write down on post-it notes what you think the purpose of the BDI method is; for example, 'to make work more efficient' or 'to increase the value of the brand'. With the group, stick the post-its on one sheet and discuss them. See if you can make clusters of meaning, for example of 'process efficiency' or 'brand meaning'.

2

With the group, brainstorm all the ingredients you would need to reach the objectives of step 1; for example, 'a shared vision' or 'R&D and marketing in the same boat'. Write each idea on a post-it and paste them on one or several sheets.

3

Discuss all the ingredients with the group and see if you can find clusters of ingredients; for example, 'creating a shared language' or 'generating ideas'. Create a sheet for each cluster by moving the post-its around.

4

See if you can find a logical order to the clusters; can you find a sequence in which they follow naturally on from one another? Do two clusters take place at the same time, perhaps? Paste the sheets onto the wall in the order that looks logical. On each cluster sheet, write down a concise summary of what takes place in that cluster.

5

Cut arrows from some other sheets that indicate how clusters follow on from each other. It may be the case that some arrows go back in time. In each arrow, write down what is needed to go from one cluster to the next.

You're done! You've created your own brand-driven innovation method. Take a high-resolution picture, post it onto <www.branddriveninnovation.com/book/create-your-own-method> and take part in the discussion!

CHAPTER 3

Building a human-centred brand

The people playing a role in the first stage of the BDI method must have a shared vision of their performance and of the impact that they want to have. They must also fully understand the users and what they like. What's more, they must understand what the users like, better than they could ever articulate it themselves.

The first stage in the brand-driven innovation method is called 'human-centred branding' because it looks at the brand as an instrument that is used by people to create innovations that are valued by people. It's branding with a human purpose, both in terms of the usability of the brand (much like a physical tool or instrument must be designed for usability) and in terms of relevance (the way that the brand connects to a human audience).

This chapter describes what is needed to start innovating, with the brand acting as the foundation. It is a lot like setting the stage on which brand-driven innovation takes place. It's about the stage itself, which must be sturdy and big enough. It's about the props that will be used during the play. But most of all it's about the people who will perform the play and those who will be enjoying it: the performers and their audience. The performers must have respect for each other's role. They must love working together, and they must blindly trust each other.

3.1 **The role of the brand in brand-driven innovation**

Brands in the innovation function

In order for a brand to be able to form a foundation for innovation, it often needs to benefit from some special attention. Sometimes, organisations have their brand lined up in such a way that you can go straight to work (meaning that you can immediately use it to drive innovation). But mostly this is not the case. This is due to the simple fact that within organisations the brand also has a role in the marketing function. This role is fundamentally different from the role of the brand in the innovation function. We looked earlier at the different roles that brands play in the introductory essay to part I (pages 10–15). In this section, we'll discover what's different about brands that play a role in the innovation function.

1 | The brand in the innovation function has to have certain **qualities** that are frequently not assigned to it. For example, it has to inspire the ideation of new product ideas, while usually its role is more concerned with capturing and marketing the story around those product ideas.

2 | The brand in the innovation function has to perform a certain **role** that it's often not performing. For example, it has to play the role of a shared strategic vision on which decisions about the organisation's future can be based. Usually, it is there merely to add intangible value to a sales proposition.

3 | The brand in the innovation function is a building block in a **process** that it's usually not a part of. For example, it has become part of the fuzzy front end of the innovation process – that part of the process where there is no design brief yet, only ideas, possible directions and information (Koen et al, 2002), while usually it is part of the marketing and sales effort that comes after the innovation process (Buijs and Valkenburg, 2005).

4 | The brand in the innovation function will be used by **people** who are not accustomed to working with it. For example, it will be used by R&D teams consisting of more technical, rational people, while it's more common for less technically oriented marketeers to work with brands.

These four criteria together form an assessment checklist that will help to assess the condition of the brand one encounters when embarking on the brand-driven innovation journey (see pages 200–201 for such a checklist).

There are roughly three entry levels for the human-centred branding stage of BDI, depending on the overall condition that follows from the assessment checklist (see pages 200–201), as follows:

– If more than 15 answers are in the 'a bit' and 'yes' columns,
  then your brand falls into category A

– If 10–15 answers are in the 'a bit' and 'yes' columns,
  then your brand falls into category B

– If less than 10 answers are in the 'a bit' and 'yes' columns,
  then your brand falls into category C

Category A

The brand is in very good condition, very suitable for brand-driven innovation, and not much work is needed.

As we've noted before, sometimes brands in organisations already function in this way, or are very close to doing so. This is often the case in highly professional technology firms such as Festo (read the case study in chapter 4, pages 130–133). It is also the case in fast-moving-consumer-goods (FMCG) companies that have a strong R&D base (such as Procter & Gamble or the Sara Lee-owned Dutch coffee manufacturer, Douwe Egberts).

Category B

The brand is in mixed condition, and needs some work to become suitable for its role in brand-driven innovation.

This is most often the case. The brand will have to be enhanced and brought up to the level required. Although the brand has been made explicit and is used by some, it has not yet come to embody the shared vision that can be used by all in their initial processes. In such cases, stage 1 of the BDI method entails overcoming the resistance of those who were involved in creating the existing brand. The only way to deal with this is to explain to them what their brand could potentially become with some additional work, and to involve them right from the start in doing that extra work.

Category C

There simply isn't a brand explicitly present in the organisation.

This is often the case with smaller companies, or companies that have been founded by and are led by strong personalities with an intuitive way of doing business. They might posses a logo or brand identity, and maybe even a list of values or a mission statement, but there is not yet a well-defined brand in existence – let alone one that is able to drive innovation.

This chapter was written with all possible situations in mind. However, the steps described in section 3.4 (pages 90–99) are based on a C-level brand. Obviously, in scenarios A and B, less energy is needed to complete the human-centred branding stage. Use the checklists (pages 200–201) to assess where your brand stands, and then adapt the steps accordingly.

3.2 **The brand as resource**

In brand-driven innovation, the brand is envisioned as a resource: it is not an end in itself, but it is a means towards that end. It's not the result of a process but is rather an input to a process. Strategy literature tells us that resources comprise the tangible (such as raw materials and machines), the intangible (such as intellectual property) and human assets (such as the skills and general know-how) of an organisation (Grant, 2002). In BDI, the brand is the intangible resource that drives innovation (see figure 1, below). It can do this in three ways:

1 | It can be a source of inspiration: ideas for new products or services can be derived from it. It can even inspire the entry of new markets, the creation of a new business model, the formation of partnerships or the acquisition of a new technology.

2 | It can guide ideation: through the use of brand guidelines (see chapters 4 and 5) it can channel the ideation and make sure that it stays 'on brand'.

3 | It can filter ideas and directions for innovation through the use of brand criteria and checklists.

Strategy literature further tells us that valuable resources must be:
– rare
– imperfectly imitable
– non-substitutable

For the brand, this means that it has to be unique (a generic brand is not rare); it has to be based on unique insights (which makes it imperfectly imitable); and it has to be connected to the organisation itself (which makes it non-substitutable). That a resource has to be rare in order to be valuable does not also mean that it should be rare within the organisation. On the contrary: computer chips are expensive because they require gold and very complex machines to be made – both gold and very complex machines are hard to obtain, being rare, and thus are valuable resources. But in the manufacturing processes of a chip manufacturer such as Intel, these machines, and the gold, should not be rare at all: they should be readily available, in sufficient capacities and quantities to allow for an uninterrupted manufacturing process. The exact same holds true for the brand as resource: it should be readily available in an accessible format to all those who need the resource to do their job. In terms of material resources, this paradox between rareness and availability can be readily resolved through good procurement and stock keeping.

When seeing the brand as a resource, this paradox is less easy to resolve. Nevertheless, it is still crucial: on the one hand, the brand needs to be unique, rare and insightful; on the other, it needs to be accessible to all. How do you avoid hollowing out the meaning of a brand as a result of making it accessible? Or, how do you avoid decreasing its accessibility as a result of adding depth and uniqueness to it? How do you build something that is both complex and easy to use? Let's go on to explore 'brand usability' a little more.

1   HOW BRANDS DRIVE INNOVATION
Brands can drive innovation in three distinct ways: as inspiration, as a guideline and as a filter.

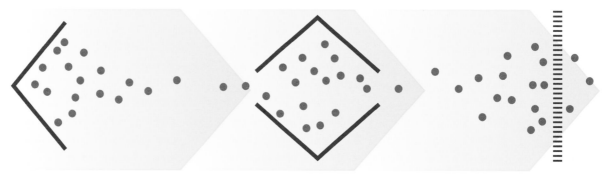

OPTION 1 THE BRAND AS INSPIRATION   OPTION 2 THE BRAND AS GUIDELINE   OPTION 3 THE BRAND AS FILTER

In practice: brand usability

Purpose

This exercise will help you to explore the concept of brand usability in a practical way, and to learn to understand the complexity of creating a brand that is sufficiently deep and inspiring, while at the same time offering easy access to all those who need to work with it.

Required

A group of five fellow students, colleagues or friends, a couple of sheets on a flip chart, post-its, felt pens.

1

Pick a corporate brand that you know very well, perhaps from a company that you've worked for. In turns, share the brand with the group, and tell the group how you know it. Write the brand on post-its and add them onto the flip chart.

2

Then, take turns in explaining what the brand stands for. Try to go as deep and wide as possible, really delving into the full meaning of the brand. Look at it from an internal point of view (the values and vision of the organisation) as well as from an external point of view (i.e. the meaning and attachment that users derive from it). Have another group member map your thoughts on post-its and paste them around the central brand post-it.

3

Lastly, discuss how that brand content could be made accessible, usable, inspiring and understandable to the organisation's employees. In turns, explain how this was done in practice and then brainstorm how this process could have been applied better. Keep taking notes on post-its and map them around the present circles on the flip chart.

4

Try to draw some conclusions: what does it take for a brand to be used by an organisation? What are the paradoxes that have to be resolved (for example, inspiring vs. concrete)?

3.3 **Brand usability**

Brand usability is the extent to which a brand, as it is found in an organisation, can be used by those who need it to do their work. Usability in products depends on the user (what's hard for some might be easy for others) and the purpose of the object (an aeroplane is harder to operate than a car). The object is the interface between the user and the purpose he or she uses it for. Usability in branding is very similar: it depends on the target group that will be using the brand and the purpose of that use.

In the traditional use of brands, it will be the marketing department using it, mostly for marketing communication purposes. In this context of use, brand usability demands that the brand can be used by people with marketing training. It also requires that it is suitable for use in advertising campaigns, packaging graphics, and public relations activities.

In brand-driven innovation's use of brands, it will be designers, developers, researchers and engineers using it, as a resource to develop new products and services. In this context of use, brand usability demands that the brand can be used by people with a more technical or creative design background. It also demands that it is suitable for use in product, service and environmental design, as well as for research and development activities.

Because the users of the brand as well as the purpose they use it for are special in BDI, brand usability in this context presents a special challenge. This is especially true given the paradox we discussed in section 3.2 (pages 80–81): the easier it is to use a brand and the more accessible it is, the harder it is to safeguard its depth, complexity and richness of insights. Resolving this paradox is what brand usability is about. In section 1.4 (pages 34–35), we previously discussed that in order for the brand to drive innovation, the content, form and process with which brands are built and captured all need to have certain attributes. These attributes can be summarised in the three golden rules of brand usability, as follows:

1 | Process – involve as many users of the brand in the creation and capturing of the brand as possible. Share and explore your findings with as many people as you can.

2 | Content – make sure that the brand content is authentic and meaningful, inspiring and understandable (see section 1.4, pages 34–35).

3 | Form –

    a | Layered: make the brand accessible in a layered manner. Show the conclusions of the process, but leave the option open for your client to delve into the process that led to those conclusions if they wish.

    b | Visual: don't just use words to illustrate your findings, use images too.

    c | Connected: don't simply use lists of words but rather indicate the relationship between those words.

2 BRAND USAGE The way in which brand-driven innovation makes use of the brand is different from how it is traditionally used, as shown in this table.		Traditional use of the brand	Brand-driven innovation's use of the brand
	What	To add value to the core offering of an organisation	To inspire the creation of the core offering of an organisation
	How	By the use of language and 2D forms and colour	By the use of 3D products and 4D services and experiences
	Who	By the marketing department	By R&D, development and design

In BDI, the brand has to be constructed in a special way: as a resource that's unique and deeply layered, but also accessible for people with a creative, technical, or research background, for purposes that involve research, design and development.

In brand-driven innovation, the brand is a resource that's unique and deeply layered, but it also has to be accessible for people with a creative, technical, or research background, for purposes that involve research, design and development. This requires a brand that has been carefully constructed, in a manner and form that's specifically suited to innovation. We will discuss this precise manner and form in greater detail shortly, in section 3.4 (pages 90–99).

SHARE AND INVOLVE	TO GENERATE CONTENT THAT'S...	AND PRESENT IT

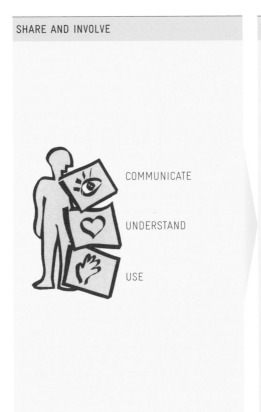

COMMUNICATE

UNDERSTAND

USE

AUTHENTIC   MEANINGFUL

USABLE

INSPIRING

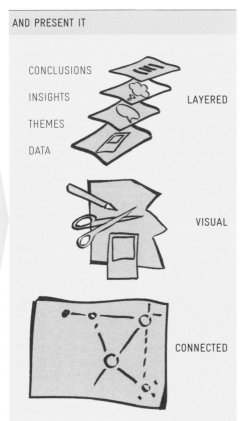

CONCLUSIONS

INSIGHTS

THEMES

DATA

LAYERED

VISUAL

CONNECTED

THE THREE GOLDEN RULES OF BRAND USABILITY
These rules refer to the way in which the brand is built (process), what it's about (content) and how it is captured (form) (see page 84).

Case study: Océ

The purpose of this case study

The following case study will help you to understand how the brand can drive innovation in a high-technology, business-to-business (B2B) organisation, and to explore how organisational culture and branding are connected.

About Océ

Océ is one of the world's leading providers of document management and printing for professionals. The broad Océ offering includes office printing and copying systems, high-speed, digital-production printers and wide-format printing systems for both technical documentation and colour-display graphics. Océ is also a foremost supplier of document-management outsourcing. The company was founded in 1877. With headquarters in Venlo, the Netherlands, Océ is active in about 100 countries and employs some 23,000 people worldwide. Total revenues in 2008 amounted to €2.9 billion (US $3.8 billion dollars – figure obtained March 2010). For more information on Océ, visit <www.oce.com>.

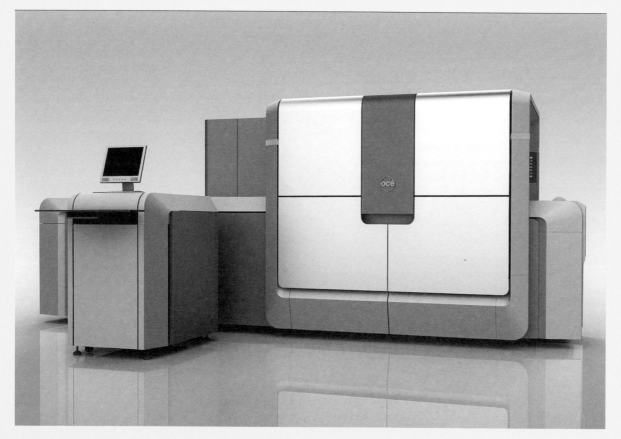

THE OCÉ
COLORSTREAM 10000
One of Océ's thoroughbred printers, for high-speed, high-volume jobs like printing brochures, books, manuals and direct mailings. It boasts Oce's distinct brand design language.

Guido Stompff, Océ

By making the embedded brand explicit, the brand starts to serve as a lighthouse for developers to orient themselves by. The artefacts we produce are ingrained with the unwritten assumptions we derive from being part of the Océ culture.

Innovation at Océ

Océ is a typical high-technology, capital-goods manufacturer: its products are highly complex, based on proprietary technology, and are aimed at a very demanding professional market. Océ's machines often play a role in their customers' core business (printing drawings for architectural firms, local editions for newspapers or account statements for banks). This puts very high demands on the durability and reliability of Océ's products. Typically, companies like these are very technology focused. This holds true for Océ, which has nine research and development sites, and more than 2000 people active in R&D (out of which one per cent are active in design).

It's unsurprising to see that Océ's innovation process starts with technology development. When we look at Océ's product portfolio, we see a tremendous attention to design and a keen focus on usability and productivity. These 'soft' values are not part of the R&D team's explicit brief, and yet they are still recognised and valued by Océ's users (Convent, 2008). How does this work? How can a company that is so focused on developing new technology introduce products to the market that have such a strong sense of consistency and which seem to stem from a powerful vision of user-centred design and attention to all stakeholders (Keus, 2008)?

Let's ask Guido Stompff, senior designer at Océ, who has been involved in researching what he calls Océ's 'embedded brand' (Stompff, 2008). Stompff has discovered that various brand-building exercises with his design and R&D teams over the years have yielded surprisingly consistent results. When it comes to framing what Océ's all about, Stompff has found that values clustered around the themes of 'involvement', 'drive', 'pragmatism' and 'independence' have consistently appeared.

Stompff says that he was 'surprised to find such consistent brand results over the years, while no one ever stated these values explicitly to my colleagues, who seemed to know what Océ was about without having to have it spelled out for them. This has led my research into the realms of organisational culture, through which I became acquainted with the seminal work of E.H. Schein (*Organisational Culture and Leadership*, 3rd ed. 2004). Schein found that within any organisation many tacit assumptions exist about what is considered "good" and "not good". These assumptions are the result of shared learning from a common past, or put differently: the result of successes and failures previously experienced. As an example, when an organisation experiences great success due to the use of innovative technology, it will assume that in order to be successful, one needs to innovate. If an organisation experiences great success in reselling and repositioning the products of others, it will assume that good marketing and not innovation will do the job.

'Schein derived the following significant relation: artefacts (such as buildings, dress code, but also employee behaviour) are a result of these underlying tacit beliefs. To make this more explicit: the products that an organisation develops and/or sells are the enacted beliefs of this organisation. Whether or not organisations like it, the beliefs of the organisation manifest themselves "authentically" in all sorts of artefacts (Gilmore and Pine II, 2007), and therefore contribute strongly to the brand as it is experienced by users. For organisations like Océ, in which the brand and the organisation strongly reflect each other (as is also the case for Apple, Microsoft, BMW and Sony), the brand should fall in line with this belief system.'

Stompff continues: 'It is easy to relate Schein's "levels of culture" to brand-related topics. (The model in figure 3 (below) clearly demonstrates the parallels that exist.) According to Schein, culture has three levels: a primary level of basic assumptions that are taken for granted (for instance, Singapore Airlines believes that the best way to differentiate is through pampering clients travelling on their planes, above all through personal contact); a further level of espoused beliefs and values that are made explicit (the service manual for the stewardesses, which details the values that they should endeavour to communicate); and a final level of artefacts, the physical manifestations of these beliefs (the behaviour of the stewardesses, the seats in Singapore Airlines business class, the food that is served). Brand touchpoints are fully in keeping with these cultural artefacts (a passenger will experience Singapore Airlines through its food, the kind stewardesses, the chairs); and the espoused values are similar to "formal" brand descriptions, such as the brand personality.

'These "lower" two levels can also be evidenced in the brand at Océ, and this teaches us a lot about how our brand drives what we do with design and R&D. However, the level of assumptions had no counterpart in branding until recently, so at Océ I started to name this the "embedded brand". Our brand is "embedded" in our organisation much like assumptions are: after working at Océ for a couple of years, it becomes part of our own way of doing things. Sometimes, this embedded brand is made explicit. The brand-building exercises were designed to enhance awareness of these underlying assumptions and to articulate their positive aspects. By doing so, the brand starts to serve as a lighthouse for the developers to orient themselves by and so align their work. But, regardless of this step, the artefacts we produce are ingrained with the unwritten assumptions we derive from being part of the Océ culture. This not only applies for Océ: any organisation that develops products has a belief system and a frame of reference about what is "good", and these beliefs always shine through in the products it develops.'

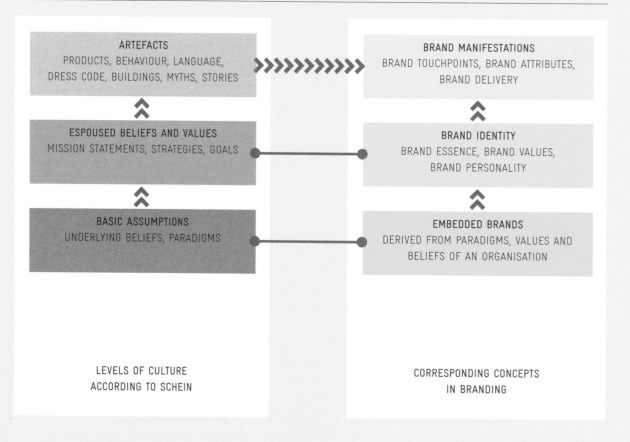

3   LEVELS OF CULTURE AND BRANDING
     The levels of culture as Schein (2004) distinguishes them correspond with the levels in branding as distinguished by Guido Stompff.

Very often, the way in which brands are presented to the organisation does not contribute towards a shared understanding. Only when they are experienced as authentic will they serve as a source of the organisation's identity.

It appears that for Océ, the act of articulating the brand drives the innovation process by helping engineers and designers decide on how to do things and what to focus on. But this is a process that seems to fit only small teams of designers and developers, due to the efforts that it requires. How should a manufacturer employing 25, 000 people articulate its tacit assumptions? And is it then possible that users appreciate these products consistently because of ease of use, productivity and ergonomics?

Guido Stompff considers that this is 'precisely why the concept of the brand is so relevant. Though Schein is widely acclaimed to be the founding father of organisational culture, he focused on defining and demonstrating it, but didn't make it operational. Put differently: he understood culture, but left it up to others how to manage, change or even transform it. I think branding could serve as an excellent platform from which to articulate, discuss, explore, change and even manage what the underlying assumptions of developers are. By discussing the brand one can discover what is "good" and why it is considered such. In my experience, in cases of contesting requirements – let's consider the classic cost price versus product quality discussions – the brand often serves as a perfect tool with which to align actions. By just asking the simple and straightforward question, "Is this an Océ solution?", or "Is it worthy of becoming an Océ product?", team members quickly come to conclusions that go beyond the realms of their usual turf. It provides a platform, a larger common goal, that enables the balancing of often complex matters.'

But if the organisation's beliefs and assumptions crystallise into good products (because development teams similarly hold these beliefs and assumptions), why the need to explain them by means of the brand? It seems that you could potentially leave them 'embedded'.

Guido Stompff argues that this is true, but that 'it ignores the nature of modern product development. Most – maybe even all – products that Océ develops are co-developed in some way. Océ has eight sites, and some products are developed by four sites: parts or modules are outsourced to external parties; some products truly are co-developed by a group of companies. In short, whereas until a decade or so ago organisational culture could serve as a source for alignment, nowadays teams are comprised of people who do not share the same organisational background, yet still need to align their actions. Explaining what the brand stands for, telling the mythical stories of past successes, demonstrating which existing products are real brand ambassadors, designing future products that show what the brand is about; these are all ways to speed up the process of teaching and learning what the "tacit" assumptions and beliefs are. And make no mistake: as Schein argued, very often the espoused formal values (the way in which brands are mostly presented to the organisation) do not contribute towards this shared understanding. Only when the brand is experienced as genuine and authentic will it serve as a source of the organisation's identity.'

Conclusions to be gained from the Océ case study

1 | The brand at Océ is 'embedded', much like cultural assumptions are.

2 | Branding, in the context of innovation, is closely connected to organisational culture.

3 | Innovations at Océ are brand-driven in a tacit way: Océ's culture gravitates around high ambitions regarding ease of use and productivity and this manifests itself in all of Océ's touchpoints.

4 | A brand that is shaped by history and is ingrained within the skin of the organisation is more likely to drive innovation than a brand that was constructed from scratch.

5 | The brand is a way to make assumptions and beliefs explicit, and thus shareable between teams.

3.4 **The human-centred branding stage**

Human-centred branding is the name for a brand-building method that places the human side of branding central to its approach: it looks closely at brand usability to ensure that it is accessible and inspiring to those who work with the brand. But it also looks at users, and how they can derive value from the brand if it manages to translate the brand vision into valuable products, services and experiences. The method combines all the branding insights of the previous chapters into one framework, which has been tested at several organisations in different markets.

There are a number of principles that underpin the human-centred branding framework:

1 | Reasoning from the concrete to the abstract and back again.

2 | Building the brand from the inside out, as well as from the outside in.

3 | Using iterations instead of a linear process. After each step in the process, the validity of the previous step is checked and – if necessary – adapted to the new insights.

4 | Using creative workshops and generative techniques to gather information.

5 | Involving as many people as practically possible and thoroughly documenting each step in a visual format (such as video and photos).

The human-centred branding stage is outlined step-by-step on pages 91–95, involving a first phase (A), iterating second and third phases (B and C) and a fourth phase (D). (See figure 5 on page 92 for the process in model form.)

4   THE BRAND AS RELATIONSHIP
The brand establishes and captures the relationship between a company's internal stakeholders and external stakeholders. The brand is both fed by, and feeds the needs and desires of both groups of stakeholders.

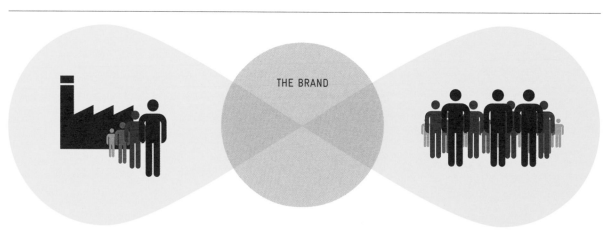

INTERNAL BRAND STAKEHOLDERS
DESIGNERS
ENGINEERS
RESEARCHERS
MARKETERS

THE BRAND

EXTERNAL BRAND STAKEHOLDERS
USERS
BUYERS
DEALERS
SERVICE PERSONNEL

Phase A: plan the project

This phase is important because embarking on a branding project such as this can often stir up both discussion and controversy. Digging into 'the soul' of an organisation can be confrontational. Therefore, it is extremely important to carefully explain why the organisation should embark on this process, what it will look like, what kinds of results are to be expected and what kind of individual commitment may be required. The preparation phase should be designed to get everyone on board and to carefully manage expectations.

Form a team of stakeholders

Look at who will be working with the brand. Whose task will it be to deliver on the brand promise? Involve these people! Form a team of designers, researchers, marketers and developers and explain to them what you are planning to do and why. Try to go as high up as possible (involve the boss or the owner of the company), but also involve people that stand out on the work floor. And involve some external partners as well, such as dealers, service personnel or agents. If the group becomes too big, you can always consider forming a core team who will be present at all the sessions and a separate group of additional people to attend special sessions.

Discuss and fill out the brand-assessment checklist

See pages 200–201 for a full version of this list. It's vital that many internal stakeholders fill out this list. The process and discussions that occur while filling it in are more important than the result. So don't send out the list as a questionnaire, but instead form small discussion groups to work on it together. Also be sure to document any discussions or arguments that arise while the groups work on the assessment.

Plan the project

A good human-centred branding process involves many creative sessions with large groups of people. These sessions take time to prepare (at least a day per session but often longer), conduct (half a day or a full day per session) and document (editing video material, transcribing audio recordings and selecting images easily require a day per session). Getting external stakeholders (such as users) involved also takes a lot of time (for example, it may take a week to recruit ten users). Afterwards, the data that is harvested during these sessions needs to be analysed and organised (this will take one or two days per session). The specialists that may be required to facilitate workshops and conduct user research also have to be booked in advance. So plan ahead and reserve enough time. A human-centred branding project for a company that is 500 people strong may take half a year or more. For a ten-person start-up, it may take three months.

5 THE
HUMAN-CENTRED
BRANDING STAGE
The human-centred
branding stage
consists of four
steps: plan the
project, research
internal brand
context, research
external brand
context and create
the brand promise.

D
CREATE BRAND PROMISE

B
RESEARCH INTERNAL
BRAND CONTEXT

C
RESEARCH EXTERNAL
BRAND CONTEXT

A
PLAN THE PROJECT

INTERNAL BRAND STAKEHOLDERS
DESIGNERS
ENGINEERS
RESEARCHERS
MARKETERS

EXTERNAL BRAND STAKEHOLDERS
USERS
BUYERS
DEALERS
SERVICE PERSONNEL

Phase B: research internal brand context

This phase starts by analysing the brand as it is present in the organisation. It goes from the very concrete brand touchpoints to the abstract, 'embedded', cultural brand assumptions (see the Océ case study on pages 84–87). At this level, the brand is reconstructed, resulting in an internal vision statement. This phase may take place in parallel with phase C: external brand research. The internal insights can enrich the external research, and the external insights can likewise enrich the internal research. If the company is a start-up and there are no brand touchpoints or statements yet, the phase can instead start at the third step.

Analyse current brand touchpoints

Analyse the organisation's current artefacts, communications, buildings and environments, services and behaviour. Look at them from a branding perspective: what meaning do they convey? What implicit choices do they represent? If, for example, an organisation reserves guest parking places right next to the entrance, this tells us something about that organisation's hospitality. If an organisation's products have a life-long warranty, this in turn tells us something about that organisation's esteem for durability and quality. It can also be a worthwhile exercise to look at the competitors' touchpoints and analyse what they convey as a point of reference.

Analyse current explicit brand statements

Analyse all brand statements that are explicitly made and presented on paper (or online): the brand vision, mission statements, personality traits, brand promises, brand values, and so on. Analyse what meaning is conveyed and what tone of voice is deployed. Compare results with the touchpoints and try to explain the differences. It may be that certain statements are hard to put into practice, while some practices are hard to put into words.

Analyse 'embedded' organisational culture, norms and values

Explore and analyse the organisation's 'embedded' brand by looking at typical manifestations of 'how we do things around here'. Use design research to get to the bottom of things. Try to take a complete overview of organisational 'assumptions': those beliefs and paradigms that seem to be such an integral part of the company that they are taken for granted. For an organisation such as innocent smoothies (pages 20–23) for example, this might be the belief that work and fun go hand in hand. For Icebreaker (pages 26–29), it might be the notion that environmentalism is stylish. This phase can be conducted using the techniques that are further discussed on pages 97–98.

Recreate explicit brand statements

Take what you've learned in the previous step and try to boil everything down to a number of clear diagrams explaining the organisation's values, personality, vision and mission. Revisit the explicit brand statements as studied before, adapt them according to your newly gained insights and capture them in diagrams. The use of diagrams and models in this step is important for two reasons. First, explicit brand statements should be visual to be remembered well. Secondly, they should indicate the connections between individual insights or the processes by which individual elements of the brand are derived from each other. For example, our founder was an inventor. Inventiveness is in our heritage. Therefore, we are naturally drawn to inventive and curious people. So being innovative comes naturally to us.

Create internal vision statement

This statement can again be presented in the form of a diagram or model and should contain answers to the questions: 'Why do we do what we do?' ('What moves us?'); 'How do we do it?' ('What's our way of working?'); and 'What do we do?' ('What business are we in?'). The answers to these questions can be distilled from the previous steps.

Phase C: research external brand context

This phase can take place in parallel with phase B: internal research. In the external research phase, we go outside to meet our external stakeholders: these are mainly users, but depending on the organisation, the business it's in and the brand it is developing, these can also be dealers, service personnel, agents, store personnel and buyers. In short, the brand's external stakeholders are all those people that somehow derive value from the brand and are impacted in their behaviour and choices by it. It is vital to get to know and to deeply understand these people, their motivations and behaviour and the contexts in which they come into contact with the brand.

Define most representative target group segments

This is a tricky one. How can you decide which target group to research, if you don't sufficiently know your target group in the first place? The advice here is to use the iterations we discussed earlier about design thinking: first, use what you already know from previous research, or from your organisation's retailers or dealers. Start the research and refine and redefine as you go.

Define contextual research questions and themes

In contextual research, it is important to frame the research in such a way that a sufficiently broad context is researched, without losing focus. For example, when doing research for a fashion brand for urban youngsters you may want to look into their behaviour with regards to how they live, how they study or go to school, how they go out and which cultural activities they undertake. Because the brand for these people is not an isolated entity that is 'consumed' in isolation, becoming aware of the context in which the brand is experienced is thus very important.

Set up context-mapping research

Setting up a context-mapping research programme (see section 3.5, pages 100–105) requires time. It is not easy to frame the right questions and design the right workshop activities based on the themes of the previous step. What's more, a sufficiently large group of target-group representatives will have to be recruited for the research. There are specialised agencies who can help you out with this but they will also require time (and a budget) to provide this help. In general, a series of contact moments (workshops, house visits) is advisable in order to allow the external stakeholder to become more aware of, and more explicit about their own motivations and behaviour.

Perform context-mapping research

Again, it is important to involve as many internal stakeholders in the process as possible. If experienced people facilitate the workshops and house visits, other internal stakeholders who are not experienced researchers can accompany them. Because, ultimately, nothing beats meeting a user for yourself, in their own context. Be sure to document each stage carefully and visually. Again, the research order goes from the concrete behaviour involving artefacts that surround the user, to his or her more abstract opinions and ideas. From here, your research moves on to explore the user's visions and values. In the next step, these form the basis from which you can re-interpret the more concrete layers.

Harvest context-mapping results

Don't let the quantity and enormous variety of data that emerges from these kinds of research scare you. If you take enough time, and gather enough curious and creative people together to analyse the results, harvesting will occur by itself: patterns will emerge and insights will naturally occur to you.

Create external vision statement

This statement should again be presented in the form of a diagram or model and should contain answers to the following questions: 'Why do they do what they do?' ('What moves them?'); 'How do they do it?' ('What's their way of working?' or, 'What are the processes in which they use our offering?'); and 'What do they do?' ('How do they behave?', 'What does their life in the context of our offering look like?').

Phase D: create brand promise

This is the final phase of the first stage of the brand-driven innovation process, and it's the stepping-stone to the next stage. In this phase, all the findings of the internal and external research are combined into one place. As we've already discussed in section 1.1 (pages 18–23), the brand defines the relationship between the organisation's internal and external stakeholders. It is in this phase that the relationship is made explicit in the form of a brand promise, as discussed on page 32.

Combine insights from internal and external research

Compare notes. See if and how the insights from the internal research match those from the external research. What are the key differences? In the case of the fashion brand it might be, for example, that internally people are very proud of the brand and regard it as the best brand on the market, while externally people might like it, but only as one of many fashion brands from which they create their outfits.

Define the relationship

What sort of relationship would naturally evolve from the insights that resulted from the internal and external research? How does that compare to the actual relationship between the organisation and its users? For example, the fashion company may want to lock its users into the brand by selling them entire outfits and giving them discounts when they buy more than one item; but users may not appreciate this 'possessive behaviour' and prefer a more 'open' relationship.

Define the brand promise

This statement should again be presented in the form of a diagram or visual and should describe what the target group's values are, explain why and how the organisation will deliver those values, before then describing what the organisation will do to deliver those values.

Case study: Priva

The purpose of this case study

The following case study will give you the opportunity to understand the process of human-centred branding in practice, and to learn to realise the potential effects that a branding project like this may have on an organisation. This case study focuses not so much on *what* to do in a human-centred branding project (see section 3.4, pages 90–95 for more on that), but more on *how* to do it.

About Priva

Priva is a Dutch company that develops and markets hardware, software and services for climate and process control, both in the horticultural and in the building intelligence market. Priva started up in the 1960s selling heating systems for greenhouses. The CO_2 that escaped from the gas-heaters proved to have a tremendous beneficial effect on the crops. Soon, Priva managed to leverage from this gain in growing efficiency by broadening their scope: they moved from selling heating to selling expertise on the entire climate management of greenhouses. Their next step was to move from horticulture and greenhouses to climate-control systems in buildings. This presented a very different market, with comparable climate challenges. The company became international, expanded and is now a 400-person strong organisation which is active in 72 countries. Priva is a family-owned company that attaches the utmost importance to dealing respectfully with people and the environment.

Priva CEO, Meiny Prins, explains: 'Priva considers it a duty and a responsibility to use and manage resources, nature and the environment with the utmost care. That is why innovation with a view to sustainability will be a high priority in the years to come. Priva's own recently completed company headquarters, the Priva Campus (in De Lier, the Netherlands), provides a good example of this, being one of the few CO_2-neutral office buildings in the world.'

The challenge

As a company, Priva has experienced two major changes over the last five years: first, the founder, Jan Prins, stepped back in 2006 and left the leadership of the company to his daughter, Meiny Prins; secondly, the building intelligence business unit increased rapidly in size and turnover. Although some of Priva's greenhouse products proved to work well in buildings, the building intelligence market proved to be completely different, both in terms of business model and value chain, and also in terms of technology, product portfolio, installation and service. The building market was serviced through a separate business unit that slowly but steadily developed their own way of doing things.

What Meiny soon noticed was that the norms and values her father had instilled in the company through years of commitment and hard work needed to be practised by everyone, not just the original horticulture business unit (BU). The quick development and learning curve of the building BU needed to benefit the rest of the company. Meiny did not want to lose the synergy between the two BUs, and she wanted them to act on the basis of only one set of values and beliefs. Why? Because she knew that if a company wants to focus on innovation and show leadership in sustainability, it needs to have strong beliefs, a clear vision and a determined will to act on them.

The project

In early 2009, Meiny asked Zilver innovation to set up a project for making the organisation's embedded values and beliefs explicit, and to assess to what extent these were shared across the layers and departments of Priva. The initial hypothesis proposed that underneath the two BUs of 'Agro' and 'Building' (A and B in the illustration on page 98) was one set of shared beliefs, based on the organisation's heritage and family DNA. The trick was to uncover them, make them explicit and make them easy to act upon. Priva realised that this shared vision formed their core brand identity, and that this brand could guide everyday decisions and long-term strategic planning if it was made accessible and usable.

If a company wants to focus on innovation and show leadership in sustainability, it needs to have strong beliefs, a strong vision, and a strong will to act by it.

Step one: Uncovering values through internal workshops

The project started with a number of workshops to uncover latent and embedded values within Priva's management team and leaders. The setting of the workshops was informal and creative and went from exploring concrete artefacts and behaviour to more abstract beliefs and values, before then turning back to concrete actions. This process was enhanced through a number of creative exercises, as follows:

– Prepare a short presentation of what you love about your work at Priva using an image brought from home.

– Write about important events in the history of Priva on a postcard and hang them on a clothes line. Work together with people in your group to put them in the right order.

– Create an important event for Priva, such as a dealer day: what would you do?

– If you were to go on a field trip with someone from another department within the company, what would that trip be like? What would you do together and how would you learn from each other?

– Within your department, make a collage of your customer. How is your customer different from other customers?

The workshop was repeated in a number of iterations. The first group (top management) facilitated the second group (middle management) who in turn reported on the findings of the workshops to their teams.

Step two: Analysing data and finding patterns

The various workshops generated an enormous amount of data, captured in the form of exercise results (such as collages), photos, notes and film. The complete research team (two consultants, the design manager and a team manager) spent several days analysing the data in search for patterns: idiosyncrasies, structures, processes, contradictions, similarities and hierarchies. Patterns such as these help to make sense of the data, and to summarise it in clear insights that can be communicated and remembered. There is no rulebook for this type of analysis: it's an iterative cycle of discovering individual snippets of information and clustering them together in groups that make sense. Between these groups (and within them) new patterns emerge. It's a bit like a child organising its Lego collection: clustering the bricks according to size, colour, or type and then organising these clusters so that they make sense in further play.

What emerged from the data analysis were some very clear patterns regarding Priva's way of creating value, Priva's way of building partnerships, their understanding of their customers and of how they create value.

Step three: Getting everyone involved

The patterns that were discovered and a summary of the findings in the form of a new brand promise were sketched on large sheets and presented first to the board of managers, and later to the entire company in a quarterly meeting. They were consciously presented as sketches, not as final results: it's important that insights like these are owned by everyone, and that everyone can have their say on them. The research team did not present the sketches as something that they had uniquely 'created' or 'discovered', but purely as renditions of what was said during the sessions, and as a visual record of them. Again, this was done to create a sense of shared ownership of the results.

Meiny Prins, CEO

The process has helped tremendously in making our shared vision explicit. It needs time, but what we see now is people applying the vision to how they deal with customers, to how they innovate, to how they do business.

Step four: Presenting results

After management and the rest of the organisation had approved the initial insights, the research team made a booklet to present them in the right order and in a more final format. The booklet presented the findings but also the hurdles that had to be overcome. It was distributed amongst the entire organisation, including sales offices abroad.

Step five: The brand ambassadors

With the booklet finished and the insights shared, it was time to start building on the brand. A team of 'brand ambassadors' was assembled, on a voluntary basis, with representatives from all layers and departments of the organisation. Their task was to discuss ways in which the brand vision could be put into practice, and to determine how things encountered in everyday work may help or prevent people from 'living the brand'. Their mission was to implement their findings in their own work environment, and to help colleagues follow their lead. Management received dedicated brand training from the research team to better coach the brand ambassadors.

Step six: Follow up

The Priva brand vision formed the foundation for a refined innovation roadmap, a renewed focus on user-centred design, as well as design guidelines for the organisation's products, communications and environments. We asked Meiny Prins about her experience of the process, and she stated that: 'We see entrepreneurship returning to the work floor. Our culture has become one of initiatives, taken from the bottom up, with an emphasis on people finding their own inner strength. It is hard to maintain this culture in a rapidly changing world with much insecurity. But I believe that the efforts we are putting into this internal branding project are really paying off. We are taking our brand values very seriously and applying them to everything we do, both internally and externally.'

We also asked Judith van Zanten, Priva's design manager, how she experienced the changes. Judith replied: 'What this process has achieved for us is a more external focus on our product-development activities: because we are more certain about who we really are, we have become even more curious about who our customers really are. This has already led to customer panels, which we consult to explore new opportunities and to discover where we share our innovations and ask for feedback. The "brand in progress" programme has been an internal programme; the next step is to take it outside and enrich the relationships we have with our dealers, partners, installers and end-users with the Priva way of doing things.'

TWO PEAKS, ONE BASE
The challenge of this case was to uncover the shared vision underneath the surface of the two business units of Priva.

Conclusions to be gained from the Priva case

1 | With dedication, it is possible to create a brand vision that is owned, understood and cherished by everyone.

2 | Creative exercises in workshop format help to make embedded values and assumptions explicit.

3 | Building a brand that works is about three things: sharing, sharing and sharing.

4 | A brand that is based on an organisation's history, norms and values isn't created, it's discovered and made explicit.

5 | At some point, external consultants have to step back: ownership of, and leverage from the brand can only take off when the brand is the organisation's responsibility.

workshop 1

workshop 2

analyse the findings

quarterly employee meeting

starting to build the future

the 'booklet'

and now it is up to you

a call for participation

THE PRIVA 'BRAND IN PROGRESS' PROCESS
The brand-building process involves many steps and many stakeholders (top).

DOCUMENTING RESULTS
In projects like these, it is vital to document everything that is said during workshops and interviews very carefully, and to allow time to play with the results: it takes patience to cluster into relevant groups, find connections, and see parallels (left).

BRAND AMBASSADOR WORKSHOP
Brand ambassadors are people from all layers and departments of Priva, who discuss together how they've used the brand in their work, and what challenges they encounter in implementing its values (above).

3.5 Skills for human-centred branding: an overview of tools and methods

As we discussed earlier in chapter 2 (pages 40–67), design research is very effective for building brands. Design research is an immensely interesting field with many truly inspiring techniques and a rich set of cases. What follows is only the tip of the iceberg, but it will give you some insight into why design research is relevant to brand-driven innovation.

A small design research toolbox

What follows are some basic design research tools that you will frequently encounter in projects. There are many, many more (Laurel, 2003), but this will provide you with a good first overview.

Consumer journeys

Purpose: to create an understanding of the experience a user of a product or service has over time.

Consumer journeys are a visual map of a user's experience over time. Typically, it shows time on a horizontal axis, while on the vertical axis it may map different users or different levels of experience (e.g. functional or emotional). The consumer journey includes the timeframes before and after actually using the product or service. Personas often serve as input for the consumer journey, demonstrating that the journey is different for each consumer.

Personas

Purpose: to create empathy for the stakeholders in a project by prototyping archetypical stakeholders.

Personas are visual and anecdotal profiles of people, based on 'real people' from research or 'made-up' in brainstorming sessions. Personas are constructed from elements that are relevant to the project at hand, but usually contain some demographic information; something about their social lives and something about their work lives. Usually, several personas are created, each representing one group of stakeholders. The form of the persona depends on who will work with them, but in general it can be said that the more visual and richly detailed they are, the better they will work.

CONSUMER
JOURNEY EXAMPLE
An example of a consumer journey map, by service designer Lauren Currie, for the service 'say women', a voluntary organisation that offers accommodation for young women who are survivors of childhood sexual abuse, and who are threatened with homelessness.

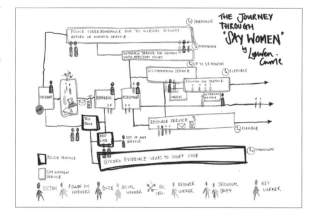

PERSONA EXAMPLE
An example of a persona that was created based on research into the lifestyles of the users of a fashion brand.

Cultural probes (Gaver et al, 1999)

Purpose: to gather data without intrusion, by playfully leading users to self-reflection and self-expression.

Design research is often aimed at learning things about users that are often hard to bring to the surface. Cultural probes are tools that help users to reflect on their own lives and to express themselves visually. This way, the researcher doesn't need to be present when the data is captured. Cultural probes typically consist of a diary booklet, which the user fills out over a period of time. Cultural probes are often followed by an interview or a house visit.

7daysinmylife.com

Purpose: gathering user insights in an easy way.

<www.7daysinmylife.com> is an online research tool that is designed to provide those who will work with the brand with inspiring insights into the life of the user of the product or service. <www.7daysinmylife.com> consists of a collection of online diaries assembled by respondents, who fill the diaries with their own images and text over the course of seven days, in response to various assignments and questions. Researchers can follow the progress of the diaries and comment upon them. The dialogue that evolves from this forms the basis for deep diving into the data.

Generative sessions

Purpose: to allow research participants to better express themselves, by making things rather than merely talking.

In many cases, interviews or questionnaires are not the best way to learn to understand users, simply because users aren't accustomed to talking about their own experiences or emotions. Generative sessions, as pioneered by people like Liz Sanders (<www.maketools.com>), circumvent this by letting users create collages, artefacts, prototypes or models in response to an assignment or question. The user talks while creating, or uses the artefact as a basis for their story, which removes inhibitions and often uncovers deeper insights.

CULTURAL PROBES
An example of a cultural probe, in the form of a diary booklet that is filled in by the user of a product or service. In this case, designer André Weenink did the research for a Dutch fashion brand.

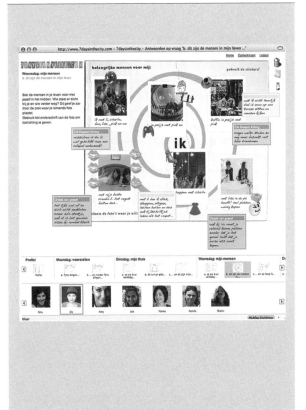

7DAYSINMYLIFE.COM
A screenshot of a page from <www.7daysinmylife.com>, an online diary environment for researching into the daily lives, desires and aspirations of users of products or services.

GENERATIVE SESSION
An example of a generative session, where users create artefacts and collages to help them talk about their experiences and needs. The creations are not a goal in themselves; instead they are used as a basis for storytelling.

Storyboards

Purpose: to capture the various aspects of a brand experience or sequence of product/service interactions in a visual way.

Storyboarding is a narrative technique adopted from the film industry and adapted to suit the needs of designers interested in ways to communicate the various features of a particular design. Storyboarding can be used to test and evaluate ideas, as well as to communicate them to others (‹www.enginegroup. co.uk›). Storyboards are normally presented as a series of 'frames' that communicate a sequence of events, such as a customer journey.

Contextual inquiry

Purpose: to learn to understand users in their own context (often their homes) and to collect richly visual data about this context.

Contextual inquiry involves spending time with a person in their own territory (such as their home, social environment or workspace) combining loosely structured interviews and observations. This technique can be seen as a form of 'ethnography for design', with less strict rules than ethnography and producing an output that's more suitable for designers. Contextual inquiry involves collecting detailed information about user's life at home or work by observing and interviewing the user while they go about their business.

Context mapping

Purpose: to gain a deep and rich understanding of people and their relationships to the products and services that they use, by involving them in a combined research and design process.

Context mapping, a combination of the various techniques and tools mentioned above, was developed at the Delft University of Technology by the department of Design for Interaction, part of the School for Industrial Design Engineering. Context mapping is a procedure for conducting contextual research with users, where tacit knowledge is gained about the context of the use of products. It aims to inform and inspire design teams, where users and stakeholders actively participate in the design process to ensure a good fit between the design and the use of a product. It makes use of cultural probes, generative sessions, various mapping techniques and storyboards, with one important over-riding principle: it sees the user as the specialist in his or her own life. It also tries to provide the user with the necessary creative tools to enable them to express themselves as such.

STORYBOARDS
Storyboards are a great way to visualise a sequence of events. This one was created by Delft University of Technology Strategic Product Design students for a study assignment.

Pause for thought: reflections on research

Purpose

In this section, you will start to develop a toolbox of research techniques to help you think about building human-centred brands. We've now explored a number of ways to conduct both internal and external research for branding. We've discovered that research techniques in which stakeholders are isolated from their context are less suitable for this purpose.

Contextual inquiry, context mapping and various forms of design research and design ethnography are more suitable. It's a good habit to develop your own toolbox of exercises for this purpose.

Let's start now!

CONTEXTUAL INQUIRY
Contextual inquiry research involves spending time with users in their own environment and context. A detailed documentation of this context and the way the user behaves in it and talks about it can be very inspiring for designers.

1

First, think of the objective: for example, what is it that you want to know? (What hidden values ultimately lie behind our current brand touchpoints?)

2

Think of how you might get to know this (for example, give people the role of guide, and let them give the team a guided tour around the building, explaining why things are the way they are).

3

Think of what might go wrong (for instance, people might be shy to guide a group around).

4

Solve those issues (perhaps by forming small teams that guide each other around, recording the tour on video).

5

Go through these steps for a number of brand questions and then design your own toolbox!

If you want to share your findings, or see what others have made of it, please go to <www.branddriveninnovation.com/book/toolbox> and join in the discussion!

A conversation between specialists: design research and contextmapping for branding

The following conversation between Liz Sanders and Froukje Sleeswijk Visser discusses user insight research methods. It explores how user insight studies can help to define an organisation's vision and the extent to which the tools and methods of contextmapping are suitable to develop visionary brands.

Liz Sanders is a pioneer in the use of participatory research methods for the design of products, systems, services and spaces. Liz teaches at Ohio State University's Design Department, the School of Design at the University of Dundee and the School of Design at Carnegie Mellon University. She is the founder of MakeTools, who explore generative tools for collective creativity. Liz has a PhD in Experimental and Quantitative Psychology from Ohio State University.
‹www.maketools.com›

Froukje Sleeswijk Visser studied Industrial Design Engineering at the Delft University of Technology. She missed the human side implicit to designing products and so embarked on a PhD project (2004–2009) that revolved around contextmapping and how to communicate and share user insight research results amongst multidisciplinary design teams. Froukje divides her time between teaching in Delft, and practising contextmapping for clients.
‹www.contextqueen.nl›

Froukje, you finished your PhD in 'contextmapping'. How would you describe this research method in a nutshell?

Froukje: Contextmapping is a research approach useful for collecting everyday user experiences and for informing and inspiring the design process. It is set up as a procedure combining several qualitative research methods such as interviews, observations, generative techniques and elements from probes. A typical contextmapping study has three basic components:

1 | Users are sensitised in their own environment and time before they participate in a session or interview. By means of self-documentation, they map their everyday life and what the product use or a routine means to them.

2 | During interview sessions (individually or in a group) users make use of generative techniques to express themselves.

3 | The results are used to inform and inspire the design process. This means that the results should not be represented in a standard research report, but rather in a way that makes them useful in creative activities.

Liz, what would you say is the essential benefit of the type of research you practise and in what situations is it applicable?

Liz: I say that design research that is practised with a participatory mindset at the front end of the design process is most beneficial for learning what we as designers can do or make (or not make in some cases) to improve the lives of the people that we serve through design.

You might refer to the design research we are doing as "usefulness and desirability" research. For example, what will people find useful, meaningful and desirable in their future ways of living? Contextmapping is most often used in the early front end of the design process – in the pre-design phase. So this means that you might not know, when you are doing this type of research, what it is that you will be designing. Your objective is to learn what people will need or what will improve their lives in the future. It is often more about identifying and describing opportunities for design versus solving a problem through design.

My hypothesis is that your way of working is also suitable to help organisations develop a guiding brand vision. What's your take on this?

Froukje: Yes, contextmapping can be used to develop a brand vision. But the method was originally developed to inform and inspire the development of new products and services. When using contextmapping for brand development, however, one needs to be aware of the following: contextmapping techniques consider the user as a central element, and everything he/she experiences (for example, routines, motivations, feelings, contextual aspects, meanings, needs, dreams) forms the focus. In contextmapping studies, we explicitly stay away from imposing certain norms and values onto users. So in my opinion, this kind of design research should be done with a very open mind and with genuine curiosity; not in order to impose or verify certain predefined values.

Liz: Exactly. This way of working is suitable to help organisations develop a guiding brand vision and I have been involved with a number of such projects in the past. The optimal application of generative tools to branding, however, requires that you understand the brand as the interface between the company and the people that the company serves. That interface should have equal contributions from each side, and not be something that is pushed from the company onto the people. Brands have been seen that way in the past, but fortunately the conversation has shifted now.

Froukje: But researching user experience is usually not the same as researching brand experience. For example, when a telecoms company wants to design an innovative service, the design team could conduct explorative research about how people communicate in their daily lives and what kind of role mobile phones play in their lives. Research about brand experience focuses more on asking users what kind of mental associations they have with a certain brand, rather than trying to discover and understand what motivates people and what they desire and need. That's why I don't usually associate research techniques like contextmapping with building brands.

However, insights into the everyday experiences of individual users are in fact very useful for developing brand vision: they can be used to check the relevance of the brand vision that a company wants to convey. They could also serve to assess whether their products and services are congruent with their brand vision, from the user's perspective. Opening up to the actual everyday experiences of their end users can help a company to build a more relevant brand vision, and to set out strategies for product and service developments that will ultimately lead to a stronger relationship with its users.

For the full conversation, go to <www.branddriveninnovation.com/book/conversations>.

3.6 Conclusion: the brand in brand-driven innovation

In this chapter, we've explored the first stage of the brand-driven innovation method: human-centred branding. We've looked at how the brand as driver for innovation is different from the brand in marketing communication: it is different in terms of its content, the processes in which it is used, the role it plays within the organisation, and the people who use it, and it therefore requires some special attention. The most important aspect we've uncovered in building a suitable brand for innovation is the aspect of brand usability: the notion of making sure that the brand is both accessible and usable for those who will develop innovations upon it. The step-by-step human-centred branding process we've charted takes this usability into account; through the process it follows (involving and sharing), through the content it generates (authentic, meaningful, inspiring and understandable) and through the way in which it finally presents this content (visual, connected and layered).

Designers can offer a valuable contribution to the building of human-centred brands: their way of doing research uncovers latent values and beliefs, their empathy for people ensures that the brand is usable and meaningful, their way of structuring information brings order to complex research findings, and their way of visualising information helps to create brands that will be remembered and understood.

Designers can offer a valuable contribution to the building of human-centred brands: their way of doing research uncovers latent values and beliefs, their human empathy ensures that the brand is usable, their way of structuring information brings order to complexity, and their way of visualising information helps to create brands that will be remembered.

Summary insights
from chapter 3

1	The brand as a driver for innovation is different from the brand in marketing communication.
2	It is different in terms of its process, content, people and role.
3	Brands in brand-driven innovation function as inspiration, guideline and filter to the ideas in the innovation funnel.
4	The brand in brand-driven innovation is a resource for the organisation, just like its people, its intellectual property and its production facilities.
5	Brand usability is vital in building brands that can drive innovation. Brand usability is the extent to which a brand, as it is found in an organisation, can be used by those who need it to do their work.
6	Human-centred branding is a process for building brands that drive innovation. It's an iterative process, it combines inside-out and outside-in thinking, goes from the concrete to the abstract and back again, is based on the format of creative workshops and design research, and involves as many people as possible.
7	The human-centred branding phases are preparation, internal and external research and creating the brand promise.
8	Various forms of design research techniques are suitable for building a human-centred brand.
9	Context mapping is a design research technique that can be especially suitable for building human-centred brands because it helps to generate deep insights, is contextual and is also richly visual.

CHAPTER 4

Building a brand-driven innovation strategy

The core idea behind brand-driven innovation is that the brand can in fact drive innovation. This implies that the brand is suitable as a driver for innovation, and that innovation can use it as both input and inspiration. In chapter 3, we worked on making the brand suitable as a driver. In chapter 4, we will profit from our groundwork and look at how we can build innovation strategies that use the brand as both input and inspiration.

In this chapter, we will develop a structured approach to building an innovation strategy on the foundations that were laid down by the human-centred brand in chapter 3. In order to do this, we will first look at the role of this second stage in the whole BDI process, and we will discover what an innovation strategy actually is. The detailed framework will then provide you with the step-by-step process required to successfully build a brand-driven innovation strategy.

This chapter involves performing a tricky balancing act. Building an innovation strategy is partly about strategy and structure, and partly about creative visionary ideation and imagination. If, after reading this chapter, you understand that one doesn't necessarily rule out the other, and that the two can in fact push each other to huge heights, you are a true design thinker, ready to work through the last two chapters of this book.

4.1 The role of innovation strategy in brand-driven innovation

In this chapter, we will look more closely at innovation strategy and its role in brand-driven innovation. This second stage in the BDI method is all about strategically devising ways to fulfil the brand promise. It's a way of saying: 'If this is what we promise to our users, then this is what we will do in the future to fulfil that promise.' It builds on a combination of what the organisation's external stakeholders desire, and what the organisation's internal stakeholders can deliver. It takes the relationship as it was established in the human-centred branding stage, and projects that relationship into the future, looking for ways to nurture and grow it. It looks for opportunities to turn internal values and beliefs into concrete plans for action, at the same time fulfilling external aspirations and needs.

Making sense of the future

The challenge of the innovation strategy stage is to take decisions about a future that hasn't yet arrived. The only way to effectively deal with this challenge is to envision this possible future, by taking what's known and building on it. Extrapolating from the here and now into what might be is called 'forecasting' and it's an art form in itself. How do you know if you are extrapolating in the right direction? Innovation strategies are ambiguous in their essence. One way to decrease this ambiguity is to build up several scenarios of what might be, so that you have a range of possible futures on which to base decisions. But then you still won't know which scenario is the right one.

In brand-driven innovation, it's the brand vision that directs. This also implies that the brand guides the forecasting process. There's a common saying that suggests that 'the only way to predict the future is to create it yourself.' This makes sense in BDI, where the organisation's values and vision drive growth. In BDI, this saying could translate as: 'The future is too complex to figure out what it will look like exactly. The only way to get a grip on it is to decide which role you want to play in it.' This question of 'What role do we want to play in the future, and what relationships do we want to build?' is a much less ambiguous one than 'What will the future look like?' The brand takes away uncertainty in envisioning potential futures for organisations.

The future is too complex to predict what it will look like exactly. The only way to get a grip on it is to decide which role you, as an organisation, want to play in it. And this role should have a strong foundation in your brand's values.

Making strategic business choices

But the innovation strategy phase is not only about dreaming up possible futures, it is also about making strategic business choices: essentially, innovation strategy is about making conscious decisions about when, how and to what extent you are willing to take calculated risks. Jos Oberdorf from the Dutch design firm NPK explains this calculated risk taking as involving the following formulation: innovation concerns a new product and/or a new market and/or a new technology. Creating only a new product can be risky, but combining it with a new market or even a new technology is much riskier. Innovation strategy starts with consciously making choices about what changes and what stays the same.

If these choices aren't made consciously, as Oberdorf has noted during many projects, the risk will increase in the course of the project, because it will be tempting to enter a new market with the new product or to add the newest technology to it. You can learn more about managing risks from innovation products from looking at Oberdorf's diagram (page 112), which demonstrates how the risk for a new product in an existing market using existing technology is much smaller than that for a new product in a new market using new technology.

Innovation strategy is about making choices, it's about focus, and it's about the courage and constraint to innovate within the realms of the risks one is willing to take. This means one has to be conscious of one's ambition and potential as well as one's ability to take risks, taking into consideration the organisation's culture and the needs and desires of its users. Seen in this light, the brand is again a solid guide in innovation strategy.

In the brand-driven innovation method, the innovation strategy stage is about making plans for what to do: 'What kind of products and services will we deliver in the future and in what markets?' But it's also about how to get there: 'How will we innovate?' 'Will we lead or follow?' 'Will we innovate radically or more incrementally?' 'Will we create an internal climate for innovation and hire the best designers, researchers and engineers, or will we out-source and build partnerships with external parties?' 'What will our innovation pulse be?' 'Do we strive for a regular, yearly pulse or do we enter the market when it suits us?' 'Do we strive for patents and other intellectual property or do we focus on first-mover advantage and move on from there?' (see pages 200–201 for an overview of these questions). All of these questions form part of the roadmap when moving towards a solid innovation strategy. And, from a BDI perspective, they can and should be answered with the brand in mind.

But before we move on, what *is* an innovation strategy?

4.2 **What is innovation strategy?**

Innovation strategy is that part of strategy which deals particularly with the growth of an organisation through the development of new products, services, processes or business models. A strategy is a long-term plan for action that defines choices on how to reach certain objectives. A strategy is not a goal. Saying: 'Our strategy is to become the market leader in Western Europe' makes no sense. You can say, however: 'Our objective is to become market leader in Western Europe. Our strategy to reach that objective is to compete on the basis of differentiation through innovation and design.'

An innovation strategy then becomes a plan of how to use the development of new products, services, processes or business models to achieve certain objectives. In the case of BDI, the innovation strategy is a plan of how to use the development of new products, services, processes or business models to fulfil the brand's promise.

We've looked at people through the lens of human-centred branding, defining who we are as an organisation, and who the people are that we aspire to create value for. The result of this inquiry was the brand promise: a clear objective as to the value that we want to deliver as a company. Now we've come to the question of strategy: the plan that will help us to reach that objective. The last two stages, design strategy and touchpoint orchestration, gradually move us towards an awareness of the tools, technologies and 'instruments' that will be needed to execute this strategy. Together, these ingredients (people, objectives, strategy and tools) form the POST framework, as devised by Li and Bernoff (2008), which we will return to in chapter 5.

1   MANAGING RISKS IN INNOVATION PROJECTS
The risk for a new product (P) in an existing market (M), using existing technology (T), is much smaller than a new product in a new market using new technology. Image courtesy of NPK design, the Netherlands.

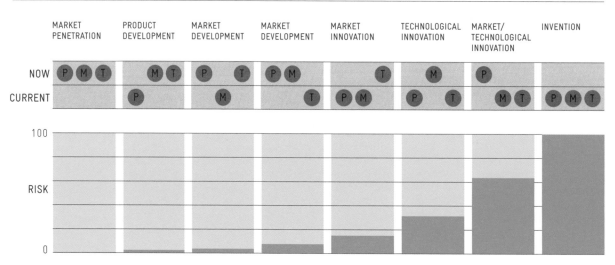

In brand-driven innovation, the innovation strategy is the plan that establishes how to use the development of new products, services, processes or business models to fulfil the brand's promise.

In practice: distilling strategy from innovations

Purpose

This exercise will enable you to learn to see the strategic objectives behind innovations.

Required

A group of four–six people. You will also need a set of six cards depicting innovations that stand out because they are surprisingly successful, unexpected, a big failure, or surprisingly clever. You could re-use the cards that you used earlier, for the exercise on page 25. Each group member draws a card and then each in turn follows the steps outlined here.

Example

The creation of the Volkswagen Phaeton appears to be a strange move by Volkswagen. Wouldn't it make much more sense to service that particular target group with the Audi A8, which is also in the Volkswagen group's portfolio? What could be the reason for introducing such a car under the Volkswagen brand? To explore new technologies? Was it perhaps a pet project of a proud CEO? Well, it appears that in order to gain and keep leasing contracts with large corporations, Volkswagen has to be able to offer a full range of cars, from the compact, for the toiling masses, to the super luxurious for the management board. Hence, the creation of the Phaeton, that, knowing this, all of a sudden makes so much more sense.

1

Take two minutes to explain the nature of the innovation, and what makes it special. Is it a success? For whom? Does it strike you as a logical innovation for the brand that it stems from?

2

Take five minutes to describe what you think the purpose of the innovation has been. Was it to open up a new market? To leverage from a new technology? To shield off competition? And what strategy was employed to reach those objectives? Are these objectives connected?

3

Take 15 minutes to discuss your thoughts with the group. Try to explore different viewpoints and possible scenarios.

After each round of cards, take a few minutes to check the internet for stories about the innovation. Can you find support for your viewpoints? Or is the story altogether different?

4.3 Brand-driven innovation strategies

A brand-driven innovation strategy is one in which the innovation strategy (as discussed in the previous chapter) is based on the brand: it takes the brand as input for the strategy, and the fulfilment of its promise as the objective. Other more common drivers for innovation strategy were previously discussed. They are, for example, the desire to leverage from a new technology, the need to stay up to speed with the competition, the potential of a new market segment, or the opportunities that arise from new legislature.

In terms of objectives, these drivers would translate as follows:

– Technology
'Our objective is to benefit as much as possible from the investments we made in our new technology. Our innovation strategy is to use the technology as a platform innovation, on which we can base many products in many markets.'

– Competition
'Our objective is to be number one or two in our market in terms of market segment. Our innovation strategy is to develop new products made at a higher volume, at the cost of the profit margin.'

– New market segment
'Our objective is to enter the Russian market. Our innovation strategy is to adapt our product as little as possible, so that we can save our resources for penetrating the market and gaining market share.'

– New legislature
'Our objective is to benefit as much as possible from the new law that makes winter tyres obligatory in the Netherlands. Our innovation strategy is to develop a service system that makes it easy and attractive for drivers to comply with this law.'

You may notice two things here:

1 | These are all very valid reasons for innovation. All of the drivers make sense and, from an entrepreneurial point of view, should be taken into account. Brand-driven innovation doesn't stipulate that you should 'use your brand to innovate and ignore all other drivers'. On the contrary. It just says: 'Look at these drivers in a certain way.' Which neatly brings us on to point two.

2 | None of the drivers really tells you what to do. They function as an impulse, as a push in a certain direction. How you, as an organisation, choose to react to that push depends entirely upon your organisation's culture, values, beliefs and norms. Where have we heard that list of words before? Right! How you react to a driver for innovation depends on your brand!

These two findings teach us that no matter what drives your innovation, it's your brand that helps you decide on how to react to that driver. So, in that sense, every innovation strategy should be at least 'brand directed'. Otherwise, the objective may make sense but your strategy to reach that objective will not: if an organisation does not act according to its own norms and values, it will lose its focus and ability to plan and strategise (Schein, 2004). But if the brand directs you in everything you do, wouldn't it make more sense to define it as a driver? If you think in terms of your personal career, would you read every job vacancy going and then decide which one suits you the best? Or would you look at your education, your interests and ambitions first and then decide where to look for the right opportunities?

The brand as a lens

That's why in the innovation strategy stage of the BDI method, we've turned things around: rather than have all sorts of objectives for innovation and have the brand as a guide for your reaction, we've taken the fulfilment of the brand's promise as the core objective, and positioned the 'classical' drivers as guides to enable you to reach that objective. In this set-up, influences in markets, technologies, legislation, trends, competition and so on have become opportunities for shaping the innovation strategy.

In brand-driven innovation strategy, the brand can be compared to a lens (built on Davis and Dunn, 2002). It's a lens through which internal influences can be projected outward. Internal influences, such as resources and capabilities, may be meaningless to the outside world: it's quite hard for a user to distinguish between companies on the basis of internal qualities alone. But by combining these internal qualities with the brand, they become unique. By projecting them outward through the brand lens, they suddenly acquire focus and meaning.

But the brand is also the lens through which to look at external influences, to see whether they can be used to fulfil the brand promise. Without the lens, they are just facts, without focus or meaning. By looking at them through the brand lens, they get connected to what makes the organisation tick, and so they gather focus and meaning. The external facts become interpreted and internalised. To see the brand in this way helps to make innovation more proactive and less reactive. It helps to start with ambition, and to then take into account the internal and external context in which that ambition must be brought to life.

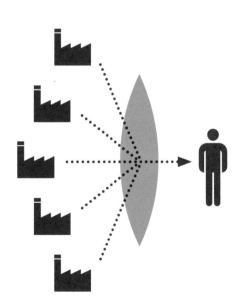

THE BRAND AS PROJECTOR
INTERNAL INFLUENCES BECOME
FOCUSED AND MEANINGFUL

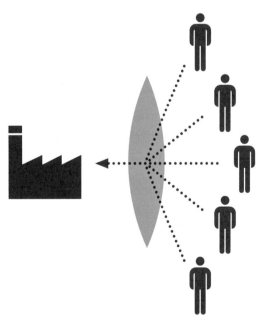

THE BRAND AS LENS
EXTERNAL INFLUENCES BECOME
FOCUSED AND MEANINGFUL

2 THE BRAND AS PROJECTOR AND AS LENS The brand focuses internal influences and projects them to the user in a meaningful way, but it also helps the organisation to focus outside influences and see them clearly.

A conversation between specialists: building brand-driven innovation strategies

You're probably curious about how building brand-driven innovation strategies works in practice, and want to know how design managers in particular deal with this challenge. The following conversation with Philippe Picaud and Pierre-Yves Panis focuses on the practice of building innovation strategies that build on the brand. We also discuss the role of the design manager in large organisations, bridging R&D and marketing.

Philippe Picaud graduated from ENSAD Paris and also holds an MA in Industrial Design from Syracuse University, New York. He began his professional career in Paris followed by two years in South Africa. On his return to France he held various jobs as design director for large companies, the latest two being Decathlon and, since 2009, Carrefour. Philippe is an active member of the international design management community and is presently on the Advisory Boards for the Design Management Institute, Renault, and the IFM in Paris.

Pierre-Yves (PY) Panis is design director for Legrand, a manufacturer of electrical wiring devices and electrical systems in France. He has worked for product design consultancies in the US and in France. Before working in the corporate sector, Pierre-Yves spent eight years in Southern Africa where he created Design Co Operation (DCO), a non-profit design structure aimed at improving urban informal sector production in Zimbabwe. He is a graduate of Les Ateliers (the French National School of Industrial Design) in Paris.

You are both design managers at large corporations. To what extent are you involved in innovation strategy and brand strategy at your company?

Pierre-Yves: My involvement in brand strategy is becoming more hands-on. I've recently been given the authority and responsibility to develop what we have called 'art direction' for the Legrand brand. That means that I have to cover packaging, print, web design as well as space design.

It doesn't mean that the expertise for all those different aspects is located within design. But design is now responsible for drafting guidelines, for making recommendations and building strategy which pertains to the brand. And design must ensure that whatever is being implemented is in accordance with those guidelines.

Philippe: My involvement in the brand strategy is threefold. One is to develop the new identity of Carrefour through different applications such as corporate guidelines, packaging, internet and in-store communication. The second area is the product portfolio. This involves the creation of product lines under the Carrefour brand, which represent about 30 per cent of the volume sold by Carrefour. The third area involves all design activities that are aimed at supporting the shopping experience of the consumer.

Pierre-Yves: With regard to innovation: design is more and more involved in innovation at Legrand. Over the last six years, design has been a key driver for innovation, and we have been given the mandate for that role. For example, when I arrived at Legrand I introduced a policy of spending 15 per cent of our time on long-term innovation projects. This was something that was fully accepted and adhered to. In its implementation we have to be honest and realise that over the years we have been devoting between 10–12 per cent of our time on long-term innovation and not 15, but still.

Philippe: In the past, innovation was housed within R&D in many companies. Which means that it was very much driven from within and very often by engineers. This is changing because companies are realising that truly valuable innovation is more social, more user-oriented and more usage based. This is why innovation is turning more to design competencies. However, in big companies like ours, we still have specialised innovation managers, who are not involved with design at all. Their job is to carry the flag of innovation, and maybe to teach the organisation how to innovate.

But when it comes to actual innovation projects, where you have a target in terms of deliverables, design always makes an essential contribution. So design may not really carry the flag of innovation, but there is no innovation project without design today.

Is your work 'brand-driven' in the sense that you see it as your task to fulfil the brand's promise in your designs and innovations?

Pierre-Yves: Yes, I do see it as my task (our task) to fulfil the brand promise – but design also has to be a part of shaping that brand promise. We definitely have been doing that through product design.

And now we'll have better opportunities to bring an overall coherence between the brand promise built into the products themselves and all the touchpoints that would be created to support that brand promise.

Philippe: As an in-house designer my task is to fulfil the brand promise. Sometimes we can influence or modify the content of that promise, but most of my input is to fulfil it, through the different domains of design such as communication, products, and services. I believe that there is convergence between innovation, brand development and design. Because the strategy of a company to evolve and to grow, through design and innovation, impacts the company's brand image. So, one impacts upon the other. Brand development, innovation and design converge around a company's strategy for growth.

Is the design function explicitly part of defining your company's innovation strategy and do you think it should be?

Pierre-Yves: Yes, and I believe it should be. Why? Because nobody else is taking the lead in doing it. We can bring tremendous value in terms of making innovation more user-focused, more palpable, more concrete and usable. But design shouldn't be the sole origin of our innovation strategy. There are business roadmaps and ambitions within the divisions that need to be taken into consideration. These divisions know how to deliver value to their specific markets, both at a product and at a systems level, and we need to work together with them on defining opportunities for innovation.

Philippe: I agree that design is part of the innovation strategy and it should be. Even when it's not initiating innovation, it's adding value at the end. I think it is because design has a different approach to innovation than, let's say, engineering. Design is about asking questions and not applying fixed rules to the solution of a problem. It thereby opens the borders of the problem. Design is good at understanding users, and at observing social aspects of behaviour. And it translates this understanding into innovative solutions for complex problems.

For the full conversation, go to ‹www.branddriveninnovation.com/book/conversations›.

4.4 **The innovation strategy stage**

The innovation strategy stage is the second stage in the brand-driven innovation method and builds on the first stage: the human-centred branding stage. The innovation strategy stage in BDI is different from other innovation strategy methods or processes, in that it takes the brand as input. Still, this does not mean that it disregards what is there to be learned from all the innovation strategy tools that are available. But it does add a twist.

Building a brand-driven innovation strategy is about taking the brand promise and devising ways to fulfil that promise in the future. It starts with the future creation phase, in which an ideal situation is envisioned. Next, it uses the brand as a lens. First, to project one's own resources and capacities outwards: to scout for ways to leverage from them in order to fulfil the brand promise. Secondly to look at external changes and developments: to use them as opportunities with which to build the desired future. Then, in a much more practical final phase, the results from the previous phases are mapped into a concrete innovation strategy.

The same principles that underlie the human-centred branding stage are valid in the innovation strategy stage (see pages 90–99). However, some extra rules do apply, as set out below:

1 | Postpone judgment. When crafting an innovation strategy it's tempting to discard potentially great directions, saying 'We've tried that, it won't work.' Give room to ideas, in order to let them grow.

2 | Look around. Building an innovation strategy based on your brand does not imply that you don't look at external factors such as competition, market developments, trends and so forth.

3 | Don't rest on your laurels. An innovation strategy is not something that is fixed in time. Revisit your strategy frequently to check whether it's still up to date.

4 | Design the strategy. Crafting an innovation strategy is a creative process. Use creative techniques, involve design thinkers and visualise!

The innovation strategy stage in step-by-step form is outlined on pages 119–122. See figure 3 (below) for the process in model form, again involving a first phase (A), an iterating second and third phase (B and C) and a fourth phase (D).

3   BUILDING AN INNOVATION STRATEGY
The innovation strategy stage consists of four steps: create the future, scout for internal opportunities, scout for external opportunities and create the innovation strategy.

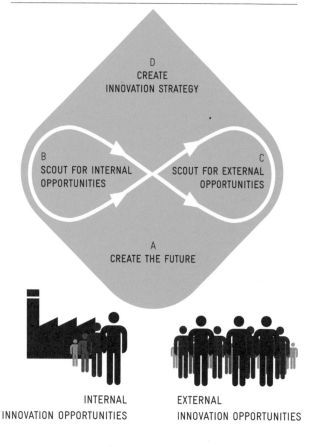

D
CREATE
INNOVATION STRATEGY

B
SCOUT FOR INTERNAL
OPPORTUNITIES

C
SCOUT FOR EXTERNAL
OPPORTUNITIES

A
CREATE THE FUTURE

INTERNAL
INNOVATION OPPORTUNITIES

EXTERNAL
INNOVATION OPPORTUNITIES

In brand-driven innovation, where your organisation tries to act upon its values and the user tries to act upon theirs, aspiration and ambition are driving forces to be reckoned with.

Phase A: create the future

This phase is about envisioning a future for your organisation and its stakeholders, in which the brand promise is completely fulfilled. What would that world look like? What kind of value would your organisation deliver to the user, and how would that match your internal brand?

Get the right people involved

Since you are about to embark on a very creative visionary process you will probably want right-brain thinkers on board. You are going to need visionary people who can visualise and 'prototype' possible futures. But you will also have to be able to make this vision land again. After dreaming, comes doing. So make sure that you also include people who know how to get things done in your team. Make sure you are clear that building an innovation strategy is a stage in the BDI process, whereas in reality it might be an activity that is repeated frequently or that is even ongoing. It might even be an idea to create a yearly event around it.

Immerse in stage one

Take the results from the human-centred branding phase and make sure that everyone in the team understands what they mean. If they weren't part of the process, show them what has been done to get to the results. Make sure they become involved. If the team stays the same, you're all set!

Define brand aspirations

Based on the internal and external brand vision, define brand aspirations. If this is the internal brand vision, then what is it that we would really like to achieve? What is our aspiration, based on our values and vision? And what is it that our user would really like to achieve? What is his or her aspiration, based on his or her values and vision? Build several options. Don't stick to only one aspiration, but define several possible ideals or several variants of them. Dare to think ahead a number of years. Don't think in terms of 'Where do we want to be next year?', but rather in terms of 'Where do we want to be five years from now?'

Build future brand scenarios

In the case of BDI, the forces to be used in the scenarios are the aspirations of the previous step (see section 4.5, pages 128–133). The thinking behind this is that aspirations are in fact very strong forces that influence what your future may look like, because these aspirations stem directly from what you value and believe in. In brand-driven innovation, where your organisation tries to act upon its values and the user tries to act upon theirs, the aspirations and ambitions are driving forces to be reckoned with.

Bring the scenarios to life

Visualise those scenarios and make them real. Maybe use the personas that were created in the first stage and take them through the scenarios. What do they experience? What do they love? What do they miss? What kind of products and services do they encounter? Create a day in the life of your organisation, in the future scenario. What does the work look like, what are you focusing on, and what are the metrics that judge the quality of your work? What are the new partnerships and what are the new competitors?

Phase B: scout for internal opportunities

This phase can take place parallel to phase C and is about finding internal opportunities to make the scenarios come true. It scouts for internal drivers for innovation and projects them outwards through the brand lens to assess whether they can contribute to the scenarios of phase A.

Map internal resources and capabilities

Make an overview of your organisation's resources (which must be unique, imperfectly imitable, non-substitutable, and appropriable) and map how they lead to capabilities (for example, you have precision manufacturing equipment as a resource, which gives you the capability to manufacture very high-quality products).

Map changes in internal resources and capabilities

Make an overview of how your organisation's resources and capabilities are changing. These might be a newly developed technology, new manufacturing equipment, the acquisition of another company, shifts in the demographics of your colleagues, more financial pressure because of a public stock notation, a different focus because the son of the boss is taking over, and such like.

Map the future of your internal resources and capabilities

Project the changes you've mapped so far into the future: what is the direction your resources and capabilities are developing in? What trends and developments can you see? For example, 'We are moving towards setting the standard in high-tech solutions,' or 'We are moving towards having a young and highly educated staff force' or 'We are moving towards an open structure where we're partnering more and more with our suppliers.'

Combine these with the brand to build opportunities

Take the brand promise. Use combinations of the brand's promise and your future resources and capabilities, and see how they match up. Make several interesting matches. Let's create an example. Let's imagine that your brand's promise is about providing services to disabled people. Suppose the future of one of your resources/capabilities is that your staff is becoming more highly educated and as such can perform more complex tasks. An interesting combination might then be to provide more complex services, such as financial services or education, perhaps. The brand is the lens through which you project the resources or capability outwards to make them relevant.

Use the combinations to build scenarios

See how the various combinations you've built contribute to the scenarios in phase A. Map the combinations on an axis from 'contributing a lot' to 'not contributing very much'.

The brand is the lens through which you look at the influencer and connect them to your system of beliefs and values.

Phase C: scout for external opportunities

This phase can take place in parallel to phase B and is about finding external opportunities to make the scenarios developed in phase A a reality. It scouts for external drivers for innovation and projects them inwards through the brand lens to determine whether they can contribute to the scenarios.

Map external influencers

Produce an overview of your organisation's external influencers. These can be based on the classic demographic, economic, political, environmental, social and technological issues (or DEPEST factors); but there are always more things at stake than these factors alone, and there are always influencers that are specific to your organisation. Also map the competitive field.

Map changes in external influencers

Compose an overview of how these influencers are changing. Is there more environmental pressure? Is your target group becoming older? Are your competitors moving in certain directions? Is technology becoming commoditised?

Map the future of the external influencers

Project the changes you've mapped in the previous step into the future: in which directions are your organisation's influences developing? What trends and developments can you see? For example, 'Our users are becoming more design conscious,' or 'Our competitors are moving into retail' or 'Touch-screen technology will be commonplace.'

Combine these with the brand to build opportunities

Use combinations of the brand's promise and the future influencers, and see how they match. Make several interesting matches. Let's return to our earlier example and to the brand promise about providing services to disabled people. Suppose the future of one of the influencers is that high-speed mobile connectivity is becoming commonplace. An interesting combination with the brand might then be to provide a mobile monitoring and assistance service. The brand is the lens through which you look at the influencer and connect them to your system of beliefs and values.

Use the combinations to build scenarios

See how the various combinations you've built contribute to the scenarios in phase A. Map the combinations on an axis from 'contributing a lot' to 'not contributing very much'.

Phase D: create the innovation strategy

This phase is about coming back to a concrete level. It uses existing innovation strategy techniques to map the findings from the previous three phases in concrete plans for the near and distant future.

Build branded search areas

Combine the most promising internal and external opportunities into branded 'search areas'. Search areas are combinations of internal strengths with external opportunities (translated from the Dutch *zoek velden*, Roozenburg en Eekels, 1995). Branded search areas in this case are where internal resources and capabilities combined together with the brand then meet external influencers combined with the brand. Branded search areas define the places where you should look for opportunities to fulfil the brand promise in a way that matches your organisation's DNA and the aspirations of the user.

Build innovation strategy criteria

Use the assessment checklist for defining innovation strategy criteria (on pages 200–201) to assess what kind of innovation criteria you should use. Based on the outcome of the checklist and the discussion that ensues from working with it, build a list of innovation strategy criteria for your company. For example: 'Our innovation strategy should be more user-centred than it was in the past' or 'It should focus on services as well as products.'

Assess brand search areas

Take the branded search areas and assess them on the basis of the innovation criteria that you have already developed. Rank the branded search areas from 'very fitting to the current innovation climate' to 'not fitting to the current innovation climate' (indicated as 'now' in the assessment checklist on page 200). Also rank them from 'very fitting to our desired innovation climate' to 'not fitting to the desired innovation climate' (indicated as 'in the future' in the assessment checklist on page 200).

There will now be four general categories of branded search areas:

1 | Attractive now and attractive in the future

2 | Attractive now but not attractive in the future

3 | Not attractive now but attractive in the future

4 | Not attractive now and not attractive in the future

Discuss and choose

Categories 1 and 2 deserve priority. Category 2 needs some further scrutiny: why are these search areas no longer attractive in the future? What changes? Can we change them so that they stay attractive or become even more attractive? Category 3 has no priority now but will be an opportunity for the future. What needs to be done in order to be ready for it? Category 4 has no priority but needs to be studied carefully: what made these branded search areas evolve from phases A, B and C, but perish in phase D? Maybe they merit some further exploration, given that they are brand-driven opportunities. Perhaps the assessment criteria we selected don't match our brand vision?

Fill the search areas

Use each selected search area to ideate possible future products and services. During the ideation, keep in mind that each branded search area combines the brand promise with internal capabilities and external opportunities, and that the individual ideas in the search area should do the same.

Build the roadmap

Map the selected branded search areas and the ideas within them on a horizontal time axis to build what is called a roadmap (see section 4.5, pages 128–133). Try to add depth to the roadmap by adding a vertical axis that can portray various markets, target groups, innovation themes, product categories, and so on. Use the roadmap for detailed innovation planning, allocating staff and resources to specific timeframes, and pinpointing the need for research, ideation, prototyping and testing activities along the way. Indicate relationships on the roadmap between the individual ideas and look for ways to build up your earlier ideas into more developed, later ones. Make sure to visualise the roadmap well and spread it as widely throughout the organisation as you can – maintaining confidentiality where necessary, of course.

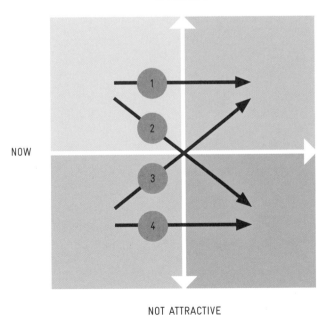

ATTRACTIVE

NOW

IN THE FUTURE

NOT ATTRACTIVE

4   ASSESSING BRANDED SEARCH AREAS
Branded search areas should be assessed on their attractiveness now and in the future. Those that are attractive now deserve immediate attention (1 and 2); those that become unattractive (2) should be scrutinised – why is this so? Organisations should be prepared for those that will become attractive (3).

Case study: ETNA kitchen appliances

The purpose of this case study

The following case study will demonstrate how a human-centred brand can inspire an innovation strategy that matches an organisation's resources and capabilities and caters to the needs and aspirations of its target group.

About ETNA

ETNA is a Dutch brand of kitchen appliances that creates ovens, dishwashers, microwave ovens, steam ovens, refrigerators, range hoods and induction, gas and electric cookers. ETNA was originally an iron foundry, founded in 1856. Manufacturing all kinds of ironware, varying from coal heaters to agricultural machines, ETNA found its focus when gas replaced coal in heating and cooking at the end of the 1920s. The 150-year-old brand kept growing when electricity became the main energy resource, and has stopped manufacturing heaters, to focus on their domain: the kitchen. ETNA's products are partly designed in-house (those parts the user sees and touches) and partly procured through a network of OEM suppliers. ETNA is part of Atag Nederland bv, and distribute their products in Belgium and the Netherlands.

The challenge

ETNA is a typically Dutch brand: no-nonsense, light-hearted and very accessible. The accessibility of the brand has many facets: a well-structured portfolio, clean and easy to understand products, a loyal and well-informed dealer network and an open and informal tone of voice in communication. But most of all, ETNA's products are cheap, only slightly more expensive than the price-fighters at the bottom of the market. As Martin van der Zanden, ETNA's business manager, puts it: 'We want to be the A-brand everyone can afford.' This position has a significant consequence: in order to keep its A-brand status, ETNA has to innovate. But ETNA has to keep these innovations affordable for their target group. This means that ETNA has to do two things:

1 | ETNA has to find opportunities for innovation that are highly relevant to their target group, connecting to their lifestyle and to what they have come to expect of the brand. This will induce them to spend a little more, on a brand they trust and a product that is relevant to them, and thus to choose ETNA over competing price-propositions at the bottom end of the market.

2 | ETNA has to find opportunities for innovation that are highly accessible to their target group, allowing them the benefits of added functionality, comfort, or design at a low price. This means ETNA has to be very smart about how they innovate, working closely with their suppliers, and developing a keen awareness of how to lower the cost of new technologies.

Based on conversations with brand-driven innovation consultancy, Zilver, ETNA felt that it was time to get a grip on these innovation challenges, and saw that a sharp focus on ETNA's brand and users was essential to achieve this. They asked the consultancy to take them through a process of exploring the target group and their consumer journey (page 100), refocusing the brand, getting a grip on innovation opportunities and developing guidelines for design.

USER RESEARCH
The online user research tool ‹7daysinmylife. com› (page 101) was used to better learn to understand the users of ETNA products. Users were asked to keep a diary for a week to share their use of the kitchen and its context with the research team. The users were then visited in their house by the research team. This poster summarises the insights from one of these users.

The project

The consultants and the company set out on a journey that roughly followed the methodology as described in this book. The following process steps were taken:

Step one: Assessment of status quo

An assessment was performed of all existing data concerning market, target group, brand, strategy, innovation, portfolio, design and value chain. The conclusion of this assessment was that there was a lot of data available but that it lacked usability. The market research data, for example, was very quantitative and didn't give ETNA's designers sufficient foundation to work on. The brand was quite extensively captured for communication purposes, but considerably less so for product design and innovation purposes.

Step two: 7daysinmylife.com

A <7daysinmylife.com> context mapping research (pages 100–101) was performed, to get to know the target group's needs and desires concerning cooking and eating. The online diaries ETNA consumers kept for a week centred on their cooking and eating rituals and habits, but also explored their interior tastes and life styles. After the online diaries, house visits took place to deepen the insights and to enable the team to ask additional questions and photograph the ETNA users and products in their home contexts.

Step three: User data workshop

A first workshop was held with all company stakeholders, to explore the <7daysinmylife.com> research data and to build personas and consumer journeys (page 100) with them. The purpose of the workshop was to familiarise the internal team with the user insights, to create empathy for the users, and to make sure that the insights could be used by the team in their daily jobs.

Step four: Brand usability

The brand, as it was formulated for communication purposes, was enriched with the user research and workshop insights. It was captured as the relationship between the company, with its resources and capabilities, and the user, with his or her needs and aspirations. The team had discovered that the company combined two opposing qualities, namely a sober no-nonsense attitude and an attitude of enthusiasm and passion. In parallel, it was discovered that the user also combined two interesting sets of character traits, namely a need for daily order and routine, as well as a need for rituals and meaning. Mapping these opposing qualities on two axes led to four interesting combinations of company and user traits. These four combinations were more 'active' and inspiring than the original traits, and since they represented the possible manifestations of the relationship between user and company, they were used as a springboard for innovation.

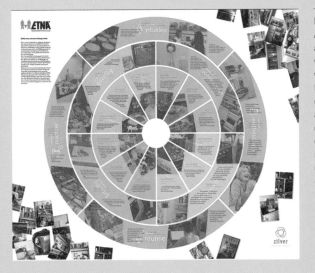

ETNA BRAND CIRCLE
After the user research and the first company workshop, the insights were bundled in a brand circle. This circle combines the rational and emotional internal qualities that were discovered, with the rational and emotional user qualities that emerged from the research (the outside ring). The combinations between company and user qualities (the brand as relationship, page 18) are mapped on the internal ring, and are called innovation values. They form the input for further exploration.

TREND CARDS
In innovation strategy,
the brand vision needs
to be connected to
what's going on in the
outside world. The brand
functions as a lens to
filter and focus these
external developments
(page 115). These 'Trend
Cards' map current trends
in kitchens, cooking and
dining. They were used
to explore brand-driven
innovation opportunities
in the second ETNA
workshop.

Step five: Innovation workshop

A second workshop with all company stakeholders was held to explore market trends and innovation opportunities in the context of the newly focused brand and its user group. As input for the workshop, the brand insights as discovered by the team were presented, as well as a set of current market trends pertaining to kitchens and cooking. The four combinations of company and user traits were used to assess the trends, their relevance for ETNA and the consequences for product and service innovation. The many new product and service ideas that evolved from this assessment were then screened to see where they would fit on a timeline of innovation. The timeline itself was not the purpose of this exercise. The purpose was to find out what criteria the team used to assess whether an idea had high or low priority, was attainable or challenging, and whether it was typically ETNA or not.

Step six: Innovation guidelines

The results of the second workshop were combined with the research data in order to develop a set of innovation guidelines. The guidelines were based on the combined knowledge that was gathered in the course of the project, and presented in a highly visual format, giving concrete examples with the guidelines and linking back to the original research data (quotes and examples from users) and workshop results (quotes from participants).

Step seven: Consumer journey and design workshop

A third workshop with all company stakeholders was held to explore the consumer journey and the strategic role of design in the different stages of the journey. Both the current situation and the future directions evolving from the roadmap were mapped in the consumer journey that was sketched out in step 3. Each possible future direction was mapped to correspond with a stage in the journey and with one of the four innovation values. Based on this, the designers in the team were asked to define their role and contribution and to sketch out design directions for each step in the journey. Additionally, in order to add depth to the map, the four questions of what, who, when and where were answered for each stage in the journey.

Step eight: Design guidelines

The results of the third workshop were used to develop a set of design guidelines related to the innovation values from step 4. Again, a very visual format was chosen, with lots of examples, original research data and workshop materials.

Step nine: Presentation

A final presentation to the company board and all internal stakeholders was held to create buy-in for the project, and to ensure that the results would be understood and accepted by all involved. A scheme of check-up meetings was arranged, to make sure the results of the project were implemented and that the insights found their way into the newly developed ETNA touchpoints.

Brands can be strong foundations for innovation if you see them as the relationship between the organisation's vision, culture, resources and capabilities on the one hand, and the user's needs, desires, dreams and aspirations on the other.

Conclusions to be gained from the ETNA case

1 | Brands, as they are present in organisations, are often created for the purpose of marketing communication. They are not immediately usable for innovation and design. This requires a process as described in this case and in chapter 3.

2 | One aspect in making a brand usable for innovation and design is to strongly connect it to the lives, needs and aspirations of the users of the organisation's products and services. This can be done through a method called contextmapping (pages 102–105).

3 | Brands can be strong foundations for innovation if you see them as the relationship between the organisation's vision, culture, resources and capabilities on the one hand, and the user's needs, desires, dreams and aspirations on the other. Building a brand-based innovation strategy requires a usable brand that functions as a lens to view and interpret external influences, and as projector to focus and filter internal influences (page 115).

4 | Innovation roadmaps and guidelines can form a good basis for design guidelines. Once you have decided what to do, you can start thinking about how to do it.

5 | Consumer journey mapping is a great way to combine brand thinking, user centred thinking and design thinking, enabling you to employ design strategically in every stage of the user's experience.

6 | In projects like these, the process is as important as the result. Getting stakeholders around the table, discussing research results, doing creative workshops together and developing a shared vision on the future are great ways to align teams and create innovative potential.

7 | Visualise results! An image says more than a thousand words.

INNOVATION AND DESIGN GUIDELINES
The innovation and design guidelines will help ETNA to design their future products and services in a way that connects their DNA to the needs and desires of their users.

CONSUMER JOURNEY MAP
The consumer journey map is a visual representation of the way that the user experiences the ETNA brand over time, through various touchpoints. Creating a consumer journey map helps us to understand the brand experience from the user's point of view, and to see the product in the context of the surrounding services.

4.5 Skills for brand-driven innovation strategies: an overview of tools and methods

Future scenarios

Purpose: to get a grip on the future by visualising it and making it as realistic as possible.

A scenario can be defined as 'a rich and detailed portrait of a plausible future world, one sufficiently vivid that a planner can clearly see and comprehend the problems, challenges and opportunities that such an environment would present' (Wikipedia). A scenario is not a specific forecast of the future, but rather a plausible description of what might happen. Part of the benefit of building scenarios lies in pinpointing the forces and trends that shape possible futures. Another great benefit of scenarios is the visualisation that they involve: by making it as richly detailed and real as possible, designers are triggered to discuss the implications of possible futures. Scenarios are often followed by a 'back-casting' exercise in which the team tries to construct the future by looking back from it: defining the events that have led to a desirable future.

Scenarios are usually built on the basis of two axes, each representing two opposing outcomes of an important trend or force. The scenarios are then made by filling in the two-by-two matrix that is built from those axes.

The concept car strategy

Purpose: to explore the future by making it visible, and by making it tangible.

See the case study on Festo (on pages 130–133) for an extensive discussion of this strategy (also known as future concept strategy). As noted there, concept cars as used by the automobile industry are great brand-driven innovation strategy tools: they visualise in the form of an innovative concept, they make that vision tangible, they align designers, researchers, engineers and marketers, and they provide a great source of user feedback. One could consider a concept car the embodiment of a future scenario.

FUTURE SCENARIOS
Students of the Delft University of Technology made these two future scenarios for a bus and coach company. The students visualised two possible future bus concepts within a social context, in order to trigger dialogue about future developments and what these might mean for the client.

scenario 'harmony'

scenario 'rush'

CONCEPT CAR
The BMW Gina concept car (above) is a great example of how car companies use the development of future concepts to stretch their imagination. The Gina concept car uses a flexible skin, which radically changes the car's construction and design language.

Creativity tools

Purpose: to harness the creativity that's present within a group of people, in order to solve a problem or to explore many different solutions to that problem.

When you search for innovation strategy tools on the internet, you will mostly find creativity tools. Apparently, it's not the strategy part of defining innovation strategies that is considered the hardest, but the creativity part. And let's admit it; within a business context, where problems are complex, the future is uncertain, team dynamics can be challenging and there's always a to-do list waiting on your desk, it is very hard to be really, truly creative. That's why quite a number of people have studied this problem and have devised ways of enhancing creativity in the work context just described above. Some of these creativity tools are very systematic and structured, such as Systematic Inventive Thinking, or SIT (<www.sitsite.com>). Others are based more on human facilitation and coaching, such as the work of Marc Tassoul (2009). Yet others are based on the principles that lead to new technologies as found in patent literature, like the Russian TRIZ methodology (<http://www.creax.com/index.htm>). However, all these creativity tools have one thing in common: they are based on the premise that creativity is not something that one either has or doesn't have. Creativity is a state of being that can be enhanced and stimulated, coached and practised, in a business context as much as in any other. It is way too important to be left to coincidental bouts of inspiration, or random bursts of genius.

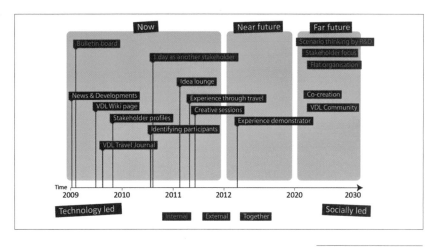

Roadmapping

Purpose: to create a visual map of different innovations or innovation steps in time.

A roadmap is a graphical representation of an organisation's future (typically the next five years) in a map. The primary purpose of a roadmap is to create a clear overview of an organisation's innovation plans by visualising how individual ideas are planned and connected in time.

Typically, a roadmap will consist of a horizontal axis representing time, and a vertical axis representing, for example, the stakeholders in the innovation process, innovation themes, markets, target groups, product categories or supporting processes, depending on the purpose of the specific roadmap. In addition to mapping ideas in time, the roadmap should indicate the relationship between those ideas and how they build on each other. A roadmap can be applied to different levels: the organisation, a specific department or business unit, a market segment, or even a product range. This also implies that having made a general roadmap on the level of branded search areas, for example, it may be advisable to then develop more detailed roadmaps at an ideas level or at a departmental level.

Check out <www.branddriveninnovation.com/book/innovation-tools> for examples of more tools that you may find helpful.

ROADMAP
Students of the Delft University of Technology made this roadmap for a bus and coach company. The roadmap features a horizontal timeline on which various directions for innovation (from the technology-led to the socially-led) are mapped, and colour coded in three different themes ('internal', 'external' and 'together').

Case study: Festo

FESTO

The purpose of this case study

This case study with Festo is designed to show you
what a brand-driven innovation strategy might look
like in practice. It will enable you to learn how to
work with future concepts as part of a sustainable
innovation strategy. It will also demonstrate how
brand-driven innovation strategies are by no means
limited to consumer goods industries but can be just
as applicable for business-to-business high-technology
organisations, too.

About Festo

Festo is a worldwide leading supplier of pneumatic and
electrical automation technology, with its headquarters
in Esslingen, Germany. Automation technology is
applied in manufacturing facilities and machines to
automate production. Festo specialises in rapidly
moving, intricately complex machines sliding along
rails, pivoting around axes, picking up parts and
dropping them, guiding machine parts to operate at
exactly the right spot, and transporting goods through
manufacturing facilities on highly efficient conveyor
belts. The globally operating, independent family
enterprise is known for its top-quality, high-precision
products, which evolve from a continuous process
of innovation. Festo also offers vocational training
and education, and is renowned for its professional,
industry-oriented qualification solutions in the fields
of industrial training and consulting.

BIONIC PENGUINS
These penguins are in
fact robotic swimming
machines that can be
remotely controlled,
but also react to their
environment and to each
other. Festo develops
these bionic creatures to
explore new technologies
and partnerships.

Festo's brand vision

Festo's brand vision posits that in order to make perfect machinery, you have to look ahead and invent the future today. Future concepts are the link between the known present and the as yet unknown future. They visualise new ideas so that they can be experienced and discussed by customers, employees and network partners.

A sustainable innovation strategy always involves the question: what makes us different? One way to find a unique brand expression is to look very closely at nature. Efficiency is key for industrial automation, and this is where nature has had quite some practice. Festo believes that they can create perfectly efficient automated motion sequences if they learn and adapt from nature. This ambition to recreate via technology what nature has created by evolution over the course of many millennia is called bionics. Festo's vision of company development through the use of bionics is essential to the brand. It reflects a deeply embedded respect for nature and a thorough understanding of the relevance of efficiency to the company's customers.

The Festo Bionic Learning Network

What sets Festo apart from other high-tech industrial companies is its bionic innovation approach. Festo initiated its first bionic projects in the 1990s. Since 2006, Festo has been running a programme called 'The Festo Bionic Learning Network'. The Festo Bionic Learning Network is a yearly cycle of explorative innovation projects that take place in close cooperation with universities, schools, research institutes and specialists in specific fields. The projects don't have a short-term commercial objective: they are not meant to be directly taken into production, nor are they meant to be sold to customers right away. What the projects aim to do is explore Festo's vision through the development of tangible working prototypes, in order to learn from them.

The future concepts strategy at Festo

Festo's innovation strategy revolves around 'future concepts', just as the automotive industry works with 'concept cars'. Dr Peter Post, head of research and programme strategy at Festo, describes how future concepts reflect an organisation's, R&D team's or design team's vision of the future, and its aspiration as to how that vision can be turned into reality: 'The future concepts are not meant to hit the market, they are meant to demonstrate where the company is heading. The prototypes are displayed at fairs and trade shows. They trigger dialogue and test reactions.'

But they are much more than marketing instruments:

1 | They interpret the brand and make it tangible. Teams working on future concepts have to decide what the brand's aspiration means in practice: 'Where do we go from here, given that these are our values and beliefs?' Future concepts help take those values off the paper, and make them real. The fact that the concepts don't have to be commercially viable in the short term helps to remove inhibitions and limitations in the design process. They are part of the first phase of the innovation strategy stage as described earlier.

2 | They help decisions to be made on possible directions for innovation. By exploring potential directions for the future, and actually prototyping those directions, deciding on where to go becomes easier and less risky. Once a future concept has been formed, it is much clearer to see how hard it was to build certain new solutions, how certain decisions turn out in reality and how the audience reacted to the results.

3 | They help to test and set design directions. They are instruments for a team to test its common design vision. They help to provide alignment on how to translate the brand into 3D design. And they help match trend forecasts on design with the design team's agreed design direction.

In essence, future concepts are the perfect brand-driven innovation instruments.

Festo's innovation strategy

Over the past few years, the Festo Bionic Learning Network – a cooperation between Festo and renowned universities, institutes and development companies – has become established as an integral part of Festo's innovation processes.

The Bionic Learning Network thus reflects Festo's solutions competence for evaluating new approaches in sustainable product development. 'We intend to be the innovation leader in our sector. To this end, we must repeatedly travel down new, in other words entirely different, paths in order to provide our customers with added value,' says Markus Fischer, manager of the Bionic Learning Network at Festo.

At Festo, in the region of four to six future concepts are built within the Bionic Learning Network each year. Festo's visionary approach to bionics is taken as a starting point for each year's Bionic Learning Network projects: 'How can we learn from nature to make our products better?' Each year, different movements in nature are chosen as a source of inspiration; the motion of a bird's wing in flight, the motion of the tails of a swimming jellyfish, or the motion of a manta ray gliding through water. Teams of Festo engineers, researchers and designers, together with students and specialists from the field, study these motions in great detail. They are then redesigned using bionic technology and Festo automation products, and built into working 3D prototypes. The results are stunningly beautiful: they vary from a remote-controlled flying jellyfish, to swimming penguins demonstrating swarm behaviour, to a robotic manta ray that dives into the deep. The results steal the show at every trade fair where Festo is represented. 'We want to inspire our customers and together strike a new path in close partnership,' adds Markus Fischer.

For each future concept, special solution groups had to be formed. Researchers from Festo's R&D department work together with designers, universities, students and independent development companies. Designers are perfectly suited to play the role of translator between the brand and technological innovation.

The benefits of the Bionic Learning Network

Markus Fischer explains the uses of the programme, saying: 'The Bionic Learning Network has a tremendous scope in terms of benefits: it is good for us as a company but it is also good for our clients. We learn from its results, but we learn even more from its processes. We use it as a vehicle for innovation and design, but it is as much a brand communication tool.' Fischer documents the ten main benefits of the Bionic Learning Network as follows:

1 | It positions and communicates the Festo brand much more effectively than traditional brand communication would do, evidenced by the impact that Festo makes on trade fairs.

2 | It demonstrates Festo's capabilities in a very convincing way. We have our bionic prototypes to tell the story.

3 | It aligns engineers, designers, marketers and sales people: it gives them a shared understanding of what the Festo brand is about – in designing, building and demonstrating the projects.

4 | It attracts talent to the company: it is a recruiting magnet. We use it to attract new employees, but also technology and research partners.

5 | It stimulates young people to develop an interest in technology: this is a very important aspect for Festo, because we believe that technology can improve the world we live in if it's in the hands of the right people.

6 | It explores possible future directions for innovation and assesses their feasibility and potential. Much of what we try out in the Network reaches production in one way or the other.

7 | It helps explore new markets. It's a risk-free area of exploration in which to assess whether we can add value in a certain new market.

8 | It creates and maintains value networks through cooperation with technology specialists and academics in an explorative, experimental setting.

9 | It is a platform to introduce new products to the market in a very compelling way. We use the Network to promote new products and demonstrate what they are capable of.

10 | It helps to fill the innovation funnel with new ideas, which are spin-offs from the work done within the programme itself. While working on the prototypes, we solve many problems that we also often encounter in commercial projects.

Markus Fischer continues: 'What fascinates me about our Future Concepts approach is not only the impressive result, but also the process, the mental exercise. It is a very practical brand-driven innovation strategy. You can turn your brand into a driver for innovation through asking yourself the questions: 'How would we fulfil our brand's promise if we were free to create what we want, without restrictions? What products would really bring our vision to life? And how could we then learn from those products? How can we create spin-offs from these future concepts that will be meaningful and profitable tomorrow?'

Conclusions to be gained from the Festo case

1 | Brand-driven innovation strategies are not limited to applications in the consumer-lifestyle industry. They can also be applied in industrial B2B environments.

2 | Future Concepts are perfect brand-driven innovation instruments.

3 | In order to explore your brand's innovation potential, it helps to define some long-term, not primarily commercially oriented projects, or better still, a programme of recurring projects.

4 | This strategy belongs in the first phase of BDI's stage two, the innovation strategy, where future explorations based on the brand are made.

5 | Building an innovation strategy like this aligns teams, creates a shared understanding of the brand and the organisation's direction, and results in a perfect communication instrument that helps to both trigger and assess customers' reactions.

RESULTS FROM FESTO'S BIONIC LEARNING NETWORK
The results from Festo's Bionic Learning Network are always elegant and exciting, as well as integral to Festo's innovation strategy: the Air-penguin (above); the Air-jelly (left). To see Festo's movies for yourself, search for 'Festo' on YouTube.

4.6 Embedding innovation strategy in the organisation

The creation of an innovation strategy has to be supported throughout the organisation. Therefore, you have to make sure that you have a team that can carry the weight of the process, and that you gather support and understanding outside the team, too.

The team

When you embark on an innovation trajectory as described in section 4.4 (pages 118–127), you have to realise that you are entering an area of uncertainty. In exploring the future, foundations for everyday decisions no longer count, anything is possible and nothing is certain any more. For some people, this is a great relief and they will cherish the freedom to explore. But for others, this uncertainty will be threatening and confrontational. It is too easy to leave these people out of your project team because they're not the extrovert visionaries that you might be looking for. Very often, these people have other skills that you need in your team just as badly. They may be more rational and skilled at bringing ideas into reality. They may also be critical or sensible with regards to the viability of ideas.

When you develop an innovation strategy, be it through concept cars or future scenarios, you are in fact prototyping the future and testing it. Make it very clear that the possible futures that are sketched and prototyped in the process are just ideas, possibilities to be explored and rejected when they don't suit the objective. Share with your team the information that you are not haphazardly deciding on your organisation's future; you are carefully designing and prototyping possibilities, so that making decisions on future directions can be done smartly and with calculated risk. Keep your team informed on any decision that is taken, any direction that is rejected, or any new impulse that is taken into account. Create an open innovation lab in which anything is possible – except, of course, turning your back on team members.

The rest of the organisation

The first tip is: make the rest of the organisation as small as possible. That is: include as many people in the innovation strategy formation as humanly possible. On the other hand, you do have to keep the team sessions manageable so, in larger organisations, there will always be people who aren't directly involved. Make sure you keep these people in the loop by telling them what you are doing and why you are doing it. Or, when you choose not to bother them with details about the process, make sure they are well-informed about the end results. That implies also communicating the considerations that led to the innovation strategy team's proposals for directions to follow. Build up your story to the organisation in the same way that the decision was built up by the team.

At the fuzzy front end of innovation, there are no specialists who own and control the entire process. Everyone can have a great sense of future opportunities, and a keen understanding of where brand, internal capabilities and external needs have a perfect fit. Winning ideas are often combinations of different expertise areas. That's why it is smart to involve many different people in the innovation strategy stage of BDI.

At the fuzzy front end of innovation, no one owns the process. Everyone can have a sense of future opportunities, internal capabilities and external needs. That's why many different people should be involved in innovation strategy.

Pause for thought: reflections on the limitations of user-driven innovation

Purpose

This section will enable you to critically reflect on user-driven innovation and to understand its limitations.

1

In current innovation practice, there has been a shift from technology-driven innovation to user-driven innovation. This is a very good thing. It's much smarter to look carefully at what users need and to adapt your technology to that than to force your technology into the market. Still, there is a catch to user-driven innovation: just as with the other drivers for innovation that were discussed previously, the user doesn't tell you what to do. Users can be great sources of inspiration for innovation, but how you react to these sources of inspiration is up to you. Again, this reaction is framed by your organisation's culture, values, beliefs and norms. Even user-driven innovation needs the brand to interpret.

2

Thus, the catch with user-driven innovation is that doing user research in itself doesn't drive innovation. The research results will not be unique to your organisation. Another organisation, doing the same kind of research with the same users, may arrive at the same data. It's what you do with the data, how you internalise it and interpret it based on your own values and norms, that turns 'generic' user data into your own user insights. And insights have the capacity to drive innovation.

3

Next time you hear people talk about user-driven innovation, ask them if it's the user that drove the innovation or if it was the organisation's interpretation of that user. Join in the discussion on the pros and cons of user-driven innovation on <www.branddriveninnovation.com/book/user-driven> and share your own insights.

4.7 Conclusion: innovation strategy in brand-driven innovation

In this chapter, in which we've explored the second stage of the brand-driven innovation process, we've looked at building brand-driven innovation strategies. Innovation strategies set out to fulfil certain strategic objectives through the development of new products, services, business models and processes. In that sense, the innovation strategy stage of BDI is the most creatively challenging and exciting to work in: it explores, designs and prototypes possible futures, in order to judge whether they are worthwhile pursuing.

Brand-driven innovation strategies are special because they take the fulfilment of the brand as the strategic objective of the innovation, and they take the brand as driver. Brand-driven innovation strategies use more classical drivers such as changes in technology, markets and user trends as opportunities and guides to realise the fulfilment of the brand promise.

Although we discussed a process for building brand-driven innovation strategies in this chapter, and also covered some of the techniques that may be helpful in doing so, the real essence of the innovation strategy phase lies in taking your brand seriously: 'If this is what we promise with our brand, this is what we should do to deliver on that promise.' What you then do to turn this pledge into reality is largely up to you. The processes and techniques in this chapter have been designed to guide you along the way.

The real essence of the innovation strategy phase lies in taking your brand seriously: 'If this is what we promise with our brand, this is what we should do to deliver on that promise.'

Summary insights from chapter 4

1	Innovation strategy is about how to reach strategic objectives through growth and change. It is a plan of how to use the development of new products, services, processes or business models to attain certain objectives.
2	A brand-driven innovation strategy sets out to fulfil the brand promise through growth and change. It is a plan of how to use the development of new products, services, processes or business models to fulfil the brand's promise.
3	It builds on the combination of what the organisation's external stakeholders desire, and what the organisation's internal stakeholders can deliver.
4	The brand takes away uncertainty and ambiguity in building innovation strategies.
5	No matter what drives your innovation, it's your brand that helps you decide on how to react to that driver. So, in that sense, every innovation strategy should be at least 'brand directed'. Even in user-driven innovation, the user may inspire innovation, but it's an organisation's vision and values that direct the innovation.
6	In a brand-driven innovation strategy, the fulfilment of the brand's promise is the objective and the 'classical' innovation drivers are guides to reach that objective.
7	In brand-driven innovation strategy, the brand can be compared to a lens: a lens to project internal capabilities outwards in a focused manner, and a lens through which to look at external opportunities and internalise them.
8	The same principles that underlie the human-centred branding stage are valid in the innovation strategy stage, but it also has its own specific rules.
9	The phases in the innovation strategy stage are: create the future, scout for internal opportunities, scout for external opportunities, create the innovation strategy.
10	Tools for building innovation strategies include future scenarios, concept car strategies, creativity tools and road mapping.
11	The creation of an innovation strategy has to be supported throughout the organisation. Therefore, you have to make sure that you have a team that can carry the weight of the process, and that you gather support and understanding outside the team.

CHAPTER 5

Building a brand-driven design strategy

This chapter is built on the premise that design is essential in bringing brands to life through meaningful touchpoints that deliver on the brand's promise. But this can only be achieved successfully if design is used in the right way. That means that design must be seen as an adaptable capability that can be put to use as a strategic instrument to reach certain objectives.

This chapter focuses on the third stage in the brand-driven innovation process: building a brand-driven design strategy. It builds on chapters 3 and 4, and takes the innovation strategy that was crafted in chapter 4 as its starting point. Design has a huge role to play in brand-driven innovation, as we saw in chapter 2. But this can only be achieved successfully if design is used in the right way. There is not one right way in which to use design: design has many different faces and there are many purposes that design may fulfil.

When using design strategically, the trick is to choose the right type of design for the purpose at hand, in the same way that a carpenter chooses exactly the right tool for the task that they need to perform. In this chapter, we explore what a design strategy is and what it means to use design strategically in the context of branding and innovation. We then go on to explore the different faces of design and what different functions it can have, particularly in bringing brands to life. Next, we will look at the processes and skills that help build brand-driven design strategies.

5.1 The role of design strategy in brand-driven innovation

Turning vision into value

Brand-driven innovation, the creation of meaningful innovations based on a strong brand vision, would be nowhere without design. As we will see, BDI needs design to turn vision into reality, to give shape to meaning, to connect silos in the organisation around a shared goal, and to make innovations both usable and attractive. So, to put it even more strongly, the role of design in BDI is of such importance that it requires a thoroughly strategic approach: before we can use design, we must first craft a design strategy. Before we explore what a design strategy entails, let's first look at why design is of such strategic importance for BDI, and accordingly, what the role of the third stage of BDI is.

The first two stages of BDI are about crafting a visionary, shared-brand platform and the innovation strategy that builds on it. They are both stages that require visionary thinking, human-centredness and a focus on the future. They are also both stages in which time and energy is invested in planning and preparation. They're about creating the set on which the play can be performed. With stage 3, we have arrived at the next level: the set is in place, now the play needs to take shape. The role of the third stage of BDI is much more practical, convergent, short term and externally focused than the previous two. It deals with the question of how to create value for a certain group of people through new products and services, which find their roots in the innovation strategy that set out to fulfil the brand promise. As such, the third stage is about turning plans into reality, taking into account the people that the organisation targets and the sort of products, services and experiences that they might value.

As discussed earlier in chapter 2 (pages 40–67), design is vital in this process of turning plans into reality. Not necessarily because design alone can turn the abstract into the concrete. No, what's unique about design, and what makes it such a versatile and vital ingredient of BDI, is its ability to turn vision into value. And turning vision into value might just be the precise essence of BDI. Design can do this through sleek aesthetics, through surprising usability, or through creating overwhelming experiences. Internally within the organisation, design can also be the engine behind the processes that turn vision into value, too: it can bridge silos within the organisation that have separate agendas and different performance indicators; it can make plans and ideas concrete and tangible; it can envision possible futures for the organisation and prototype and test them; it can make organisations more empathetic towards their users; and it can encourage creativity and innovative thinking within organisations.

In short, design has many roles, as showcased in figure 1 (opposite).

Function of design	Example
To enhance creativity and innovation	In the Fatboy case study (pages 44–47) design thinking, design research and design-led ways of visualising opportunities are used to channel creativity and to get a grip on possibilities for innovation. Although the founder of the company is creative enough, he surrounds himself with designers to focus his creativity and to turn it into exciting branded innovations that make sense to the organisation and its users.
To enhance empathy and user-centredness	In the BALTIC case study (pages 62–65) it was service design agency live|work that helped museum staff develop a structural interest in and empathy for their visitors. Good designers are interested in users and are accustomed to projecting themselves into the lives of the people that they design for. Live|work used this natural tendency and managed to infect their client with their enthusiasm for it through the use of low-threshold, user-insight research techniques.
To bridge silos and connect departments with different agendas	In the Priva case study (pages 96–99), it was a design manager initiating and leading the process: she was able to understand each department's agenda and to connect them through a shared vision. Design research methods and visualisation techniques helped make the different visions explicit so that they could be discussed.
To envision possible futures for the organisation	In the Festo case study (pages 130–133), the Bionic Learning Network is an exploration of the company's future directions in innovation, led by a design manager and executed by designers, in close cooperation with scientists and engineers.
To resolve conflicting interests and demands into one fitting solution	In the NLISIS case study (pages 188–191), many paradoxes are resolved. Innovation processes are often full of these paradoxes, created by conflicting demands and the differing interests of the stakeholders involved in the innovation. How can you make a small company look big? How can you be modern and cutting edge in a very conservative market, while still gaining trust?
To make plans and ideas tangible and concrete	On the Masters programme of Strategic Product Design within the school for Industrial Design Engineering at the Delft University of Technology, around 100 students every year are challenged by a company to bring their plans to life in a concrete and compelling way. Client companies have included TomTom, Océ, Philips, Johnson Controls Inc. and Mexx.
To make innovations usable and relevant for end users	Household equipment manufacturer, Oxo, solves issues of ergonomics and usability through clever and appealing design. Oxo treats every hand-operated product with a meticulous attention to usability, resulting in great performance, ease of use and aesthetics.
To create coherent experiences that satisfy all the senses	In the Virgin Atlantic case study (pages 172–175), we come to understand how a brand can create an overall experience through all brand touchpoints, in which the whole is more than the sum of the parts. Design management and design coordination enable this process, through the careful crafting of a consumer journey that builds up the overall experience touchpoint by touchpoint.
To create aesthetics that communicate the right story to the right people	In the Trespa case study (pages 162–165), design is used to create product prototypes, environments and communications that speak directly to the imagination of the architect. The company consciously chooses aesthetics that invite dialogue and challenge leading architects to stretch their conception of facade cladding, thereby enhancing their brand's position.

1 THE DIFFERENT ROLES OF DESIGN IN ORGANISATIONS
This table explores the diverse functions that design may play within different organisations, with examples of each taken from the case studies featured within this book.

5.2 **Setting objectives for design**

As discussed earlier in section 2.1 (pages 42–49), a design strategy describes how design is used within an organisation as a strategic instrument to achieve a set of given objectives, aiming to reach a certain target group or market. As such, a design strategy is comparable in its nature to other strategies. For example, a marketing strategy that focuses on the use of marketing as a strategic instrument to reach a set of given objectives, a financial strategy using financial instruments, or a human resources strategy using people, and so on. The only thing that makes a design strategy unique is the fact that it focuses on design.

In section 4.2 (pages 112–113), we discussed how it's important not to confuse the goal with the road towards that goal in strategy. A strategy is a description of the road, not a description of the goal. But the goal is obviously a fundamental part of defining a strategy: a route description has no function without a clear set goal to be reached. The same holds true for describing a design strategy. That's why in this chapter we will include the goal of the strategy in our discussion. Furthermore, the target group of the strategy is vital, especially when it comes to design strategies. To know whom you design for is vital to design's success. And lastly, when it comes to crafting a design strategy, it is important to choose the right design instruments and tools.

Together these ingredients (people, objectives, strategy and tools) form the POST framework, as devised by Li and Bernoff (2008) and discussed earlier (on page 112). So within the larger POST sequence of the four stages of BDI, the design strategy stage has its own explicit POST iteration, a sequence within a sequence. It is this POST sequence that will form the backbone of section 5.4 (pages 148–153) in which we discuss how to build a design strategy. In crafting design strategies, it is very important to understand how design can be used to reach different objectives. In defining these objectives and getting to the bottom of its implications, a design team can't be zealous enough: the objective of the use of design influences (or should influence) every decision that will be taken along the way. Let's spend some time exploring those different objectives.

Why should we use design?

When we try to answer the question 'Why should we use design?' we are questioning the objective of design. The tricky thing about objectives is that they are 'nested'. For every objective, there is a larger objective that can be defined. Let's look at the example of a hammer to explain how objectives are nested. The first objective of a hammer is to drive a nail into wood. This might be called the 'purpose' of the hammer, and is comparable to the roles of design that we discussed in the previous paragraph. These roles are in fact the 'purposes' of design. But although the purpose of the hammer might be to drive a nail into wood, this is not the objective of using it. This might rather be to hang up a painting, or to fix a chair. In turn, this objective is nested in the larger objective of decorating one's home or sitting comfortably. And so, in this way, every objective is nested in a larger, more abstract one.

Objectives for the use of design are numerous and varied, and can differ from organisation to organisation, situation to situation, market to market and even touchpoint to touchpoint. An example of how design objectives are nested might be represented by the conversation in figure 2 (opposite). As you can see, at the start the answers to the questions are specific to the design challenge at hand (that is, to increase the percentage of returning customers through one of design's primary purposes, that is the design of a better service experience); whereas towards the end they become more and more generic and universally applicable. When discussing design objectives, it's important to be aware of more abstract, generic purposes like increasing margins and safeguarding the continuity of the organisation; but it will provide clearer guidance to focus on the more concrete, 'lower order' objectives. Designers will be triggered more by an objective such as 'to design our service experience so that more customers return', than by an objective like 'to design our services so that they will safeguard the continuity of our organisation'.

Keep asking how and why

A good way to guide the discussion towards these lower-order objectives is to simply keep asking 'how?' after each answer. How do we safeguard continuity? By improving financial performance. How? By increasing overall margin. How? By increasing the margin per customer. How? By making sure they keep returning to us. How? By designing a better service experience.

It is important for design as a profession to take design objectives very seriously and to lead the discussion in setting them. Every time design is called in to make a product a bit better looking, the immediate question should be 'why?'. What is the strategic purpose of making a product more aesthetically pleasing? To reach a different target group, to be able to charge a higher price, to gain market share, to out-compete a rival, to reposition the brand or to be able to change retail channels? All of these are valid reasons for using design, but a choice needs to be made.

At the same time, designers will need to ask 'how?' when a manager shouts out 'We need design to increase our margins!'. How? Do we want people to pay more, stay longer, come back more often, or buy more of our products? And is the role of design then to increase usability, improve aesthetics, raise performance, enhance interaction, or improve the overall experience of our product or services?

All of these questions need to be answered in order to set a sharp objective for design that guides the plethora of decisions that will need to be taken in the course of the design process that will follow.

Why do we need to take care of our service design?	Because we want our users to have a more positive service experience.
Why do we want our users to have a more positive service experience?	Because we need to increase the percentage of returning customers.
Why do we need to increase the percentage of returning customers?	Because we need to increase the margin per customer.
Why do we need to increase the margin per customer?	Because we need to increase our overall margin.
Why do we need to increase our overall margin?	Because we need to improve the financial performance of our organisation.
Why do we need to improve the financial performance of our organisation?	Because we need to safeguard its continuity and satisfy its shareholders.

2   DESIGN OBJECTIVES
Design objectives are 'nested', meaning that each objective fits into a larger, more abstract objective. To reach a higher abstraction level, ask 'why?'. To become more concrete, ask 'how?'.

5.3 Design's role in brand-driven design strategies

Design as an instrument has many possible functions (see page 141) and it can fulfil many possible objectives (as discussed on pages 142–3). So there are many different design strategies that can potentially be adopted (see the discussion of POST on page 142 and figure 3, below). Brand-driven design strategies are a special breed. They are the design strategies that help organisations use their brand to not only inspire innovation but also to turn their innovation efforts into meaningful user experiences that exceed the expectations that were created by the brand's promise. In these brand-driven design strategies, design has a specific nature and is used to reach specified objectives.

In brand-driven design strategies, design's objective is to create solutions, interactions and experiences that stem from the brand's vision and that make tangible and meaningful what the brand promises in abstract form. Take the car brand, Volvo, for example: the Volvo brand promises that they produce cars 'for life'. The innovation strategy that stems from this brand promise focuses on enhancing and protecting life in the context of mobility. This leads to innovation efforts in safety, in sustainability and in gearing to the needs of different age groups and demographics.

Volvo's design objective is then to turn this 'for life' vision and the innovations that stem from it into an overall experience that generates trust, comfort and joy for its users, so that the mobility solutions lead to a rich involvement in what life has to offer rather than distract from it.

It does this through the use of various design functions: usability through in-car ergonomics, aesthetics that communicate safety (Volvo's 'shoulders' indicate its Side Impact Protection System), and through coherent experiences over various touchpoints such as dealers, websites, brochures and advertisements. (For an extensive design case study about Volvo, read Toni Matti Karjalainen's *Semantic Transformation in Design*, 2003.)

3   PEOPLE, OBJECTIVES, STRATEGIES, TECHNOLOGIES Originally devised for social media strategy, this sequence by Li and Bernoff (2008) also proves helpful to develop design strategies.

P   O   S   T

PEOPLE   OBJECTIVES   STRATEGIES   TECHNOLOGIES

In brand-driven design strategies, design's objective is to create solutions, interactions and experiences that stem from the brand's vision and that make tangible and meaningful what the brand promises in abstract form.

Design's final objective

So we can now begin to see how, in brand-driven design strategies, design's final objective might be the ultimate fulfilment of the brand promise; but that nested in this objective are more concrete objectives that will resemble the different roles or purposes of design (as discussed on page 141).

What role design will play, and to what purpose it will be used, will depend on the content of the brand promise as defined in the first stage of the BDI process. This is what makes the design strategy brand-driven. But, as we have seen in the Volvo example, design will often be used in many different roles, each to highlight a particular aspect of the brand, or to bring the brand promise to life through a specific interaction.

Volvo's safety is expressed aesthetically through its broad 'shoulders' and ergonomically through its seat design, for example. But design at Volvo is also used to resolve the paradox between Volvo's aesthetic heritage (its expressions of safety perceived as 'boxiness'), and its over-riding ambition to express a more agile, dynamic lifestyle.

Holistic brand design

When crafting brand-driven design strategies, it is important to look at how the different roles of design can help to fulfil the brand's promise. The experience will be richer and the solution more convincing if design gets to play several of its roles simultaneously.

Sadly, in many brand-driven design strategies, design only gets to play the one role: that of dressing the offering up in the visual identity of the brand. The product will get the organisation's key colour, a logo in the right place, maybe a characteristic form element, but that will be it. The store where the product is sold will be nicely designed to match the brand's visual identity, with colours and logos to match, but again, that will be it.

Design's only role in such strategies is a purely aesthetic one. And that almost always signifies an opportunity missed.

What if the product were to not only look like it matched the brand, but also behaved like it? More concretely, what if it were to fulfil the brand promise through what it did, how it did it, how you could interact with it, how it was made and how it made you feel? What if the store did not only look branded, but also lived up to the brand's promise in the way that it guided you, in the way that its staff helped to make you feel at home and find what you were looking for? It is this kind of holistic brand design that building brand-driven design strategies is all about.

A conversation between specialists: brand and design strategies

The conversation on these pages focuses on the role of the brand in designing products, communications, interactions and environments. How do design practitioners use the brand to inspire, inform or drive design decisions? And what is the influence of the brand on their design's aesthetics, performance or usability? What is design's role in building brands? We ask two professionals from the design industry – Pim Jonkman and Aldo de Jong.

Pim Jonkman is a design strategist educated at the Delft University of Technology's department of Industrial Design Engineering. Pim is owner of Scope Design Strategy, a design agency active in the medical and mobility industries. Pim is also the owner and initiator of innerbrand.nl, an online measurement tool helping companies to pinpoint their visual brand language. Pim is currently active as a designer and entrepreneur under the name of Twinckl.

Aldo de Jong holds a Masters in Chemical Engineering from the Delft university of Technology. After jobs at Procter & Gamble and General Electric, Aldo embarked on an MBA at Barcelona's IESE Business School. Aldo's career has centred on consulting in strategic innovation and design, first at Eggo innovation consultants and later at Smart Design, where he now works, consulting for clients on how to use design as a strategic tool to drive innovation.

What role does branding play in your work?

Aldo: When we start our projects we make three assessments: the first is to look at our client's brand attributes and values: who are they and who do they want to be? The second is to look at how the user of our client's products sees that brand. The third is to look at the role that the product we're designing has in bringing the brand to life. These three assessments drive us in our work. We believe that the brand resides in the minds of users, and is created through the touchpoints they encounter. It is our job to design the right touchpoints, in such a way that the brand experience has value for the user.

Pim: I also work with these different interpretations of the brand. Before I can start my design work, I have a number of sessions with the different stakeholders in the company, to assess their interpretation of the brand attributes that they brief me with: what does 'innovative' or 'user friendly' mean to them, and how can we align the different interpretations throughout the organisation? I've developed an instrument called innerbrand.nl that facilitates this dialogue and helps to make the brand attributes concrete. The brand is the central theme in new product development: it provides the common language for the various stakeholders, and it represents the authenticity of the product. Therefore, the congruence in the interpretation of this language is vital.

To what extent is the client's brand part of your briefing? Are you also involved in brand creation?

Aldo: Often our clients see the development of a new product as a means to shift their brand in a certain direction. For example, they want their brand to be more human, or more open, or to radiate more authority. Design, and new product development are ways to make this shift happen, and in that sense it's often part of our briefing. But sometimes we'll only get a single sheet of paper with the brand values on it, or in other cases, very little information about the brand at all. That's when we know that we have to deepen the discussion before we start the design work. That means we also get involved in shaping the brand. This can be done through extra research, or workshops, or with instruments like the one Pim developed.

Pim: To me products and services are the eating of the pudding. They fulfil the brand promise. When clients understand this they will let me translate their desired brand positioning, or marketing strategy, in innovation and design, to create products and services that deliver on the promise the brand makes. But it differs from client to client how explicit the brand is as part of the briefing. Sometimes it isn't there at all and we have to dig for it, and sometimes it's the foundation of the project.

I also frequently encounter situations where I find I have to deepen the brand before I can work with it. Then it's a matter of building up trust, so you can start asking the right questions.

Does the brand drive the products aesthetics only, or also the way you deal with functionality and usability?

Pim: The brand vision finds its way into all aspects of the product design. In my work the focus lies on the visual translation because the looks of a product define your love for it at first sight. The aesthetics help to communicate and explain the functionality and usability of a product through the use of design semantics. Using the innerbrand tool helps to discuss it in a sensible way.

Aldo: We are well known for our focus on product usability. But like Pim says, product aesthetics are tremendously important in explaining this usability to a user, and to give him cues as to how the product should be used. We talk about three 'reads': The first read attracts the user through the gesture and personality of a product as experienced at a distance, and communicates what the product is for.

The second read gives cues about the use of the product in a consistent manner that is appropriate to the brand. And, in doing so, gives users the confidence to buy the product. The third read happens during the actual use of the product, and will, if all's well, affirm the purchase decision and make people happy customers. When you can ensure consistency in the brand experience across those three reads, that is when you've created a cohesive and compelling user experience that connects people with the brand.

Pim: What I find interesting is the role design can play in these different reads. Obviously, in the first and second read, there is no real interaction with the product yet. But still you need to communicate the product's unique selling points. That's where aesthetic design plays a huge role. While in the third read, usability design, interaction design and functional design play a much larger role; not to communicate the USPs but to actually deliver them.

For the full conversation, go to <www.branddriveninnovation.com/book/conversations>.

5.4 **The design strategy stage**

The design strategy stage is the third stage in the brand-driven innovation method and builds on the first and second stage: the human-centred branding stage and the innovation strategy stage respectively. The design strategy stage in BDI is special because it treats design in its broadest sense as a strategic activity that connects the worlds of branding and innovation. The design strategy stage paves the road for the next stage called 'touchpoint orchestration' in which the actual multidisciplinary design will be executed.

Building a brand-driven design strategy is about taking the results of the innovation strategy stage and exploring what role design will play in bringing that strategy to life and so turn it into value and meaning for the users of the organisation's products and services. It builds on the results of the human-centred branding stage as well, by gearing towards the design needs of the people that played a key role in this stage (both internally and externally). It also looks for ways to bring the brand to life through design, and it explores how design will play a role in fulfilling the brand's promise.

As discussed earlier (in section 5.2, pages 142–143), the design strategy stage has the POST structure as its backbone: people, objectives, strategies and tools. It starts with the people and objectives phase, in which the human-centred insights that were gained in the first stage are translated into a design context, and the innovation strategy results are translated into clear design objectives. It then moves on to an internal and external design strategy phase, in which the roles of design both inside and outside the company are mapped, and choices made as to how design will be employed. In the final stage, called 'design tools', the internal and external strategies are combined into a concrete plan for action with regard to the use of design.

The same principles that underlie the human-centred branding stage and the innovation strategy stage are also valid in the design strategy stage. However, some extra rules apply:

1 | Find the patterns. The easiest way to discuss design is by using concrete examples. Still, it's important to find the patterns behind the examples. Try to define guidelines, not just examples.

2 | Ask why. Design is not a goal in itself. If you want to use design strategically, you need to be very aware of why you're using it.

3 | Be interdisciplinary. Look at design from many angles. Get different design disciplines around the table. Have different designers work together. And have them look at their work from the user's point of view.

4 | Involve. Involve designers in crafting the design strategy and the design guidelines. And if possible, involve users.

5 | Visualise. The only way to build a design strategy that will be used is to make it very visual.

The design strategy stage in step-by-step form is outlined on pages 149–153. See the figure on page 149 for the process in model form, again involving a first phase (A), an iterating second and third phase (B and C) and a fourth phase (D).

The design strategy stage in BDI is special because it treats design in its broadest sense as a strategic activity that connects the worlds of branding and innovation.

Phase A: formulate people-based design objectives

This phase is about setting very clear objectives for how your organisation wants to use design to bring the brand, and the innovation strategy that evolved from it, into life. It builds upon the belief that design is there to serve people, and at the same time it is a process that is created by people. In this first phase of setting objectives, these people play a central role.

Get the right people involved

Everyone has an opinion about design. And although the validity of some of these opinions is open to debate, it is wise to adopt an inclusive attitude when building your design strategy. You want people to understand the choices that were made and the directions that were chosen, and as we have seen in the other stages, inclusion is the best guarantee of this. The sort of people you want on board will include those involved in the previous two stages, such as design managers and designers, and maybe additionally some external designers with whom your organisation frequently partners.

Immerse in stages one and two

Take the results from the human-centred branding and the innovation strategy stages and make sure that everyone in the team understands them. If they didn't take part in the process, show them what has been done to achieve the results. Make sure they become involved. If the team stays the same, you're all set!

Define design aspirations

Based on the brand promise and the innovation strategy, define design aspirations. Ask yourself: 'If this is where we want to be with our organisation five years from now, and this is our innovation roadmap to get there, what role would we like to attach to design? Do we want to be a design leader?' Many companies say they want to be 'like Apple' when it comes to design, but try to avoid this trap: being 'like Apple' is far from easy, and for many companies it makes no sense to attach such a relentless and uncompromising role to design. Look for your own aspirations instead.

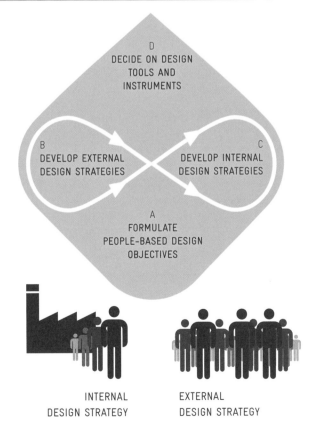

INTERNAL
DESIGN STRATEGY

EXTERNAL
DESIGN STRATEGY

4   BUILDING A DESIGN
    STRATEGY
    The design strategy
    stage consists of
    four steps: formulate
    people-based design
    objectives, develop
    external design
    strategies, develop
    internal design
    strategies and decide
    on design tools and
    instruments.

Define your organisation's design culture

Explore how your organisation has dealt with design in the past. Is it outsourced or held internally? Does it play a central role? Is design valued for its different functions as mapped out on page 141? Is design involved in projects at an early stage? How are designers valued and regarded within the organisation? In short: what is your organisation's design culture? Try not to see design as something glamorous that your organisation should actually value and place centrally, if in reality it doesn't. There's nothing wrong with saying: 'We value design and we aspire to do more with it but at this point in time we don't have the culture to support a very central design function internally.' Also, try to see design as an instrument: try to describe the purposes for which design is used within your organisation and for which purposes it isn't, and how that fits into your culture.

Define design's target group

Go back to the results of the external research in the human-centred branding stage: who will be the users of your organisation's design? What sort of people are they and what sort of design do they value? Will their needs be best served by product design, communications design, environmental design or service design? Will they be more interested in aesthetics or more concerned with performance or usability? Work with what you already know and perform extra research if necessary.

Match design aspirations with target group and culture

Match what you've learned from your exploration of your organisation's design culture and your target group's design needs, with the design aspirations you've defined so far. Are there big gaps? Are your aspirations higher than your target group's needs and those that your own design culture calls for? Is this due to healthy ambition or are you being unrealistic? Or do you aim lower than your own design culture and needs call for? Are you realistic enough or are you not sufficiently ambitious?

Define design's objectives

Working with all you've explored in the previous steps, you will have now built a pretty strong knowledge of what design could do within your organisation, for the people who will work with it and will benefit from it. Next comes the hard bit: defining what design should do to make the second stage's innovation strategy a reality. Go back and develop at least one (but preferably two) workshops around setting the right objectives for your organisation's use of design. One way to break the ice is to look at what the objectives for design were in previous projects. Play the 'why' and 'how' game to go up and down in abstraction level. Be as detailed as possible in your design objectives, and define specialised objectives for different markets, product groups and situations, where you feel this is needed.

Try not to see design as something glamorous that your organisation should actually value and place centrally, if in reality it doesn't.

Phase B: develop external design strategies

This phase can take place in parallel to phase C and focuses on developing the external design strategies that fulfil the design objectives as developed in phase A. External design strategies look at which design means, disciplines, layers and styles are required to bring value to the intended audience.

Develop a rough consumer journey framework

The purpose of the consumer journey at this point is to get a grip on the role of design in the different experiences that a user has with your product or service (see page 100 for an explanation of consumer journeys). Experiences might comprise, for example, 'orientation on the web', 'visiting the retail environment', 'installing the product' or 'asking for assistance'. The consumer journey maps these experiences along a time-axis, possibly for different groups of users and diverse types of products or services. They help to provide an overview of users' experiences, and of what the different interactions with your product or service might mean to them. The rough consumer journey framework is used to assess what design could contribute to each of these experiences. This will happen in the following steps. (Here's a tip that will make life easier for you: make the rough consumer journey framework as visual as possible, and make it big – you will need the space to add lots of information to it later on in this stage.)

Map the design objectives onto each experience

Take the experiences from the consumer journey and assess how the design objectives from phase A, can be attained in each experience. For example, when a design objective is set 'to create an open and inviting brand', this objective could be attained in the retail environment by designing an open, home-like atmosphere that is both inviting and accessible.

Map design functions onto each experience

Look at the design functions and see which function fits which experience best, given the design objectives that must be fulfilled. For example, the creation of an open and inviting retail environment might be attained by using design's aesthetic function, but also by using its usability function; for example, by looking at logical and comfortable routing, by looking at how to present the products in a clear and uncluttered manner, or by looking at a check-out system that is user friendly.

Map design disciplines on to each experience

For each experience along the consumer journey, look at how different design disciplines may be used to reach the design objectives. The different design disciplines are product design, environmental design, communication design, interaction design and service design (see page 153 for a full discussion of design disciplines). For example, in a retail environment, environmental design plays an obvious role, but for the shelving system product design may be required; for in-store communications and routing, communication design will be needed; and for in-store kiosks, interaction design will be useful.

Map design layers on to each experience

Take the Design Layer Model (page 155) and assess which design layer is most important for each experience. When buying a product, the aesthetic layer may play the most prominent role, while the interaction and performance layers are more important when using a product.

Phase C: develop internal design strategies

This phase can take place in parallel with phase B and focuses on developing internal design strategies that fulfil the design objectives as developed in phase A. Internal design strategies look at how to organise your organisation's design resources into the right structures and processes in order to facilitate the external design strategies.

Make an inventory of your organisation's design resources

It's time for a bit of self-reflection! Assess what the status quo of design is within your company in terms of the following aspects:

- people: how many and what kind of designers do you employ?

- processes: what design processes does your organisation employ, and in which situations?

- methods and tools: what kinds of design methods and tools does your organisation employ?

- partnerships: does your organisation partner with design consultancies or with design schools?

- structures: how is design organised and structured? Where is design located in the organisation?

- leadership: who leads design? Who sets the example?

- learning: how do designers learn and develop? How do they become aware of new developments?

Make a gap analysis for internal resources versus external needs

See how your internal resources match the external design needs that you've already explored in phase B. For example, your retail design requires a very strong focus on usability and interaction, while your current design partner is better at interior aesthetics.

Decide where to improve and where to outsource

Look closely at the gaps you've exposed in the previous step. Where can you hone your own resources to match external needs? Are there also redundant resources (a very well-developed graphic design studio, for instance, even though graphic design plays only a minor part in the experiences that you've mapped out)? Are there new partnerships that should be built, based on this gap-analysis? Should you, for example, find a second retail design partner that is more focused on routing and usability to work together with your existing retail designer?

Build improvements for design resources

Make a plan of how to adapt your resources to the needs that you've previously explored. Go back to the list of steps in B and C and assess which adaptations must be made and how you are going to make them for each aspect.

Phase D: decide on design tools and instruments

This phase is focused on taking the results from phases B and C in order to build a set of design guidelines and a well-structured design organisation upon these. These will function as the organisation's toolbox for the next stage, touchpoint orchestration.

Build design guidelines for each design discipline

For a discussion on design guidelines and how to build them, see figure 5, opposite. Your assessment of external design needs for each experience has given you a strong basis to work from: now reorganise what you've found for each experience into new clusters, starting with breaking an organisation down into design disciplines. Try to frame your findings into a visual document, capturing the essence of what you expect each of the five design disciplines to contribute to the consumer journey. See these documents as the start of a working relationship that sets out to fulfil the design objectives in the entire consumer journey. They may be used to brief external parties, as well as internal designers.

	Product design	Communication design	Environment design	Interaction design	Service design
Aesthetics	What the product looks like	What the communication looks like	What the environment looks like	What the interaction looks like	What the service looks like
Interaction	How the user interacts with the product	How the user interacts with the communication	How the user interacts with the environment	How the interaction feels	How the user interacts with the service
Performance	What the product does	What the communication does	What the environment does	What the interaction does	What the service does
Construction	What the product is made of and how it's made	What technologies the communication uses	What the environment is made of and how it's made	How the interaction is made/ programmed	What technologies the service uses
Meaning	What meaning the product sets out to convey	What meaning the communication sets out to convey	What meaning the environment sets out to convey	What meaning the interaction sets out to convey	What meaning the service sets out to convey

Build design guidelines for each design layer

Detail the guidelines to include the design layers for each design discipline. Try to be complete, even if it requires some imagination. Use lots of examples to illustrate what you mean. The goal is to fill in this table as completely as possible.

Make a plan for design organisation

Having completed the guidelines, make a concrete plan that clearly states how you are going to organise design in such a way that you can meet the design objectives. What steps need to be taken, what people need to be hired or trained, and what new partnerships need to be forged? Which internal team will take the design decisions and how will they work together? What timeframe is needed to reach the objectives?

Make a plan for design processes, methods and tools

Be sure to also include the design processes, methods and tools that you will use to meet the design objectives in your plan. What methods or tools need to be developed, or bought? What training and development is required? What internal and external expertise needs to be harnessed and made available? And how will you inform and involve the rest of the organisation along the way? Once you've included the answers to these questions in your plan, you've built a solid design strategy.

5   DESIGN LAYERS
AND DISCIPLINES
Design has many
layers. Users will
unravel these layers
when they encounter
a designed product,
communication,
environment,
interaction or service.
See also figure 6
on page 155.

5.5 Skills for brand-driven design strategies: an overview of tools and methods

Consumer journeys

The consumer journey as used in the first stage of brand-driven innovation can be detailed at this stage by looking at it from a design perspective. (A full discussion of consumer journeys can be found on page 100.) The consumer journey maps different experiences that diverse users may have over time interfacing with your organisation's products or services. It is useful to assess what role design can play in making these experiences truly relevant and valuable for the user.

Design Layer model

Purpose: to bring the brand to life through design in a rich and holistic manner.

This model is based on the realisation that when making a brand vision tangible, it's much more than looks that count. Think of a rich and rewarding brand experience that you've had, such as visiting the Tate Modern gallery in London, for example. Remember what your first impressions were, from approaching the building (its impressive looks), to visiting the exhibition space and admiring the artworks, to finding your way to the café or the toilet (how was the building organised?), to finally going home (what will you always remember?). The Design Layer model treats brand touchpoints as layered structures that the user 'peels off', revealing these different experiences one by one.

Design disciplines

Purpose: to allow design to have its maximum effect in terms of bringing brands to life, with all design disciplines working together – each with their own specific task, but each being based on a shared vision, with a shared goal.

Design can be divided into disciplines, not in order to cut design up into small chunks, but in order to make it as complete and multidisciplinary as possible when embarking on a strategic design project. Recall a branded experience that made a big impression on you, like buying and unwrapping a new MacBook Pro: it's the combination of many design disciplines working together that make the experience what it is for you.

In this book, a structured division of design into five disciplines has been employed, building on Wally Olins' similar compartmentalisation of the discipline in his book, *On brand* (2005). The five design disciplines are:

1 | Product design: 3D design. Includes product styling, industrial design, engineering, structural packaging and furniture design.

2 | Communication design: 2D design. Includes graphic design, advertising (online, print, outdoor media and integrated media campaigns), digital media, corporate identity, 2D packaging design and signage.

3 | Environmental design: 3D design, on a scale that can be entered by humans. Includes interior design, architecture, exhibition design and design for public spaces.

4 | Interaction design: 2D and 3D design, focused on the operation of and interaction with products. Includes on-screen interface design, but also the physical interaction design of controls, buttons and levers, and so forth.

5 | Service design: '4D' design. The stringing together of touchpoints to form a service, and the design of the human interaction between users and an organisation's representatives (Olins calls this the 'behaviour' discipline).

Needless to say, these disciplines overlap at the edges and many examples of design can be found that prove hard to fit into one of the categories listed here. Again, the purpose of this exercise is not to carve design up into thin, narrow segments, but rather to be comprehensive and multidisciplinary where possible.

Design guidelines are a means to visually capture the ways by which an organisation intends to translate its (brand) vision into design.

Design guidelines

Purpose: to brief internal or external designers so that they will perform optimally and reach the design objectives as set out in the design strategy.

Design guidelines are a means to visually capture the ways by which an organisation intends to translate its (brand) vision into design. They are intended to brief designers so that they stay within certain boundaries, without taking away their creativity and individual room for interpretation. Here are some tips on building design guidelines that work to the advantage of all parties involved.

1 | Use visual examples of what you mean.
An image says more than a thousand words.

2 | Use examples of products that are comparable to yours but also of other categories and markets.

3 | Divide the guidelines into chapters or sections using, for example, the different design layers or disciplines to create structure.

4 | Consciously use the process of building design guidelines to get people around the table discussing design: selecting images and clustering them to make visual design guidelines are great activities for an interactive workshop with internal and external designers, marketing personnel, sales people and management.

5 | Consciously use the process of briefing designers as a way to fine-tune the guidelines. For example, by letting the agency that you are briefing contribute their own images to the guidelines, this creates a better understanding of what you mean to convey, and it also creates commitment and co-ownership.

Design Format Analysis (Warell, 2001)

A Design Format Analysis (DFA) is a way to structurally assess how brand values are translated into design by the use of characteristic form elements. DFA looks at all the characteristic aesthetic elements of a brand's product portfolio; and then goes on to check the extent to which these elements are present in each individual product.

This approach produces two results:

1 | It will indicate which product is the most 'representative' for the brand because it has the most characteristic form features;

2 | It will indicate which aesthetic features are the most important for the brand's design language.

It would be very interesting to see whether this approach would also work for the other design layers of interaction, performance, construction and meaning. Go ahead and try it for yourself!

Aesthetics	The sensorial layer	What the touchpoint does to the senses: looks, smell, touch and sound
Interaction	The behavioural layer	How the user interacts with the touchpoint, and what kind of behaviour it invites
Performance	The functional layer	What the touchpoint does, the problems it solves and the functionality it brings to the user
Construction	The physical layer	How the touchpoint is made, what it's made of and what technologies are used
Meaning	The mental layer	What meaning and emotions the touchpoint conveys

6 DESIGN LAYERS
Design has more layers than just the aesthetic outer layer. A complete design strategy takes all layers into account (see also page 153).

Case study: Dapper

DAPPER

The purpose of this case study:

This case study will demonstrate how the application of design strategy works in practice. It will also enable you to get acquainted with the application of design strategy tools.

About Dapper Fashion

Dapper General Apparel Company Limited is a clothing brand based in Bangkok, Thailand, founded in 1979. Dapper is a trading firm and manufacturer of garments, shoes and accessories. The scope of operations of the brand continues to expand nationally as well as internationally, to include exclusive shops and outlet stores all over Thailand, and in several other Asian and European countries. This case study discusses a project conducted at Dapper's footwear division by Aisoon Sucharitkul, for a Masters degree in Strategic Product Design at the Delft University of Technology.

The case study

Sucharitkul set out to perform a graduation project at Dapper with the main objective of developing what he called a 'design philosophy' (Ravasi and Lojacono, 2005). A design philosophy consists of two related components: a set of 'core design principles' and a 'stylistic identity'. The first component, 'core design principles', is comprised of explicit guidelines which provide directions for designers or product developers on how to design a product. These principles are based on a set of shared beliefs influencing designers' decisions about how a product will appear and function. The latter component, 'stylistic identity', refers to the more tangible manifestation of design that is specific to a particular brand and which sets it apart from its competitors (the combination of shapes, colours, materials and patterns). As Sucharitkul notes in his paper for the D2B2 Design Management Conference in Beijing, China, in 2009 (Sucharitkul *et al*, 2009) the stylistic identity of design is closely connected to the aesthetic layer in the Design Layer model (pages 153 and 155), while the 'core design principles' closely resemble our brand-driven design strategy.

Design philosophy in the fashion system

Changes in fashion result in a continuous renewal of product aesthetics, having their primary effects on design attributes such as materials, silhouette, texture, colour and patterns. At the same time, companies that operate in the fashion system may seek to build a strong brand identity by carefully selecting those fashion trends that are in line with the brand promise. Trends irrelevant to the brand may not be followed or, if unavoidable, may only affect the design of new products at a surface aesthetic level. Brand-relevant fashions, to the contrary, may have implications for the development of deeper layers of product design, up to the conceptual layer of brand meaning.

Adapting the design layers model

In order to adapt the framework of brand-driven design to forces imposed by the fashion system, a new framework was created (opposite page, top). Within this framework, the outer layer of aesthetics is seen as being in constant flux, changing in respect to the fashion parameters of detail, colour, material, texture and silhouette. Moving inwards, each of the consecutive design layers tends to have a higher degree of constancy over time than the previous one.

The model can be better understood by visualising how liquid in a cup would rotate when stirred near the outside of the cup, the centre remaining still while the outside 'layer' rotates in accordance with the speed of the stirring. In this analogy, the core design principles act as a measure of the viscosity of the liquid. Depending on their approach to design, some companies can be like water, and be easily stirred by fashion changes; while other companies can be like syrup and therefore react to changes in fashion with more resistance and mostly at their outer layers.

Researching design principles and stylistic identity

Over a four-month research period, in which Sucharitkul worked as a design management consultant for the Thai company, Dapper's design principles and stylistic identity were uncovered. In line with the approaches outlined in this book, Sucharitkul used design research techniques to uncover deep and applicable insights into the company, its culture, its heritage, its founder and its employees; but also into the Thai fashion scene and the brand users' aspirations, lifestyles and shopping behaviours. Sucharitkul also performed a design format analysis (see page 153) to uncover the fashion brand's current design language.

The four Dapper Design Philosophy (DDP) Tools

Based on the theoretical frameworks, the on-site research and the resulting design layers, four tools were developed to enable Dapper to gain a firmer grip on their Design Philosophy, as well as to give them a practical guide to apply it in daily practice. The four tools are outlined in the following paragraphs.

DDP Key

This first tool is called the DDP key and is a mini visual booklet. It is intended for all stakeholders involved in men's footwear design from management level to brand managers and designers. The DDP key represents the relationship between the elements that make up the design philosophy. These elements are the brand promise, design principles, stylistic identity and the fashion system. Stakeholders can read the booklet, which provides brief descriptions and an overview of the framework for the design philosophy.

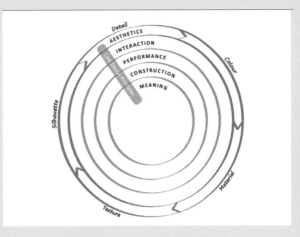

THE DESIGN LAYER MODEL REVISITED
Sucharitkul interpreted the Design Layer model of page 155 as a cup of liquid that is stirred: the outside spins faster than the inside (aesthetics change faster than meaning), the more viscous the liquid is, the slower it spins (stronger design principles will create more stability).

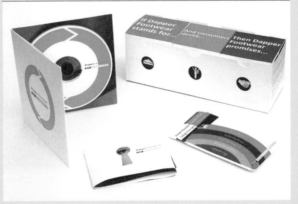

THE FOUR DDP TOOLS
Sucharitkul created four Dapper design philosophy tools as a result of the research he did at the Thai fashion company. The tools were meant to help designers incorporate the brand's core principles and stylistic identity in their work.

TOOL ONE: DDP KEY
The DDP key summarises all the elements that make up the Dapper design philosophy.

DDP 'promise cubes'

The DDP promise cubes comprise a tangible and interactive tool that represents the relationship between the Dapper brand and its consumers. They can be placed on the desktop of footwear designers and other stakeholders, thus helping them to become fully immersed into the brand promise.

They can also be used when an insight into the brand promise is required for work (for example, for use in marketing strategies, retail design and promotional activities). At the core of the design philosophy is the brand promise, which provides insight into consumers' expectations when using and buying Dapper footwear. The DDP promise cubes provide insights into this brand-consumer relationship.

DDP 'principle cards'

The principle cards are designed to help inspire, guide and inform designers and other stakeholders about the core design principles inherent in the DDP. The principle cards are built upon the Design Layer model and translate the brand promise into design execution. The cards contain two sides: the 'design principle' and 'enquiry' features.

The 'design principle' side presents an image and explanation of the principle in relation to a specific five-layer design, and informs the person using it about the guiding principles behind every pair of Dapper men's shoes.

On the other side, the 'enquiry' feature makes users think about new fashion trends that might be selected for Dapper footwear. This side can also be used for scrutinising the brand fit of Dapper's footwear designs prior to production and launch.

DDP 'style palettes'

The DDP style palettes form a digital template tool intended for use during the design of new footwear collections. The DDP Style palette is comprised of a 'past style palette' containing historical information (like images, sales data and design specifications) on all of the collections in the men's footwear line over the past three years, and a 'new style palette' that contains newly gathered information on trends, put together by designers by mixing style and fashion elements for the new collections with selected elements from the past. This allows for more consistency in design, both within and between different collections.

TOOL TWO: DDP PROMISE CUBES
The Dapper design philosophy promise cubes connect Dapper's internal values with their users' needs, to form the brand's core promise.

TOOL THREE: DDP PRINCIPLE CARDS
The Dapper design philosophy principle cards translate the brand's promise into guidelines for execution, using the Design Layer model on page 155.

At the core of Dapper's design philosophy is the brand promise, which provides insight into consumers' expectations.

Testing

The DDP tools were tested on the men's footwear line for the then-upcoming 2008 fashion collection. Overall, Dapper designers felt that the tools represented a 'new approach to designing', not only applicable for Dapper, but also for other Thai fashion brands. Moreover, their encouraging experience has now persuaded both CEO and management to initiate implementation of the tools for the women's footwear lines, and possibly even for handbags and clothing.

However, the designers mentioned that because of the innovativeness of the tools, it may take some time before everyone in the company can fully embrace and sustainably implement them as part of an approach to strategically design new, branded products for future collections going forward.

The application of the DDP tools led to a new footwear model, which has a distinctive stylistic identity in alignment with the underlying brand promise. Recent market data from the company verifies that this footwear model has a high sales performance and that its 'signature' design has made it a price premium product within the Dapper men's footwear brand.

Conclusions to be gained from the Dapper case study

1 | Design principles, stylistic identity and brand vision are closely related concepts.

2 | Design and design strategy are vital when it comes to translating brand values into relevant products.

3 | Building a brand-driven design strategy can lead to very practical, applicable tools.

4 | Brand-driven design strategies can lead to new design outputs that closely align with the brand promise.

5 | You can't build a solid design strategy without an understanding of an organisation's internal and external context.

6 | Designers are quite happy with design guidelines and tools if they are inspired by them, not constrained by them.

7 | The proposed approach and tools can be implemented under different cultural contexts.

5.6 Embedding design strategy in the organisation

The first thing to realise when you are embarking on a design strategy project within your organisation is that no one ever woke up with the urgent need for a design strategy. Many organisations are new to the idea that design is a strategic capability that can play a role in fulfilling organisational objectives, let alone the idea that design can be adapted, fine-tuned and honed to suit the fulfilment of specific objectives. For many organisations, design is still a rabbit to be pulled out of a hat when the opportunity arises, a black box that may or may not increase sales or a company's profit margin; but also something that is very hard to organise, structure, influence and control. So when you are selling a plan to develop a solid design strategy because you believe there is value to be gained from getting the maximum effect out of design, and in using it as a strategic instrument to get things done, you will, more often than not, have some preaching to do.

However, experience teaches us that when you use the various frameworks set out in this chapter, when you are capable of explaining both the rational and the more emotional benefits of design, and when you succeed in connecting them to your organisation's strategic objectives, your efforts will be welcomed. Embedding design strategy in the organisation will be easier if you take the rules of thumb outlined below into account.

Explain what you do

A design strategy is never a goal in itself. Don't get carried away. You will only gain support if you can indicate how your efforts benefit the organisation and its larger strategic objectives. A design strategy requires explanation. Many people will not understand what you are working on. Spend time on explaining what you do, how you do it and why you do it. It's fun, and it creates support.

Involve people

You might be the designer or design manager but that doesn't mean that you own design. Get those non-designers at the table and ask them what they expect from design and how design may help them. And have them collect images of examples, make collages, judge competition and assess your current design expressions. You will be amazed at how much you will learn and how much support you will gain.

Set goals and measure them

When you are 'selling' the use of a solid design strategy, don't be afraid to set some concrete goals in place and measure whether you've attained them along the way. A goal may be a more efficient design process, a better relationship with agencies, a better congruence between design and corporate strategy, or better methods and tools. It is up to you and your organisational situation what promises you make to your management. The point is not to be afraid to embed your design strategy in some solid promises, and then to stand by them and measure to what extent you succeed in fulfilling them. You will gain a lot of confidence from it, and it will give design strategy the credibility it deserves.

In practice: working with design strategy tools

Purpose

This exercise challenges you to play around with the different design strategy tools detailed in this chapter, in order to discover how they work in practice and what their value might be in strategic design projects.

Required

Two people, a roll of plain wallpaper, black, green and red felt pens, post-it notes and some time.

1

Pick an experience with a product or service you've had lately that you would like to work on as a design strategist. Choose one that includes a considerable span of the consumer journey, for example, booking and going on a holiday.

2

Take turns in telling your partner about the experience in as much detail as possible, and don't leave out your personal emotions during different stages of the experience.

3

Take about three metres of wallpaper and hang it on the wall, horizontally, one for each experience. Define the different steps in time that created the experience. Write each step on a post-it, and map them on the wallpaper. You've just created a consumer journey map!

4

Go over each step and analyse to what extent it was branded. Was the step unique to the brand, and did it reflect what the brand stands for? Was design used to reflect the brand and bring it to life?

5

Take the black felt pen and write under each post-it what the design objective of each step may have been. For example, when you booked the vacation, at some point you consulted a *Lonely Planet* travel guide for your destination. Its design objective was to give you up-to-date inside information. Later on, you may have looked for images of your destination on Flickr. Its design objective was to inspire you and help you find what you were looking for.

6

Then, under each step, write which design *functions* were used intensively (in green), and which weren't but should have been (in red), based on the table on page 141. For example, the check-in at the airport was designed well in terms of aesthetics, but the queueing and waiting and dealing with paper forms was quite old-fashioned: it could have used a bit more design as innovation.

7

Next, under each step, write which design *disciplines* were used intensively (in green), and which weren't but should have been (in red). For example, a lot of attention had been paid to the architecture of the holiday resort, but the service provided by the personnel was noticeably poor.

8

Under each step, write which design *layers* were used intensively (in green), and which weren't but should have been (in red); e.g. the rental car office's interior looked outdated but interaction with the staff was very efficient. Go over both wallpapers and marvel at the complexity of the design: do you see how building a solid design strategy would have created a more rewarding experience? How would you help the organisation behind your experience develop a design strategy? Upload a photo of your wallpaper and your comments to <www.branddriveninnovation.com/book/design-strategy-tools>.

Case study: Trespa International BV

TRESPA®

The purpose of this case study

The following case study will explore how a company can fulfil its ambition to reposition their brand through a multidisciplinary design strategy, connecting its core competences to its users' needs and aspirations.

About Trespa

Trespa International BV manufactures and markets panels for exterior cladding, decorative building facades and interior surfaces. Trespa manufactures these panels in their plant in Weert, the Netherlands, but sells them worldwide, through an international network of sales offices.

Trespa's innovation challenge

From their start in 1960, the world in which Trespa operates has been a highly dynamic one. With changing architectural trends, changing needs in the built environment, and changing legislation, Trespa always had to be innovative and flexible to stay relevant. Currently, as much as ten per cent of Trespa's turnover stems from new products. A multidisciplinary team of marketers, designers and research engineers continuously work together to create future products. But breakthrough technological innovations take a long time to reach the market: Trespa's investments in production facilities are large, meaning that R&D has to deal with strong manufacturing constraints. On top of this, the product is chemically complex and needs to meet many regulations.

Architectural trends and needs change more quickly than breakthrough innovation can keep up with. That's why Trespa has a second cycle of innovations: innovation through design. More incremental innovations that use design in all its disciplines (product, environment, communication, interaction and service) to keep connected to the architect and his or her needs.

Facing the challenge with a solid design strategy

Design for Trespa has never been a goal in itself: they have employed design in various specific ways, to reach specific strategic purposes, to face the challenges of each particular period of their history.

On the one hand one might say the meaning of design at Trespa has grown over the years, from 'design as styling' to 'design as innovation' (based on 'the design ladder', Danish Design Centre, 2003). On the other hand, the meaning of design hasn't necessarily grown, but has adapted itself to different circumstances.

Evolution in design strategy

If you look at Trespa's history of applying design, you can distinguish four periods.

Let's look at these periods a bit more closely, to explore how design has been used differently, but equally strategically, in these different periods.

7   AN EVOLUTIONARY DESIGN STRATEGY

Period	Mission	Trespa's role	Design focus
Functional development	To provide the best functionality and performance	Provider of functional benefits	Best in class panel function and performance
Panel styling	To lead in panel styling and variety	Provider of emotional benefits	On-trend panel styling
Integrated design	To understand and inspire upcoming architects through integrated design solutions	Provider of integrated solutions	Integrated facade solutions
Design leadership	To challenge leading architects through cutting-edge innovation and design	Partner in innovation and design	Expertise and co-creation

Design for Trespa has never been a goal in itself: they have employed design in various specific ways, to reach specific strategic purposes, to face the challenges of each particular period of their history.

1960–1998 functional development

Context

Trespa exterior panels are valued for their functional qualities. Trespa holds a strong competitive advantage in the market for exterior panels, based almost solely on their production technologies.

Strategy

Function is Trespa's key differentiator from competition. The Trespa collection, its communication and the applications of the Trespa exterior panels in projects all have very basic functional orientation. Trespa is focused on exploiting its technological advantage on all levels.

Design management

Design is R&D driven and focused on communicating functional benefits and demonstrating performance (durability, reliability, quality). The design management focus is on aligning design and engineering.

Brand research

Over the years, the brand image of Trespa is measured and compared to that of competitors on five dimensions: knowledge, solution provider, design, price positioning and functionality. Market research from this period shows the very functional image of Trespa. The brand is seen as professional, quality driven, reliable but not attracting any attention and not exciting.

1998–2004 panel styling

Context

Functional benefits of the Trespa panel become commoditised. Competition is closing in on the functional aspects of the Trespa products and a growing need for aesthetic facade materials among architects and real estate developers emerges. Trespa has to apply its increased manufacturing and R&D expertise to generate added value for the creative specifier, the architect.

Strategy

Trespa realises the necessity of changing from a technology-driven to a technologyand design-driven company, and implements a new competence focused on design management. A shift from a focus on the product to the customer takes place. The customer in Trespa's case is the architect who specifies the use of Trespa in the designs, and is interested in aesthetics, expression, and a more integrated approach to facades. A new collection is developed, which offers architects well-balanced colour schemes, textures and structures.

Design management

Design becomes market driven and focuses on the needs of architects, both in terms of performance and expression: a modern aesthetic is chosen. The design management focus is on aligning design and marketing.

Brand research

Market research shows that the design image improves. With functionality staying the same, the focus on price positioning decreases, enabling Trespa to become an upmarket player, to keep manufacturing in Western Europe, and to avoid price erosion.

2004–2009 integrated design

Context

The increasingly demanding building industry prefers solution providers to suppliers. Sustainability and climate control become important. Trespa develops expertise to develop integrated facades.

Strategy

Trespa's design management competence develops further, both in terms of design expertise and in terms of technical know-how. Trespa starts to explore the realisation of designs on the edge of contemporary architecture, working with design management agencies such as Zilver, and architects such as Jean Nouvel and Norman Foster. Through this new design focus, Trespa sets out to position itself as an enabler of top architecture. This also implies that its employees need to work on understanding and facilitating the architect's creativity.

Design management

Design becomes more customer-centred and experimental. Design focus: research into the aspirations of architects, and creation of future concepts (see page 128) to demonstrate Trespa's capacities and to evoke reactions. Design management focus: aligning design with the customer.

Brand research

Market research in this period shows that Trespa's design image has further improved. Also the rating on 'knowledge' and 'solution provider' increases. The rating on price focus decreases further, in line with Trespa's more premium positioning.

Trespa perspectives

Trespa's future concept strategy takes shape in a programme called 'Perspectives'. It's a multidisciplinary design, innovation and communication programme that started in 2004. Aart Jan van der Meijden, Trespa's commercial director, was involved with the programme from the start: 'Perspectives' main purpose has been to start a meaningful dialogue with architects by showcasing potential futuristic Trespa applications in a thematic way. It facilitates Trespa's role as design partner and solution provider, by demonstrating their capabilities and expertise and by triggering a discussion between peers.'

The Perspectives programme is to facade system architecture what concept cars are to the automobile industry and are in that sense comparable to the approach discussed in the Festo case on page 128: it's a way for Trespa to get internal teams aligned, to demonstrate their design philosophy to the world in a tangible way, and to trigger a response from their target audience, the architect. The Perspectives programme attracts a new audience to the brand and has spin-offs into the regular innovation cycle.

Trade fairs

One of the triggers of the Perspectives programme is Trespa's yearly trade-fair booth that travels the international circuit of building fairs. It provides an opportunity for Trespa to present their vision in full scale, in three dimensions, embedded in a carefully orchestrated experience. Van der Meijden: 'Our customers have come to expect a lot from us. But the trade-fair booth also has an important internal benefit: it aligns our marketing, R&D and sales teams and it helps us to make our dreams tangible. We have built applications that we didn't think possible at first.'

NY showroom

One of Trespa's latest ventures has been to open a showroom in New York. Teaming up with designers from the Netherlands (to leverage from the Dutch design trend) Trespa has created an 'island of Dutch design in the Big Apple'.

What's next?

Now that the Perspectives programme has been running for six years, designers and marketers at Trespa are looking for something new to challenge them. What will be next for Trespa? Van der Meijden: 'Our ambitions for the future are big, and the opportunities for innovation are endless. We need to keep innovating on functionality, but on a systems level. Facades are platforms for media, climate systems, energy harvesting and daylight systems so we need to develop expertise in these areas, both in design and R&D. We will need to partner with other facade experts. And we will have to open the door to partnerships with leading architects, co-creating with them to realise their dreams through innovation and design, and enabling us to turn our mission into reality.'

Conclusions to be gained from the Trespa case

1 ¦ A good design strategy changes over time. It adapts itself to new contexts, ambitions, target audiences, trends, capabilities or technological advances.

2 | Trespa has measured the result of the implementation of their design strategy over the years, by looking at the effect it has had on their brand. Customer satisfaction, sales, margin, repeat purchase and buyer profiles are other dimensions that can be measured to assess design effect. But what you should measure depends entirely on what your objective is. Trespa's design objective was to reposition the brand.

3 | Trespa's design strategy has been very multidisciplinary. Although it is a product company, it has consistently used communication, environments, web and service design to enhance the interaction with their customer.

4 | Companies like Trespa see the use of design as a key brand attribute. Although in these cases one has to be aware of window dressing (using design merely to make things prettier, but not to create strategic benefits for customers), Trespa genuinely interacts with customers and challenges them to get the most out of their product.

DESIGN SKETCHES
Trespa's Perspectives programme involves a continuous design effort, resulting in an ongoing architectural trend analysis and many design sketches. Each year, around ten ideas are chosen to be prototyped.

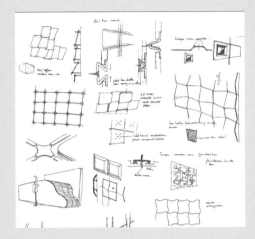

COMMUNICATION
The Perspectives programme covers products, environments and communication, all in line with the Trespa brand and the design objectives of the programme (right).

DESIGN CONCEPTS
Pictured are examples of design concepts, as used to trigger the dialogue with architects. Some of these concepts are chosen to be explored by R&D, to see how they can be brought to life in 3D.

TRADE-FAIR BOOTH
A selection of the concepts that have made it to 3D stage are showcased each year in a travelling trade-fair booth. The booth attracts many architects who come looking for inspiration and new applications.

NEW YORK SHOWROOM
In 2008, Trespa opened a showroom and meeting facility for architects in New York (above), for the continuation of the Perspectives adventure: opening a dialogue with the US market.

5.7 Conclusion: design strategy in brand-driven innovation

In this chapter, we've built a case for the strategic use of design to turn brand vision into valuable and relevant products and services. We have learned to see design as an adaptable capability that can be put to use as a strategic instrument to reach certain objectives. We've established that an important aspect of using design strategically is setting clear design objectives. Design can have many different objectives, and it can play many roles in organisations. In brand-driven innovation, many of these roles must be used in order to fulfil the brand's promise in a rich and rewarding way.

BDI's design strategy stage provides the tools and insights that will help you use design in its full multi-disciplined and multi-layered way, building a user-centred consumer journey that delivers the brand's vision through tangible experiences.

BDI's design strategy stage provides the tools and insights that will help you use design in its full multi-disciplined and multi-layered way, building a user-centred consumer journey that delivers the brand's vision through tangible experiences.

Summary insights from chapter 5

1   Design is essential in bringing brands to life through meaningful touchpoints that deliver on the brand's promise. Design is capable of turning vision into value.

2   When we try to answer the question 'Why should we use design?' we are looking for the objective of design. Design objectives are 'nested': for each defined objective, a new 'why' can be asked. The trick is to choose the right level of abstraction.

3   In brand-driven design strategies, design's objective is to create solutions, interactions and experiences that stem from the brand's vision and that make tangible and meaningful what the brand promises in abstract form.

4   Nested in this objective are more concrete objectives that will resemble the different roles or purposes of design as discussed in this chapter. What role design will play, and to what purpose it will be used, will depend on the content of the brand promise as defined in the first stage of the BDI process.

5   Design is multi-disciplined and multi layered. These disciplines and layers can be used and adapted to serve specific purposes.

6   The design strategy stage has the POST structure as its backbone: people, objectives, strategies and tools.

7   The people and objectives phase translates the human-centred insights that were gained in the first stage into a design context, and the innovation strategy results into clear design objectives.

8   The internal and external design strategy phases map the roles of design both inside and outside of the company, and facilitate choices as to how design will be employed.

9   The design tools phase combines the internal and external strategies into a concrete plan for action with regard to the use of design in the organisation.

10   Design strategy is never a goal in itself. To launch a solid design strategy within an organisation, both the rational and the more emotional benefits of design need to be explained effectively in relation to the organisation's strategic objectives.

CHAPTER 6
Orchestrating touchpoints

This chapter is about creating individual touchpoints in such a way that they function optimally, while at the same time taking care to ensure that they produce a whole that is more than the sum of the individual parts. It is about orchestrating individual instruments in an orchestra in such a way that each one plays its part perfectly – while combined, they form a symphony.

The fourth stage in the brand-driven innovation method is called 'orchestrating touchpoints'. It deals with the creation of all the different points through which a user comes into contact with a brand. These contact points, or brand touchpoints, should function individually: the advertisements, the website, the store, the salesperson, the packaging, the user manual, the product, the service person. But together, they should tell a story. Combined, they form an overall experience that will settle itself in the memory of the user and will come to represent what the brand means. This fourth stage is about creating the individual touchpoints in such a way that they function optimally, while at the same time taking care that they combine a whole that is larger than the sum of the individual parts.

As discussed at the beginning of chapter 2 (pages 42–43), execution is vital. You can build the best human-centred brand you can imagine, and have all the innovation and design strategies to hand in the world, but without turning your plans into touchpoints that have relevance, originality and value, you are merely creating a business on paper. This chapter is about execution: it deals with how to make different designers of different disciplines work together with sales, marketing, engineering, manufacturing, services and management to turn your BDI plans into a valuable and meaningful reality for your users.

The chapter starts by exploring what brand touchpoints are and how they work, and by looking into the nature of multidisciplinary design management. We then look at how to involve the user in the process of creating touchpoints that function well and combine together to form the perfect brand experience. Next, we will set out to develop a step-by-step working method for the fourth stage of BDI. We will conclude the chapter by looking at the special (and very important) emergent field of service design management, and at how to set up the orchestration of touchpoints within the organisation.

6.1 **Brand touchpoints**

In touch with the brand

Brand touchpoints are those points through which a user comes into contact with a brand. These points can be tangible (a product or environment) or intangible (a service or the 'word of mouth' discussion around it), created by the brand owner (an advertisement) or by the brand user (a blog post evaluating a service or product). A shift is taking place from the tangible to more intangible touchpoints: from products to services, and from services taking place in the physical world to services that take place online. A similar shift is taking place from brand-owner created touchpoints to user-generated touchpoints. However, a brand without any touchpoints that are put forth by the brand cannot exist: even a virtual brand like the social networking platform Facebook has to provide the website and infrastructure on which its users can generate their content. (Try to conceive of a brand that is entirely user-generated: it's a nice thought experiment.)

In 2002, Scott Davis and Michael Dunn used the concept of brand touchpoints in their book, *Building the Brand-driven Business* to describe how a user experiences a brand over time. To this end, they introduced the concept of the 'brand touchpoint wheel', in which three stages distinguish the way in which the user experiences the brand: the pre-purchase, the purchase and the post-purchase experience. We will build on this model by centring it less around the purchase, and more around the brand promise and its delivery. Since the brand touchpoint wheel is a circular representation of a consumer journey, it should be clear that every organisation has its own brand touchpoint wheel, and that this changes over time according to the specific product or service it's depicting.

Designing touchpoints

The brand touchpoints that are put forth by the organisation very often involve design of some kind. Since brand touchpoints are the only points through which actual interaction between the user and the organisation can take place, they have quite a task to fulfil: they deliver the functional and emotional benefits to the user that, combined, represent a certain value that the user is willing to pay for. As we have seen in the previous chapter, each experience in the consumer journey is equipped with its own design objective: its own task in delivering part of the value, and its own way of using design to complete that task. The same holds true for the individual touchpoints that comprise the experience: each touchpoint has a purpose and each touchpoint should be designed accordingly.

For example, a clothes shop consists of many touchpoints: the shop window, the shop name and logo, the entrance, the retail environment, the background music, the videos that are projected, the clothes racks and shelves, the changing rooms, the counter, the labels on the clothes and the clothes themselves. Each touchpoint delivers a specific value to the user. For example, the counter at the clothes shop has very specific individual functions: it needs to reflect the clothing brand's identity and it needs to stand out as the point in the shop where you can pay and get information. It also has to make paying for and packaging the goods as quick and comfortable an experience as possible. It needs to be designed so that the customer can pay in private, has room for her handbag and can receive the goods comfortably. And it needs to be designed so that the shop personnel have all they need within arm's length, in addition to a good view of the shopping customers.

1   SHIFTS IN
    TOUCHPOINTS
    Brand touchpoints
    become more and
    more intangible.
    And more and more
    often, these are
    generated by users,
    not organisations.

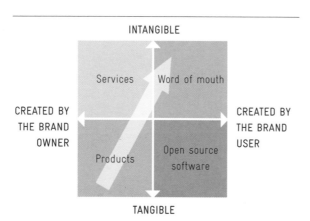

So, each touchpoint needs to be designed in such a way that it delivers this value in optimum form, fitting the user's needs and desires, fitting the organisation's strategic objectives and identity and, ultimately, fulfilling the brand's promise. But delivering a specific value to the user is not the only role that a touchpoint has. An individual touchpoint is only a building block in the formation of the total user experience. We can employ a musical metaphor to express this: if what the user experiences and will remember in the end is the symphony, all the touchpoints combined form the orchestra playing that symphony. And each individual touchpoint is one instrument in that orchestra. So, the second task of a touchpoint is to contribute to the symphony by playing its specific part in harmony with the other touchpoints.

Let's return to our example of the counter in the clothes shop: in the entire user experience, it is the one point where human interaction takes place and thus it should represent the human face of the brand. In addition, it is the place where the actual transaction takes place: clothes are obtained in exchange for money. It seals the relationship between the user and the clothing brand; therefore, it should be designed with the nature of this relationship in mind.

Each task point has a role to play in the entire journey through the touchpoints that form the brand experience for the user. Just as each instrument has a role to play in the orchestra in order to perform a symphony. To assign these roles to touchpoints and to make them play together in order to deliver the experience – in short, to orchestrate touchpoints – comprises the other half of the fourth stage of BDI.

2 THE BRAND TOUCHPOINT WHEEL Originally developed by Davis and Dunn (2002) the brand touchpoint wheel can be seen as a circular consumer journey (see page 170). This diagram gives an example, as the touchpoint wheel is different for each consumer journey.

Case study: Virgin Atlantic, UK

The purpose of this case study

In this case study you will learn more about how touchpoint orchestration works in practice; and to understand how each touchpoint has its own dedicated purpose while still working in harmony with other touchpoints to create an overall experience.

About Virgin Atlantic

Sir Richard Branson founded Virgin Atlantic Airways Limited in 1984. It was his first venture outside of the world of pop and rock music (he had formerly set up an audio record mail-order business, followed by a chain of record stores and a music label, Virgin Records). His fellow directors thought he was mad – particularly when he announced the new airline would begin operating in just over three months. Virgin Atlantic possesses every ingredient of the quintessential Virgin story: the small newcomer taking on the giant and complacent establishment; people's champion Branson being tired of the conveyor-belt attitude to passengers adopted by traditional airlines, introducing better service and lower costs for passengers, and establishing a reputation for quality and innovative product development. Starting with one leased Jumbo on an inaugural flight to Newark filled with celebrities from the music and entertainment world, Virgin Atlantic went on to be valued at £1.2 billion ($1.8 billion) in 2000; and by 2008, had become the second largest British airline, having flown six million people around the globe and with a turnover of £2.3 billion (US $3.3 billion).

Design at Virgin Atlantic

Design at Virgin Atlantic is not only about making things look good, although that is surely one of its tasks. Design is firmly rooted in the company's strategic objectives and brand values. As the diagram below indicates, the Virgin Atlantic design department operates on an organisational foundation comprised of three layers, as follows:

1 | The company manifesto, which determines the non-negotiable aspects of the day-to-day business, such as safety and on-time departure. It also determines where the focus of the business will be for a three-year period.

2 | The business objectives: in addition to the manifesto, the business sets its yearly goals with regard to the annual budget and the new markets to be tackled within that year. These goals adjust the direction of the manifesto for that particular period.

3 | A divisional plan: from the manifesto and business objectives a business plan is constructed. The divisional plan details all projects, their attached budgets, timescales and relevance to the manifesto for each division within the company.

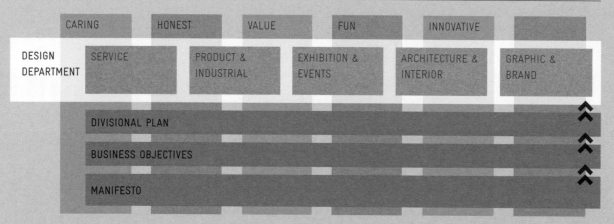

3   DESIGN MANAGEMENT AT VIRGIN ATLANTIC
The design management function at Virgin Atlantic is multidisciplinary, and builds on the company's brand manifesto and strategic business objectives.

The design department operates with the following mission: to inspire change with considered innovation. Within the Virgin Atlantic design department, five design disciplines operate: service design, product and industrial design, exhibition and event design, architecture and interior design and graphic design. Embedded within the operations of the design department and central to the business foundation are Virgin Atlantic's five brand values; to be caring, honest, value, fun and innovative.

Virgin's design department is headed by Joe Ferry, who graduated in 1996 with a Masters degree in Industrial Design Engineering from the Royal College of Art in London. Ferry's graduate project interestingly entailed the redesign of the Virgin Atlantic Upper Class sleeper seat. Joe is responsible for leading a team of internal designers who collaborate internally with engineering, as well as externally with other design experts, engineers and manufacturers. Asked by *Wallpaper* magazine about which idea or product he has been most proud of in the ten years that he has worked for Virgin, Joe Ferry replied: 'The Upper Class experience as a whole is probably what I would consider the design team's greatest achievement. It started in 2001 with our Upper Class Suite and concluded last year with the opening of our Terminal 3 Wing – I am incredibly proud of the seamless transition we have created from home to airport.'

So let's now turn to take a closer look at the redesign of Virgin Atlantic's Upper Class experience.

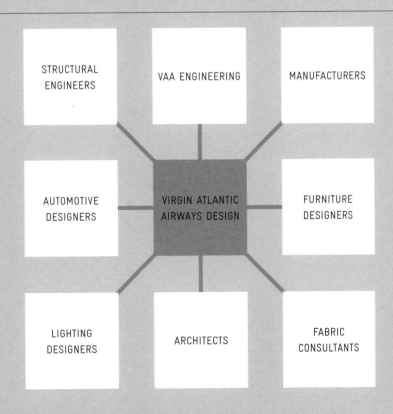

4   DESIGN AND
    THE REST OF THE
    ORGANISATION
    Design at Virgin
    Atlantic is strongly
    linked to various
    other disciplines. Its
    ability to cooperate
    with these other
    disciplines partly
    defines its success.

Redesigning the luxury air travel experience, the Virgin way

Virgin is famous for redesigning businesses by looking at them from a user's perspective, for breaking with conventions and for not taking 'no' for an answer. This is exactly what Virgin has done in redesigning their Upper Class experience. The entire consumer journey, from booking the flight, getting to the airport, checking in, boarding the plane, to the actual flight itself, has been redesigned over a time span of six years. The redesign of the entire experience started in 2001 with the development of the Upper Class suite, a super-comfortable business class seat/bed, introduced in 2003. In 2005, the new Virgin Atlantic Clubhouse at London Heathrow airport was launched and in 2007, a whole new Upper Class Drive Thru Check In system, comprising an Upper Class Wing was launched.

In an interview with the Design Council in the UK, Joe Ferry emphasised that the Upper Class Suite experience involves a holistic approach covering much more than just the seat design; involving not just the cabin ambience but also associated service elements, including limousine pick-up and a range of dining options. As such, the redesign of the Upper Class experience is a perfect example of touchpoint orchestration, where each touchpoint has a specific function, but also contributes by playing a role in the overall user experience.

Getting to the airport and checking in

A Drive Thru Check In system was developed especially for those Upper Class travellers who use Virgin's limo pick-up service: Upper Class passengers are taken in their chauffeur-driven car up a curved ramp onto a wide circular arrival area (designed by architects Foster + Partners in collaboration with the Virgin Atlantic in-house design team) where a dedicated host welcomes them. The host completes all check-in formalities before the passenger's car arrives, so all that's left for them to do is for the porter to take their bags, check the passengers in, and a host to hand them their boarding pass before they walk through the hotel-style lobby.

Relaxing at the Clubhouse

The Clubhouse was designed by SOFTROOM, a London architecture firm, in collaboration with the Virgin Atlantic team, to create interiors that feel like a private members' club. The innovative and award-winning 2500 m² layout was kept as open as possible to maximise the grand sense of scale and features a series of 'landmarks' and 'vistas' to encourage passengers to stroll around and explore their surroundings. The Clubhouse also boasts business facilities, a range of spa treatments and a choice of dining options. The Clubhouse offers busy cosmopolitans room to relax, work, play, eat, drink and be pampered.

Enjoying the flight

Once on board, the traveller will be pampered even more: the Upper Class Suite allows travellers to work, relax, share a drink with a friend in the bar area or sleep in complete comfort. Every suite is fitted with a multi-directional 10.4-inch (26.4 cm) TV screen with an abundant choice of films, TV programmes and games, and each suite has aisle access. But the best thing that Ferry and his team conjured up is the way that the seat turns into a 6'5" (two metre) bed at the touch of a button. The two sides of the seat serve completely separate functions – a fully contoured seat on one side covered in leather, while on the reverse the bed is built of firm, supportive foams covered in a breathable fabric for maximum sleeping comfort.

ARRIVAL
The Virgin Atlantic design team created a whole new arrival experience for those Upper Class customers using the limo pick-up service.

The whole consumer journey has the Virgin brand attitude embedded in it. Not by stamping Virgin logos everywhere, but by asking the same question at every point: 'What ingrained conventions can we break to serve the user better?'

Although the entire experience was developed over the course of many years, and involved many design disciplines as well as the efforts of many other experts, the whole journey is extremely well orchestrated. As Jeremy Brown, senior design manager of customer experience for Virgin Atlantic Airways notes: 'The passenger's needs are always recognised. We design environments, products and services, uniting the Virgin Atlantic brand, to fulfil these needs throughout the journey, creating a unique and memorable passenger experience.' Antoinette Nassoupoulos, architect and partner at Foster + Partners, makes the same point in a similar way: 'The design strategy focused on making an exclusive and seamless journey. The whole journey has an exclusive, luxurious, glamorous feel to it, breaking away from the feeling one normally gets in airports of being in a process space, of being someone who has to go through a series of tedious process steps to get to the aircraft. It's much more like the old age of travel where I feel I am welcomed and greeted and special.'

What's especially interesting to note is that the whole consumer journey has the Virgin brand attitude embedded in it. Not by stamping Virgin logos on every surface, but by treating every step along the journey in the typical Virgin way, by asking: 'What ingrained conventions can we break to we serve the user better?'

Conclusions to be gained from the Virgin case study

1 | To orchestrate touchpoints in such a way that a compelling overall experience is created requires strong design management skills, the ability to have many different specialists work together, the skill to convince management and the patience to execute the plan down to its tiniest detail.

2 | What connects all the touchpoints in the journey are the user's experience (of being special, being cared for and being part of cosmopolitan travel), and the Virgin brand (in taking nothing for granted, challenging every convention, and doing so in style).

3 | The Virgin Atlantic Upper Class journey is not particularly about design consistency. Every touchpoint is uniquely designed to function optimally. But it's very much about design orchestration: all the touchpoints are in tune to create a perfect service symphony.

THE CLUBHOUSE
The Clubhouse lounge area was designed to feel like a private members' club.

© Richard Davies

THE UPPER CLASS SUITE
These seats turn into beds at the touch of a button.

6.2 Multidisciplinary design management

To manage a team of designers is quite a challenge: you need them to perform a certain design task within a certain timeframe and budget. But you're not operating a machine where you pull a lever and out pops the design. Design needs careful management. It is a complex process that combines the rational with the emotional, that asks for structure and creativity and that requires both information and inspiration. And no one knows the exact outcome of a design process in advance. Next to these tricky combined attributes, designers have a slight but sticky tendency to dislike being managed. They want their freedom, their processes, their own sweet time and please, no long briefings and clients looking over their shoulders.

This requires a special kind of management that knows how to motivate and inspire this somewhat special breed within these special conditions. A kind of management that allows for freedom to explore and get inspiration, and that knows that you can't force eureka moments to happen at the snap of a finger. It's a kind of management that is about setting the right conditions for creativity to happen, and for synergies between people to occur. It's about motivating the free iteration between the rational and the emotional, the structured and the creative, between information and inspiration.

But a design team is not a kindergarten. Designers keep deadlines and work within budgets just like anybody else. And they work to meet objectives, within constraints, and know that only the best is good enough, regardless of whether they are working for an internal or an external client. So the special kind of management we mentioned before needs to be combined with all the classical management skills we learnt from business school: a strong ability to manage time and money, a sharp understanding of corporate strategy and a good knowledge of how to manage uncertainty and risk. Managing a design team requires a doubly-skilled person.

If managing a design team isn't easy, managing multidisciplinary design teams is even harder. In a project like the design of the Virgin Atlantic Upper Class experience, designers from many different disciplines clearly needed to be managed: product designers, architects, interior designers, graphic designers, service designers, textile designers and perhaps even food designers. Typically, for a touchpoint orchestration stage in a large BDI project, the team will consist of both internal designers as well as of external consultancies, agencies, and freelancers.

The shared goal for a multidisciplinary design project often includes two ingredients:

1 | To create an overall experience that is more than the sum of the individual touchpoints, and that is orchestrated in such a way that it resonates with the users' needs, desires and aspirations.

2 | To do the above in a branded way, that is, fulfilling the promise the brand set forth and delivering the experience according to the brand's unique characteristics.

Therefore, it becomes apparent that in addition to 'double skills', a manager of a multidisciplinary design team needs to be a visionary leader who understands what the user needs and wants, and what the role of the brand is in delivering that value. These are very 'broad' skills. But the design manager also needs to have a very keen understanding of each individual design discipline's potential, of its unique processes and tools, its idiosyncrasies, its heroes and foes and of how it can contribute to the whole experience. These are very 'deep' skills.

The skills of a multidisciplinary design manager have been summarised in figure 5 (facing page), building on the work on 'T-shaped skills and T-shaped professionals' by Dorothy Leonard-Barton (1995).

Design management is about setting the right conditions for creativity to happen, and for synergies between people to occur.

In practice: multidisciplinary touchpoint design

Purpose

This exercise will help you learn how to recognise the multidisciplinary design and orchestration of multi-touchpoint experiences.

Required

Go back and look at the consumer journey map you created earlier (page 161). You've divided the journey into stages that, in time, form the total experience: browsing the web, visiting the store and so on. Let's now go into a bit more detail to discover what touchpoint orchestration means for the experience that you chose to map.

1

For each stage, define which touchpoints the user comes into contact with. Really go into putting down a lot of detail here. Map them on the poster that you made when creating the consumer journey.

5 DESIGN MANAGERS
   NEED T-SHAPED
   SKILLS
   They need to have
   a broad perspective
   as well as deep
   expertise, and
   they need to
   switch between
   more rational and
   more emotional
   management
   styles (based
   on Leonard-Barton,
   1995).

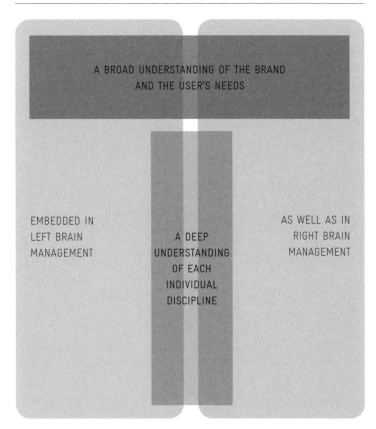

A BROAD UNDERSTANDING OF THE BRAND
AND THE USER'S NEEDS

EMBEDDED IN
LEFT BRAIN
MANAGEMENT

A DEEP
UNDERSTANDING
OF EACH
INDIVIDUAL
DISCIPLINE

AS WELL AS IN
RIGHT BRAIN
MANAGEMENT

2

How do the touchpoints work together to form the various stages in the experience? How does one touchpoint lead to the next? How do they strengthen each other? Or do they compete for the user's attention? In short, how are they orchestrated?

3

For each touchpoint, define which design disciplines (page 153) were involved and indicate them on the poster.

How do the design disciplines work together? Do they strengthen each other? What would you have done differently?

6.3 Involving users in the design management process

Involving users in innovation

Much has been written and said about the involvement of end users in the creation of new products and services. And indeed the ongoing development of co-creation, crowd sourcing and user-generated content initiatives indicates that the active involvement of users in innovation is a force to be reckoned with. Three general forces can be held responsible for this development:

1 | A social one: users have become more critical about what they buy and use, and more involved in their own behaviour as consumers.

2 | An economic one: organisations have discovered that, especially when it comes to innovation, the gate between the business and the outside world should be left open. Innovations based on real needs in the real world have more success and more economic value.

3 | A technological one: new technologies, social media and web 2.0 have provided the platforms on which organisations and users can share insights and ideas and collaboratively explore innovations.

Without going into too much detail on the rise of these developments, and referring back to the critical note on user-driven innovation on page 135, it's worthwhile exploring what these developments mean in the context of brand-driven innovation, and more specifically for the orchestration of user-generated or co-created touchpoints.

In brand-driven innovation, the brand is seen as the relationship between the organisation and the user. This relationship feeds the innovation process, and thus the partners in the relationship have equal stakes in the innovation. More practically, we have seen that this means that both the brand and the innovations that are based on it stem from combining the organisation's vision, beliefs, values and resources on the one hand, with the needs, desires and aspirations of the user on the other. Therefore, we have consequently involved the user side of the equation in our discussions on developing a brand, innovation and design strategy for BDI. We have also made it clear that in BDI it is not the user who directs innovation, but the organisation's vision of that user. From this perspective, it is only logical to involve the user in as many branding, innovation and design developments as possible, so that those involved in these developments can derive insights from their interactions with users, can stay inspired and can develop a vision that will guide them in their work.

Letting go

But things become slightly more complex when it comes to users becoming actively involved in creating touchpoints for your brand. Because this means that you have to let go of the strict rules that define how your brand is to be translated into designed touchpoints. It means that you have to replace these rules with a much more open 'stage' on which users have the liberty to interpret the brand as they wish. It means that you have to 'let go'. This requires courage, an open mind, the willingness to share and the curiosity to actually find out how your users interpret your brand. There are three levels of 'letting go'.

1 | Co-creation. This denotes the active involvementof users in the creation of new products and services, by letting them ideate, prototype and test, together with internal teams. Co-creation is exciting and it can also be confrontational; but it can take place in rather controlled settings and therefore requires a limited amount of 'letting go'. (<http://betalabs.nokia.com> is an example of co-creation that is partly public, but a lot of co-creation takes place offline or in closed environments.)

2 | Crowd sourcing. This means posing a question, an assignment or a challenge to a large number of people, based on 'the wisdom of crowds' (Surowiecki, 2005), usually making use of an online environment where participants can watch and comment on each other's entries. The sheer numbers that can be reached, the open nature of these platforms, as well as the discussions between participants, all require a considerable amount of letting go. (Design competitions, like the one at <http://www.electroluxdesignlab.com> provide a good example.)

3 | User-generated content. This means facilitating users to actually create their own content based on your brand, and allowing them to share and discuss this content publicly. Here you really have to let go and allow users to harness their own creativity. All you can do is facilitate (<http://designbyme.lego.com> is a great example).

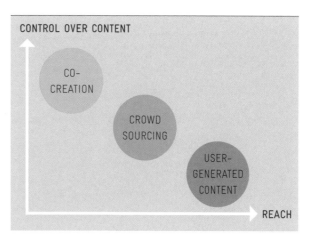

6   DESIGNING
     WITH USERS
     Involving users in
     your design efforts is
     a trade-off between
     reach and control
     over content. The
     more people you want
     to reach, the more
     you have to let go.

Again, the new brand touchpoints that evolve from these three ways of involving users play a role in creating the user experience around a brand. So again, they must be well orchestrated. As a rule, co-created touchpoints are easier to orchestrate than user-generated touchpoints. The users involved in co-creation are also easier to brief and to guide in a certain direction. But user-generated touchpoints have a much wider reach. This means you will reach a much more representative section of your target group and that the marketing spin-offs from your efforts will be considerably larger.

The above considerations imply that again, you have to study your design objectives first before you can make any decisions on how to involve users in your touchpoint creation. Do you have a very specific complex problem to solve? Consider organising a number of co-creation sessions or even develop a co-creation environment where you can ask your user for help. Do you want to inspire your users' creativity or are you curious about their ideas? Organise a crowd-sourcing initiative. Do you want your brand to play a role in the daily lives of your users and do you want to provide them with a platform to create their own content? Develop platforms for user-generated content, or make use of existing platforms (a camera manufacturer could use photography website Flickr.com for its activities, for instance). It's the design objectives that define your touchpoint orchestration.

6.4 **Touchpoint orchestration**

The touchpoint orchestration stage is the fourth stage in the BDI method and builds on the first, second and third stage: the human-centred branding stage, the innovation strategy stage and the design strategy stage respectively. The touchpoint orchestration stage is very much about execution: about designing those touchpoints that together make up the desired experience. It involves detailing the consumer journey so that each touchpoint functions optimally and so that together they fulfil the brand promise through the overall experience that they put forth.

Touchpoint orchestration is about taking the results of the design strategy stage and exploring how each individual touchpoint should function in making that strategy concrete and tangible. It also looks at how the design strategy can be filled in by detailing the consumer journey. It divides tasks amongst design disciplines and allocates design layers to the individual touchpoints. It also builds on the results of the innovation strategy stage by creating the touchpoints that deliver the innovation to the user in a functional, comprehensible and pleasant way. The extent to which an innovation actually delivers the value it promised depends largely on the way that the user interacts with it. Designing this interaction requires careful touchpoint orchestration. And the touchpoint orchestration stage builds on the results of the human-centred branding stage as well, by creating branded experiences through touchpoint interactions and by fulfilling the brand promise through tangible experiences.

The same principles that underlie the human-centred branding stage, the innovation strategy stage and the design strategy stage are valid in the touchpoint orchestration stage, but some specific rules apply:

1 | See the big picture. While 'God is in the details' (as the architect Ludwig Mies van der Rohe once claimed), it's equally important to keep track of the whole experience. Don't judge design solutions in isolation; rather, look at how they work together.

2 | Organise outside-in. Users don't care about design disciplines, silos and cultures. They care about the result. Cancel all rules that don't apply outside of your organisation.

3 | Sketch and prototype. Although you are nearing execution in this stage, keep designing. Don't jump to conclusions. Prefer a hundred mediocre sketches over one brilliant idea. Because that one idea might not make it to the end.

4 | Work together. Get all designers around the table. Have them work together, based on a shared vision, and headed towards a shared goal.

5 | Stay on track. Keep checking design solutions to see if they match the design objectives. Don't design for design's sake.

The touchpoint orchestration stage in step-by-step form is outlined on pages 181–185. See figure 7 (opposite) for the process in model form.

Individually, touchpoints fulfil specific design objectives but together, they fulfil the larger objective of creating a branded consumer journey that brings together user needs and organisational resources.

Phase A: formulate a detailed consumer journey

This phase is about detailing the consumer journey as it was first crafted in the design strategy stage, to the level where each touchpoint and its role in the journey can be identified. The trick in this first phase is to match the detailed steps of the consumer journey to the design objectives and functions as they were developed in the design strategy stage.

Get internal and external experts around the table

Form a multidisciplinary design team. Get the 'T-shaped professionals' around the table (as discussed on page 177). Make sure that you have people from all design disciplines, and don't hesitate to involve trusted external design partners; depending on the nature of your organisation, you will need marketing people, ergonomists, engineers, psychologists, retail specialists, and so on.

Immerse in stages one, two and three

Take the results from the human-centred branding, the innovation strategy and the design strategy stages and make sure everyone in the team understands them. If they didn't take part in the process, show them what has been done to get to the results. Make sure they become involved, and commit to the insights and knowledge that have been built up to now.

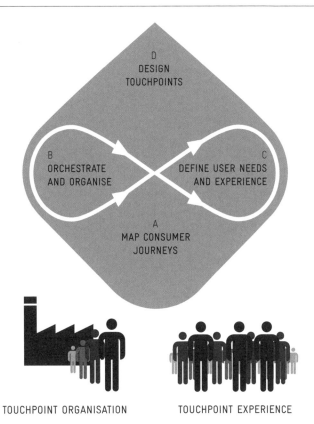

7   TOUCHPOINT
ORCHESTRATION
The touchpoint
orchestration stage
consists of four
steps: map consumer
journeys, orchestrate
and organise, define
user needs and
experience, and
design touchpoints.

Detail the consumer journey

In phase B of the design strategy stage, a rough consumer journey framework was built, based on the various experiences a user has in interacting with a brand's offer (see, for example, the three stages of the consumer journey in the Virgin Atlantic case study on page 172). It is now time to detail these experiences into the individual touchpoints that support them. In the previous chapter, we used the example of a brand delivering the experience of 'visiting the retail environment'. We will now break down this experience into its individual touchpoints: shop facade, brand logo, shop entrance, shop layout, display and shelves, in-store communication, products on display, labels, salespeople, furniture and so on.

Assign design attributes to the touchpoints

You have now mapped each touchpoint in the consumer journey and in the previous stage (building a design strategy) you've assigned design objectives, functions and disciplines to each experience. It is now time to detail these to the level of the individual touchpoints, still taking into account the overall objectives as set in the previous stage. For example, going back to the clothes shop we used as an example on page 170, we can now assign specific design attributes to a touchpoint, such as the labels on the clothing. We can say, for example, that their main design objective is to inform the user about the quality of the clothes. We can therefore say that the main function of design here is to provide clarity of information. And we will need to consult with a good graphic designer to get the job done. Of course, this sounds simpler than it actually is, and you will need several iterations to assign these design attributes to each individual touchpoint.

Phase B: define the user's needs and experience

This phase can take place in parallel with phase C and focuses on matching the detailed design attributes as defined in phase A with the exact user needs per touchpoint and the desired experience that all touchpoints form together.

Define user needs per touchpoints

In every design brief there should be a section that specifies which user needs the design should meet. What is it exactly that the design should do for the user? In this first step, your job is to look very carefully at each touchpoint and define its requirements from a user's point of view. Making a so-called programme of requirements is an important step in designing touchpoints that do what they are supposed to do.

Describe the desired user experience

Describe the experience the user would like to have when interacting with the touchpoint or a series of touchpoints. If you lack the user insights to complete this step, go back a few steps to gather these insights. You can't go on without them. Describe the desired user experience in a format that is inspiring to work with, for example, in the form of a story, a visual storyboard or a collage of images.

Assign each touchpoint a role in building the experience

For each touchpoint in the consumer journey, look at what role it can play in creating the desired user experience. Going back to the Virgin Atlantic case study (pages 172–5), for example, a person receiving an Upper Class passenger at check-in contributes to the overall experience by being efficient, comforting and business-like. A person serving a passenger at the Clubhouse, however, contributes to the experience by being relaxed, pampering and jovial.

Phase C: orchestrate and organise design resources

This phase focuses on assessing internal design requirements, assigning design tasks and planning design projects.

Define internal needs per touchpoint

Having looked in Phase B at what the user needs from each touchpoint, it is now time to complete the programme of requirements per touchpoint with a set of internal requirements and specifications. These can refer to anything from targeted cost price, required manufacturing equipment, norms and legislation, corporate identity guidelines, sustainability issues, to more visionary requirements such as the way the brand vision is to be embedded into the various touchpoints.

Assign design tasks per touchpoint.

Based on the internal and external requirements per touchpoint, define what sort of design is needed where. Different touchpoints will need different design disciplines. Translate the internal and external requirements into a table that states for each touchpoint what sort of designer, design agency, consultancy or specialist is required. Also use the plans you've made in Phase C of the design strategy stage.

Plan design projects

Define the various design and development projects that are needed to create all the touchpoints. Cluster those touchpoints that require a similar design approach, so that they can be briefed simultaneously. Plan the different design projects in terms of the needed resources (budget, time, people, extra expertise) and the expected outcome. Where possible, define the metrics that decide whether a design fulfils the requirements or not (for example, for Virgin Atlantic Upper Class passengers the time from check-in to the Clubhouse should be less than ten minutes).

Create project briefings

Combine all the knowledge you've gained into design project briefings to be used internally or externally. These briefings will include at least the following items:

1 | a summary of the previous three stages of BDI

2 | a description of the touchpoint to be designed

3 | the design guidelines that apply to the touchpoint

4 | a description of the user group that will be interacting with the touchpoint (visual and derived from user research)

5 | a description of the design objectives and functions for that touchpoint

6 | a description of the role of the touchpoint in the overall experience (in visual or narrative format)

7 | a programme of user requirements for the touchpoint

8 | a programme of internal requirements for the touchpoint

9 | a set of constraints for the project with regards to time, budget, man-hours and legal issues

Make sure that you spend the same amount of time working through the briefs that you want the designers you are briefing to spend on reading them. Where necessary, refer to back-up data such as user insights, design guidelines, design collages, personas and so on.

Phase D: design the touchpoints

This phase is about operational design management: overseeing the design of the actual touchpoints and coordinating the efforts of various disciplines, agencies, specialists and in-house design teams.

Select and brief internal and external designers

Based on your briefings and the touchpoint assessment you have done you should now be able to choose the right partners to develop the touchpoints. The process of selecting and briefing the right design partners will vary from project to project and organisation to organisation but the following general rules apply.

1 | Be critical towards (unpaid) pitches. A working relationship with a design agency should be based on more than one attempt by the agency to solve a design problem for nearly free. Building a relationship with an agency takes time from both sides, and a pitch often doesn't do justice to this.

2 | Involve internal designers when working with externals. Don't create two 'camps'. (Unless there's an explicit competition element involved as is sometimes done in the automotive industry.)

3 | Don't use the briefing as a contract. Rather, involve the other party in finishing the briefing, be open to suggestions, and even invite active participation of the other party in finishing the brief. This will create tremendous commitment and support for all the efforts you went through to get to this point.

4 | Make the briefing a living document that is adapted and detailed during the course of the project. Change requirements as they change in real life, and adapt timelines and budgets to the situation at hand. Also enrich the briefing document with insights that are discovered during the course of the project. This ensures that the briefing doesn't become obsolete after week 1, and remains a central resource for project management information.

5 | Create a list of selection criteria before you enter the conversation with an agency. What are you looking for exactly? What do you find important? The portfolio, the working method the agency uses, a sense of empathy towards the challenge at hand, the ability to listen carefully or an attitude of leadership?

Make the briefing a living document that is adapted and detailed during the course of the project.

Manage the various design projects

Once you have approved the various project proposals and your internal team has got the go-ahead, you are finally really on the way to create those touchpoints that make all the efforts of the previous stages worthwhile. Now it's important to keep track of design progress and to constantly compare intermediate design results with the original plans and strategies as laid out in the previous BDI stages. This again requires the T-shaped skills we discussed on page 177, where on the one hand, the design manager has to be completely involved in the ongoing design processes, while on the other hand, he or she has to keep an eye on the broader picture.

Measure

There's no point in devising solid strategies and setting clear design objectives if you are unwilling to measure the results of your efforts and compare them to the goals and objectives you've set in the beginning. When the first touchpoints become reality, take this measuring very seriously, but don't be afraid to be creative about it. In design metrics there is not only Return On Investment (ROI) but also Return On Expectation (ROEx) (Viladàs, 2009). It can be hard to measure concrete numeric financial results when it comes to design. But when it's possible, do it. And if not, go back to your objectives and measure those. Was your objective to redesign the store to get more people in? Measure the number of people that enter each day as compared to before the overhaul. Was your objective to create a more positive shopping experience? Ask customers what they think.

Iterate

You've come to the end of the BDI process. You've developed a human-centred brand, built an innovation strategy upon it, devised the design strategy to make it real, and finally you've orchestrated the touchpoints to bring all this to the user, and to finally make his or her experience the brand's offering in real life. Chances are that you didn't get here in a straight line. You went back and forth, skipped some steps and then went back a few, you sharpened insights gained in earlier stages to be re-used in later ones, and revisited insights that proved to be different or false in later developments. This is what design is, and it will go on. So, having introduced a series of touchpoints that string together to create the perfect branded journey, go back to the first stage and see how your brand has grown. See how your users have changed and what new ideas and visions you've developed. See how these new touchpoints affect the very nature of your brand. And then revisit your innovation strategies and adapt them to the new times. Branding, innovation and design are in constant flux. The end is only a new beginning. In a similar way to Newton's cradle, the desk device which aims to show how the conservation of momentum is effected, so too do the brand and its touchpoints constantly influence each other, in a dance of action and reaction that has no beginning or end.

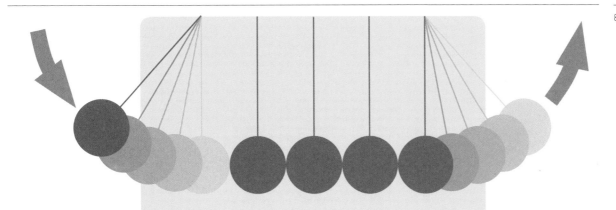

8 NEWTON'S CRADLE
Like the motion of
Newton's cradle,
brands produce
touchpoints, and
touchpoints in return
affect the brand that
they stemmed from.

6.5 **Service design management**

Although service design is 'only' one of the five design disciplines that was described on page 153, it merits special mention in a discussion on touchpoint orchestration for brand-driven innovation. This is not simply because service design is an upcoming discipline with a lot of buzz around it, but more because service design fashions the other design disciplines into a congruent story.

When designing a product or an environment in the context of brand-driven innovation, the design process can be seen as the materialisation of an abstract brand vision into the tangible embodiment of an object or a space. As we have seen in the Design Layer model (page 155), this can be done on several design layers: the brand can be translated into aesthetic design (a Bentley dealer will look different from a BMW dealer), but also into interaction design (a BMW gear shift will feel different from a Bentley gear shift), or functional design (a Bentley performs differently from a BMW). All of these layers have a direct, physical impact on the user and will help in the 'semantic attribution' (page 58) that translates these design cues back into an understanding of the brand's values and vision.

Designing services

The design of services, as opposed to the design of products and environments, lacks this materialisation into a tangible embodiment of them. Although services are often supported by a series of physical touchpoints, what you actually buy is intangible. Imagine, for example, you rent a Bentley for your birthday. The luxury car rental service your friend told you about has a website where you can check the cars, tariffs, conditions and availability. You make your choice and, when the day arrives, you go to the rental office. You wait your turn while leafing through some brochures, watching the video presentations, and taking a peek at the cars that are waiting in the car park behind.

When it's your turn, the nice girl behind the counter confirms your reservation, helps you go through the formalities and wishes you a pleasant day. Her colleague takes you to the car park, opens the door of the shiny Bentley for you and hands you the keys. As you settle yourself down into the crisp new leather, you try to pay attention to the explanation of the car's workings, while your eyes explore the matte aluminium and shiny wood and your hands go over the knobs and gear shift. When it's finally time to go, you press the start button, open the roof and rev the engine. The sound crawls up your spine while you slowly make your way out of the car park, onto the coast road, not to return until late that night. You've had the birthday of your life.

9   SERVICE DESIGN
     IN RELATIONSHIP
     TO TOUCHPOINTS
     Touchpoints
     are individually
     distinguishable
     designed entities.
     What the user
     experiences is
     their journey through
     these touchpoints.

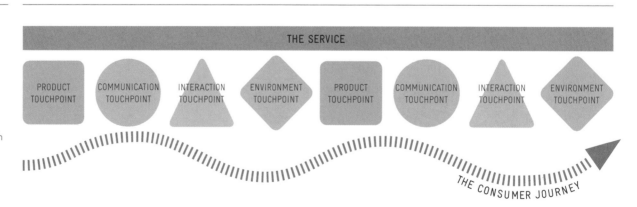

THE SERVICE

PRODUCT TOUCHPOINT · COMMUNICATION TOUCHPOINT · INTERACTION TOUCHPOINT · ENVIRONMENT TOUCHPOINT · PRODUCT TOUCHPOINT · COMMUNICATION TOUCHPONT · INTERACTION TOUCHPOINT · ENVIRONMENT TOUCHPOINT

THE CONSUMER JOURNEY

Services may just be better at fulfilling brand promises than products, environments and communications can, individually.

Touchpoint orchestration for service design

What this story tells us is that the car rental service is supported by numerous touchpoints – each and every one designed in order to support the service in a specific way, each one using specific design disciplines and design layers to fulfil its purpose. But what you actually buy is not the touchpoints. What you buy is the ability to drive the car of your dreams for one day, without any further obligations as to maintenance, payments, insurance or storage. You buy something intangible, you buy a feeling. Yet, this feeling means so much to you that you are willing to pay quite a sum for it. This is what service design is all about: the design of meaning that is supported by touchpoints, but that in the end, has a larger value than the sum of the individual touchpoints (see figure 9, opposite).

This has two implications for the touchpoint orchestration stage of BDI: service design requires very careful touchpoint orchestration, and it is a great way to form a meaningful brand experience. When designing services, very special care must be taken in designing the individual touchpoints in such a way that they support the service. This means that the process of touchpoint orchestration gets extra meaning: not only will you be designing the touchpoints so that they function individually and together form an experience; you will now also be designing them so that what the touchpoints do together actually forms a service. And this service will be at the centre of your value proposition. This requires subtle orchestration of the individual touchpoints and a solid understanding of their individual role in supporting the value that is created through the service.

The actual purpose of the touchpoint orchestration stage was to fulfil the brand's promise through the creation of meaningful and valuable interactions. Each individual touchpoint has its own purpose, but combines together with the others to create an experience. It's this experience that best resembles the embodiment of the brand's vision. Service design is a very good way of creating this experience because it also brings together the individual touchpoints to form a meaningful and coherent whole. What follows from this line of reasoning is that if you are looking for a way to embody your brand's vision in an experience that bundles all your individual touchpoints into a coherent whole, service design might just do the trick.

When Nike and Apple developed the Nike+ system (whereby a sensor in your running shoe tracks the distance you've covered, your speed and then sends this data to your iPod), they also developed the online service ecosystem around it. You can compare your data with others, keep track of your yearly progress, join global runs for charities and buy special training programmes to listen to while you run. All the touchpoints are designed to meet specific purposes: the cell, the iPod software, the running shoes, the packaging, the website. But together they support a service and, in the end, it's in this service where the two brands are brought to life and bring value, meaning and excitement to runners all over the world.

If services are such a great way to bundle individual brand touchpoints into meaningful brand experiences that resonate with users' needs, wishes and aspirations, it's no surprise to see product companies exploring product service systems, to discover retail companies looking into delivery services and online sales, and to observe advertising agencies moving into organising experiences and events. Services may just be better at fulfilling brand promises than products, environments and communications can individually.

Case study: NLISIS chromatography

The purpose of this case study

This case study will provide you with an overview of what the entire BDI method, including the fourth stage, could look like in practice. It will enable you to get a feeling for how the various BDI tools can also be applied within a small start-up company.

About NLISIS

NLISIS (pronounced 'analysis') is a Dutch high-tech start-up in the domain of gas chromatography, a chemical analysis technique. Gas chromatography is used for measuring the chemical components of substances, in laboratory environments or in the field. The food industry, the petrochemical industry and pharmaceutical companies use gas chromatography for the analysis of chemical substances on a daily basis. NLISIS was founded in 2007 as the result of a task force created by the Dutch government that was to investigate the possibilities of gas chromatography. The investigation resulted in so many ideas for new products that it led to the start-up of a new business. NLISIS is highly specialised and operates in an international business-to-business (B2B) environment. The company was founded by Wil van Egmond, a veteran in the domain, and six partners, entrepreneurs, each with their own specialisation.

The challenge

In 2007, NLISIS wanted to create a usable and inspiring brand that would help them convey their story of user-centred innovation in the very traditional and technology dominated world of chemical analysis. On the decision to build a strong brand from the start, Wil van Egmond says: 'The products and technology we offer challenge many conventions in a very conventional market. We compete with very large established companies, and our customers are big multinationals. So gaining acceptance as a small player is crucial. We have seen from the start that we needed a strong brand to position us firmly amongst our big brothers. We needed to show our customers that we were different than what they were used to, but that we could be completely trusted as well.'

But through conversations with Zilver innovation, the consultancy hired to help establish the new business, van Egmond also understood that the start-up didn't have the budgets for heavy brand communication campaigns. Instead, the brand vision needed to be embedded in everything the company would do. It was decided that the brand was to be used as a springboard to develop an innovation strategy and, based on that, a design strategy, for the coming five years. The final stage concerned the coordination of the various people and agencies that were involved in creating the design touchpoints that were used for the introduction of the brand to an international audience.

The process

The working method that was used for this project was one of the very first iterations of the full four-stage BDI method:
– human-centred branding
– building an innovation strategy
– building a design strategy
– orchestrating touchpoints

During the entire process it was made essential to continuously involve stakeholders from the gas chromatography sector (laboratory analysts, buyers, laboratory managers) in the decision-making: the sector is so heavily regulated that suppliers who deviate too much from what is customary are mistrusted. NLISIS needed to embed their innovations in the customs, working patterns and thought systems of their customers.

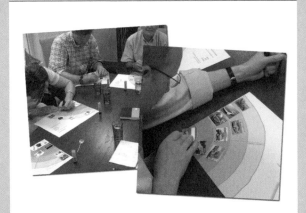

GENERATIVE
WORKSHOP SESSIONS
Generative sessions
(page 101) were held in
order to gain a deeper
understanding of the
motivation, needs and
aspirations of both
the entrepreneurs and
the lead users of their
products.

RESEARCH DIARIES
Diaries were used to
get insights into the
motivations of the
entrepreneurs and the
users. These diaries are
also called 'cultural
probes' (page 101).

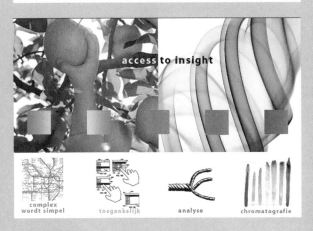

THE BRAND PROMISE
The research led to a
brand promise, captured
in a visual format and
shared with all the
company's stakeholders.

DESIGN GUIDELINES
Based on the research,
the brand promise
and discussions with
designers, design
guidelines were drafted
for various design
disciplines and layers
(pages 153–5). The
guidelines gave both
examples to follow, and
examples to avoid.

Stage 1: human-centred branding

In order to get a deep understanding of the stakeholders of the brand (the founders of the company and a selected group of lead users), Zilver employed a technique called Contextmapping (page 104). This research included lab visits, small diaries that the partners and the lead users filled in, and a number of sessions with creative exercises. The results of these exploratory efforts were shared and interpreted with the company and developed further in a series of creative sessions. This resulted in the identity and vision of the organisation and the identity and vision of the end-user merging into a brand vision and a brand promise. Again, these were shared with and refined by the entire team.

Stage 2: the innovation strategy

In this step, Zilver focused on merging the client's existing innovation strategy, which was impressively well developed, with the fresh brand insights. In informal sessions with the client, the future of the client's market was explored from the viewpoint of the brand: how can we continue to build a meaningful and authentic relationship with our end-users, given the choices we have made regarding our brand, and given the changes we forecast in the market we operate in? Also explored was the way innovation should be organised in terms of partnerships, the use of existing infrastructure, and the ways different market segments should be targeted.

Stage 3: the design strategy

In this step, Zilver translated the group's insights regarding brand and innovation into a design language comprising a design vision per discipline and a set of guidelines per layer, based on the Design Layer model (discussed on page 155). These guidelines were developed based on Zilver's experiences with multidisciplinary design projects, but were also tested with designers from different disciplines. What was tested was whether they gave direction without choking designers' creativity and whether they were easy to understand and apply.

Stage 4: touchpoint orchestration

This step entailed the briefing and orchestration of a team of designers working on the company's first flagship product, the corporate identity (including logo, stationery, presentation template, posters, brochures, spec-sheets and tone-of-voice for texts), and the website, a set of promotional videos, a trade-fair booth, and even clothing. Over several meetings, the entire design team was called together to compare notes, share ideas, discuss the brand and the briefing.

The result

The introduction of the new brand and its touchpoints was a success in a number of important aspects:

1 | NLISIS won a Design Management Europe award, the Dutch Design Award for best design client and various trade awards for innovation.

2 | NLISIS was complimented by potential clients and peers on the well-balanced, daring and inviting look and feel of the entire offering.

3 | Orders for the new product came in faster and in higher numbers than anyone dared to hope.

4 | But most importantly, NLISIS' founders were assisted in bringing their company to the market successfully, through their pride, their feeling of being part of something to be reckoned with, and radiating the right mix of being unconventional but reliable.

Conclusions to be gained from the NLISIS case study

1 | BDI is not a method that only works for multinationals or B2C companies. Start-ups and B2B companies can also benefit from adopting the same approach.

2 | Although the BDI method provides a guideline, it should not be considered to be a precise formula. The exact process steps should be adapted to the context of the specific organisation.

3 | BDI has a large organisational impact. It helps organisations be themselves, successfully.

End note: in 2009, NLISIS was acquired by Dutch chemical giant DSM. DSM will keep the brand and its design language intact, as a showcase for what branding and design can do in high-tech B2B environments.

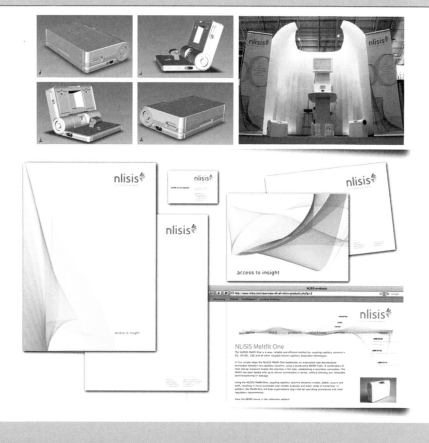

TOUCHPOINTS
Various touchpoints that evolved from the NLISIS brand. Designs for products, corporate identity, stationery, website, animations and trade-fair booth by Faes, Total Support, Nandooh, Designest, Fred Montijn, Exit 170, Tunnel-Vizion and Gaudi Hoedaya.

6.6 **Embedding touchpoint orchestration in the organisation**

Touchpoint orchestration, from an organisational perspective, is a balancing act: the design manager whose task it is to orchestrate touchpoints has to equally balance:

1 | The interests of the stakeholders in the individual touchpoint, versus the interests of the stakeholders in the overall experience.

2 | Internal design constraints versus external design requirements.

We will now turn to explore how the careful act of balancing touchpoint orchestration can be achieved.

Stakeholders' interests

We have already observed that each touchpoint has a role to play in shaping the consumer journey. Each touchpoint should function in such a way that it contributes to the total experience. When crafting the consumer journey, the design manager will carefully assign tasks to each touchpoint, so that together they can 'perform the symphony'. In the clothes shop we used in an earlier example, this might mean that the clothing labels have to provide factual information about fabrics and price, the entrance has to be open and inviting, the background music has to be uplifting and the payment counter has to provide comfort.

But what function each touchpoint should have exactly, is very often not decided by one person. Especially in large organisations, responsibilities will be divided between many individuals, each with specific ideas on what 'their' touchpoint should do, and what criteria will define its quality. The person responsible for labelling might see a huge branding opportunity in 'his' labels, not caring so much about the factual information. The person responsible for the entrance may have a different style in mind than the larger picture of the consumer journey would suggest.

To cut a long story short, not every stakeholder in an individual touchpoint sees the big picture the way you might hope. Dealing with this requires the skill to sketch the big picture and make it attractive, while at the same time respecting the stakeholder's ideas about 'his' or 'her' touchpoint and realising that the individual touchpoint falls under their responsibility. As a design manager you will very often, and by definition, tread on someone else's turf. The only way to get away with this is to do it respectfully. It will serve the bigger picture if you do.

Touchpoint orchestration is about resolving the paradoxes between individual interests and the greater picture and between external user needs and internal constraints. The truth lies where the solution is most elegant and creative.

Design constraints

The second balancing act that a design manager has to perform when orchestrating touchpoints is that between internal constraints and external design requirements. We have arrived at a point in the BDI method where it's about delivery. You are creating touchpoints for the user, in order for him or her to experience and use what you as a company have to offer. But that means that only user needs count in designing the touchpoint. Setting design objectives for a touchpoint to meet the user's need is one challenge. But also meeting all internal requirements with that same touchpoint is quite another.

One example that illustrates this very well is the Virgin Atlantic private security corridor, which was part of their Upper Class experience we discussed in the case study on pages 172–5. Virgin certainly set out to pamper their Upper Class passengers as much as possible in a stylish, cosmopolitan way that gave passengers the feeling of being very special. What a contrast with the stringent airport safety regulations we have these days. Imagine being pampered throughout the whole check-in procedure, only to find yourself having to take your shoes and belt off and being bullied by an uninterested security agent. Virgin solved this challenge by embedding the security point into their own designed environment, giving them full control over the execution of the checks while still complying with all safety regulations. But imagine how much work went into creating this elegant solution, and how much organisational skill it required!

Touchpoint orchestration is about resolving these paradoxes: between individual interests and the greater picture, and between external user needs and internal constraints. These are hard nuts to crack, but fortunately we have seen that designers are natural resolvers of paradoxes (page 50–51). The truth doesn't necessarily lie in the middle, the truth lies where the most elegant, creative and emphatic solution finds the best fertile ground to grow on. To embed touchpoint orchestration in the organisation, design managers have to work with those people who know about the individual touchpoints, how they function, what their purpose is, and what the technological, economical or legal constraints are. In order to align these different people and interests into a symphony of touchpoints that resonates with the user, design managers have to empathise with individual interests, and have the vision to see the big picture. And they have to have a relentless user-centred passion to bring the brand to life, combined with a pragmatic, hands-on attitude in dealing with constraints.

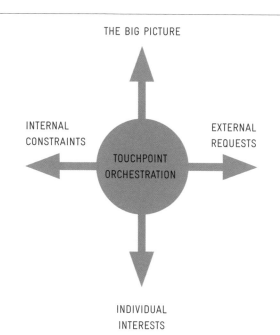

THE BIG PICTURE

INTERNAL CONSTRAINTS

TOUCHPOINT ORCHESTRATION

EXTERNAL REQUESTS

INDIVIDUAL INTERESTS

10 BALANCING ACT Managers involved with touchpoint orchestration have to perform two balancing acts: one between internal constraints and external demands, and one between seeing the big picture and individual interests.

A conversation between specialists: orchestrating touchpoints to enhance brand and design effect

In this chapter, we have come to learn that good multidisciplinary design management will help achieve the purposes for which design is employed, thus leading to stronger brands and more meaningful user experiences. In this final conversation, between Gert Kootstra and Harry Rich, we scrutinise this assumption by looking at why this is so, as well as at what it takes to actually put this into practice.

Gert Kootstra is the founder of Census design management in the Hague, the Netherlands. Gert is research fellow at the Centre for Applied Research in Brand, Reputation and Design Management within INHOLLAND University, Rotterdam. He is also the programme director of the EURIB Institute's Master of Design Management course, and he is an active contributor to research in the field of design effect and management.

Harry Rich studied law and worked as a managing director for several companies before becoming deputy chief executive of the UK Design Council, a position he held from 1999 to 2007. Harry is currently chief executive of RIBA, the Royal Institute of British Architects. He is also governor of the University of Creative Arts in the UK and council member of the Design Management Institute in the US.

Is there a known correlation between the multidisciplinary, multi-touchpoint approach of design and its effect?

Harry: A lot of the work we did at the Design Council was centred around this topic, in that it tried to help businesses to understand the impact that effective use of design could bring to them to help them compete in highly competitive marketplaces. And over the years we built up quite some data that does in fact indicate that managing design well, and using it purposefully, yields good business results.

Gert: Looking at academic support for the notion that well-managed, multidisciplinary design has a beneficial effect on users' experiences, I'd like to mention Bernd Schmitt, who has developed a scale to measure the effect of an experience in which four factors of brand experience are identified: sensory, affective, behaviour and intellectual. It is argued that design positively influences the sensory factor (Brakus, Schmitt and Zarantonello, 2009). Pine and Gilmore also point to design as a key ingredient of meaningful experiences.

If we look at these experiences, do we talk about hospitals as well as, say, the Apple store? For what kind of experiences is this relevant? What are the design objectives for which this approach is important?

Harry: I do support the notion of touchpoint design, but we must watch out that we don't look at them as isolated entities: we must keep our eyes on the whole. And that implies keeping our eyes on the user experience. Making a hospital waiting room a bit better is an incremental improvement, whereas looking at the whole experience, not taking the individual touchpoints for granted, will lead to much more radical improvements. It is in situations where this whole experience counts, where a holistic approach to design is the most beneficial.

Gert: Design can have two objectives in relation to brand objectives: to create a sensorial or aesthetic brand experience, and to create a specific brand personality. Especially the second objective has become more important in the so-called experience economy, where consumers are looking for authentic, meaningful and holistic experiences. So, I would say that this orchestration of touchpoints is especially relevant for brands that want to convey an immaterial, emotional or symbolic meaning.

What are the challenges in this multi-disciplinary, multi-touchpoint approach of design?

Gert: It's a massive task for designers to fulfil this role. I distinguish between passive design (providing structure, recognition, family resemblance, hierarchy and so on) and active design (conveying meaning and brand personality). Where traditional design management was very much about managing this passive design over all touchpoints, modern design management now faces a much more complex challenge: managing the active role of design. This challenge is complex because it requires the translation of an abstract brand vision and personality into tangible experiences, using design very actively.

Harry: I agree. And it does not only put great demands on the designer, but also on the company. Again, it has to do with being completely focused on the customer and adapting your organisation and your design efforts to them.

Gert: innocent smoothies is a good example because the design they employ is not so much about the design of the bottle or the label *per se*. It's about the experience of being included in their world, and they do a great job of conveying their brand personality of authenticity, openness and accessibility in all their touchpoints. But there are many other examples of companies that are good at this, also in SMEs.

Harry: In small SMEs, what we see is that the way they are perceived by their customers stems very much from the way the original founder or entrepreneur behaves. The brand personality is the founder's personality so you don't need any particular structures in place to convey it. It's when companies grow that the challenge starts. It is then when it becomes important to hold on to a philosophy, or a central vision.

Gert: This central vision also plays an important role in getting multidisciplinary design teams around the table. This can only be done if there is a clearly defined, elaborated and communicated design strategy that encompasses all design disciplines. I see this as a prerequisite. Following from that you need design leadership, good design programmes and proper programme management.

Harry: And then there's the people in the organisation who are vital in actually delivering the experiences we've discussed. You can design all you want but if the person behind the reception desk is unfriendly, the effect is gone.

Gert: What design can contribute to this is to help create a culture where employees understand and value their role in conveying the brand's personality. Design can make this personality explicit.

For the full conversation, go to <www.branddriveninnovation.com/book/conversations>.

6.7 Conclusion: touchpoint orchestration in brand-driven innovation

In this final chapter, we have explored how well-designed brand touchpoints will finally provide the proof of the pudding: the strategic thinking and design research that led to this point will now prove its value by forming the foundation for touchpoints that fulfil the brand's promise and are meaningful, useful, relevant and valuable.

We have seen that individually, touchpoints fulfil specific design objectives but that together, they fulfil the larger objective of creating a branded consumer journey that brings together user needs and organisational resources. This requires a special breed of 'T-shaped people', who are able to cope with the challenges of multidisciplinary design management, involving users in the design of touchpoints, and the upcoming discipline of service design.

Pause for thought: reflections on this book

Purpose

This section enables you to critically reflect on what you've learned, as well as to look forward and think about ways in which you can apply this new understanding.

1

Go back and scan the six 'summary insights' sections that complete each chapter in the book.

2

What have you picked up from this book that really resonated with you, that really landed?

3

What parts were most useful for you, and what parts less?

4

Were the more theoretical parts of more interest to you or did you like the practical applications better?

5

Can you see how you will apply the thinking, methods and the tools that were discussed in this book?

6

How do you think that brand-driven innovation will help you, in your organisation, your studies, or your consultancy?

7

Upload your comments to ‹www.brand driveninnovation. com/book/ reflections›.

Summary insights from chapter 6

1	The fourth stage of BDI is about creating the individual touchpoints in such a way that they function optimally, while at the same time taking care that they combine into a whole that is larger than the sum of the individual parts.
2	A shift is taking place from the tangible to more intangible touchpoints. A similar shift is taking place from brand-owner-created touchpoints to user-generated touchpoints.
3	Each touchpoint needs to be designed in such a way that it delivers value in optimum form, fitting the user's needs and desires, fitting the organisation's strategic objectives and identity, and ultimately, fulfilling the brand's promise.
4	Each task point also needs to be designed so that it can play a role in shaping the consumer journey that forms the brand experience for the user.
5	Multidisciplinary design management combines left- and right-brain management styles, and it requires 'T-shaped' skills: the combination of deep specialised knowledge with the ability to see the bigger picture.
6	Involving users in touchpoint orchestration is a great way to bring the brand to life. Which kind of user involvement you choose will depend on your design objectives. User involvement is a trade-off between reach and control.
7	The touchpoint orchestration process involves mapping the consumer journey, defining user needs and experience, orchestrating and organising, and the actual design of the touchpoints.
8	The brand and its touchpoints constantly influence each other back and forth: new brand insights bring forth new touchpoints. These new touchpoints will in turn impact upon your brand.
9	When designing services, very special care must be taken in designing the individual touchpoints in such a way that they support the service.
10	Service design is a very good way of creating brand experiences because it brings together the individual touchpoints to form a meaningful, coherent whole.
11	Touchpoint orchestration is about resolving the paradoxes between individual interests and the greater picture, and between external user needs and internal constraints.

APPENDIX